AF531392

WOMEN EDUCATION AND GENDER JUSTICE
A Multi-Dimensional Approach

Foreword

Shri Janardan Prasad has a long experience of working in the Department of Education (Central Institute of Education) University of Delhi. He has contributed many books in various field of education, which are being used by different Teacher Education Institutions. I am glad to see his next endeavour of writing a book on Women Education.

The writings in this book deals with a variety of issues related to women and its education starting from very traditional roles to varied changed roles due to social changes and the need for a modified women education. The book covers genesis of women education including the historical review of the slow growth of women education and significant challenges to fulfill growing need of versility in women education.

I appreciate the efforts of Mr. Janardan Prasad in successfully completing the gigantic takes in the form of this book. I am sure that the students and teacher educators in the field will find the book useful.

Date: 25th March 2006

Prof. Najma Siddique
Former Head and Dean of Education,
Department of Education,
University of Delhi, Delhi.

Preface

Man and woman are two equal familial social life partners. They have to perform more or less, though slightly equal, family life roles. According to old social traditions, the man is supposed to earn and sustain the family's whole expenses. And the woman is supposed to bring up and mould children and manage the household affairs. As such, the woman is supposed to be the epicentre of love, affection and care of the children and a source of homogeneity, sociability, hospitability, creativity and familial education. This is why the woman was given due reverence in the society in the past. And still the women are respected. All virgin girls (कन्यायें) were respected and, very often were worshipped in all Indian families. Still young girls (छोटी कन्यायें) are worshipped in Hindu families in Navratras which occur twice a year. Many elders even in the present hedonistic age do not eat food cooked by the girls, who are virgin and unmarried. The father of the writer of this book even did not accept water offered by a virgin girl. Though such a situation did not and, still does not exist in many countries. In India also people, in the present hedonistic age, do not believe in such dogmatism.

In olden times women were considered kind, pious and social human beings, being life givers and life sustainers. So women were respected in the society. Many goddesses like Durga, Vaishnav Devi, Mansa Devi, Shakumbhra Devi, Kali Devi etc., etc., are still worshipped in the country. For giving respect and recognition to women, mostly all Indian rivers, excepting few, like Bhagirathi, Ganga, Yamuna, Saraswati, Krishna, Godavari, Chambal, Gomati, Ravi, Parvati etc., etc., named after pious respected women's names. Only a few rivers like Sindhu, Satlaj, Vyas, Chenab in the West and Brahmaputra in the East are named after the names of the males. As such, generally, still women are respected throughout the Indian society.

Social change is the law of the nature. A Greek philosopher Hereclitus said that everything is in flux at every moment. All of the physical phenomena including all living beings change at every moment. So the all social infrastructure and its customs, social traits, traditions and culture change. Because of the social change all Indian social structural situations have now completely changed. The social change in the Indian society has occurred due to western cultural diffusion and consequent acculturation. With the result the old status of women in the Indian society has also changed. In olden times, the women were considered most pious and sacred human beings as they were, and still are, life givers and life protectors. Nowadays, generally women are not fairly treated. On August 26th, 2005 the father-in-law of newly married Paramjeet Kaur burnt his daughter-in-law, because bringing less dowry. Now the men, generally have become totally mad after hedonistic ends. The young women even minor girls are not safe. They cannot go out of their homes because of the fear of rape and molestation. The cases of rapes and molestations have become a common feature in the Indian society. The administration and police are helpless to stops such heinous crimes which are committed on the fair sex. Even the capital, Delhi is not free from such barbarous crimes. Rather the capital city is ahead of all cities in such heinous crimes. Such crimes against the women can only be stopped by changing the mentality of both men and women. The men should be educated about this and made humane. The girls, the would be women should be educated to be simpler and not be ostentatious. They should also be taught to learn some self-defence techniques. This can be done at the girl's schools through co-curricular activities. The girls should be taught karates and gymnastics.

The situation has become so bad for the fair sex that the girls are raped by uncles, elders, siblings, even by fathers and father-in-laws. Now, in the materialistic age the man has become totally barbarous and *jungli*. The young women and young girls cannot leave or come out of their houses for early morning walk and even for evening strolling. In capital the young girls and women are forcibly raped while they come out of their houses for walking. This crime tendency cannot be checked by law enforcement. It can be checked by educating the people and by changing their mindsets. The school education should not lay emphasis only on teaching subjects, but should also lay emphasis on life-building process. As such, our present school girl education needs reformation for its improvement. The school education should also lay emphasis on girls' psyche improvement.

In the present materialistic age the women are the victom of gender bias. This is because the women are weaker than men. Another reason is the present patriarchal society they have to go to another homes. As such, the girls are considered anta-property (परायाधन), so the interests of girls are generally ignored in the present society. Being anta-property, the custom of dowry has also added fuel to the fire of gender bias. If the desired dowry is not given by the parents of the brides, they are tortured and, even murdered in many cases. All this changes the psyche of the girls. And many of them become so self-centred and individualistic that they make their minds to achieve in their new homes, that is *Sasural* (ससुराल) what was denied to them in their parental homes. Such girls, after their marriages due to their self-centredness become the prime cause of breaking the joint family system.

Keeping all these facts in view, it has become necessary to modify the present girls education. The administrators and educationists should give attention to all these problems of fair sex while deciding about the girls' education. The girls' education should be so reformed that the girls may lead a happy married life and also perform their life roles nicely. The administrators should give the girls' school principal due rights to manage the girls school education in such a ways to achieve the objective of girls' education. The lady principles of the girl's schools should look into other life-building process of the girls. The girls' school principals should be involved in, chalking out educational programme for the girls. The present girls' education is only limited to teaching of school subjects for passing out examinations. The girls' education should cross this limit. It should be extended to life-building education of the girls, which could prepare the girls as sane, courageous and defensive. They should also be taught about their life roles.

The society as a whole should look to the proper education of the girls. Proper girls' education can only be possible when all social stigmas which go against the women can be rooted out from the society. Social stigmas, such as gender bias, considering the girls as anta-property and weaker than men are very dangerous. As a matter of fact the genesis of human existence lies in women. So the women should be given due regard in the society. They should be given equal opportunities as we give to the boys. And the girls' education should be aimed to do so.

Contents

1

Introduction

Women and men are two specific rational living beings, who constitute the social whole, that is, the society. If any of them is not fully educated and not prepared for saneful living, he or she will remain uneducated, uninculcated, unhealthy, unsaneful and underdeveloped. In such a situation saneful functioning of the society will be hampered and, will lead to the dysfunctioning of the society. So both man and woman should be treated on equal footings regarding their upbringing, nourishment, character building, enculturation and education. But it is seen, that still women are considered inferior to men and, are put on lower social footing. Right from the beginning the women education has not been as important as that of men education. Still it is seen that many people ignore women education and do not give chance to their daughters to peep in the schools. In the village of the writer similar was the position sixty/fifty years ago. But with the efforts of political fighters trio—late Shri Maharshi Harishchandraji, Pt. late Shri Babu Ram Sharma (Munda) and late Shri Babu Malkhan Singhji, a Kanya Pathshala was opened. In the beginning many people had opposed the opening of this girls' primary school. After sometime it was converted into a co-educational middle school. Now it is a Rashtriya Co-education Inter College and about one thousand girls study in it. But still in many villages and towns girls are deprived of school education. There can be many reasons for this discrepancy about the negligence of girls' education. Out of these reasons, one reason is that the girls are regarded as anta-property. Mostly families in Indian society, excepting in few tribal tracts in Kerala and in Uttaranchal, are patriarchal families. The girls when married are supposed to go with their husbands and live lifelong with the families of their in-laws. According to this custom the girls are considered outsiders and others' property, that is, 'anta-property'. Parents think this since the girls are bound to go to another's homes and live there lifelong, then what is use of educating them. They do not realise that they also require some girls to be their daughter-in-laws and live with them lifelong. Another reason is that the parents fear some sort of unfair social behaviour with their girls by some uncivilised male members of the society. In society some unethical, unsocial happenings like molestations and rape cases of the girls are often noticed. The parents of the girls fear and do not send their daughters to schools. This tendency is generally found in rural areas. Lastly the parents think that they have to spend a lot on the marriage of their daughters, as they have to give dowry. They avoid to spend on the proper education of their daughters. After all they are anothers' property to whom they will devote lifelong. As such, majority of the girls in rural areas are not sent to schools. A recent survey depicts that ten percent of the girls do not see the doors of the schools. As such, majority of the girls remain uneducated, and their roles remain limited up to giving births to the children, upbringing them and doing the household work as cooking, washing cloths, feeding cattles and managing all other household activities.

Also this fact can never be denied or ignored that the males and females are biologically totally topsy-turvy as their bodies are totally opposite to each other, but they have to live together unitedly lifelong. They are united through marriage to live together and produce the future members of the society. Though male and female are biologically heterogenic and different to each other but they live together lifelong. This may termed as "unity in bio-heterogenic diversity" which is the necessary for the future members of the society. If the male and female are not united together the social existence cannot be possible. When a man and women after getting married are united and walk on the same track, why many women are deprived of educational facilities?

Not only the women are deprived of civic and social rights, in many countries still woman are considered degraded. Generally all societies are male dominated societies and females are neglected. Even in many countries women still have no voting rights. In many societies the women are forced to cover their faces and bodies. Generally in all societies women are tortured by their husbands. In many societies the husbands divorce their wives on small problems. As such, the women have no freedom to speak and walk. In their new homes in many women are tortured by their mother-in-laws for not bringing sufficient dowry. And many cases they are murdered. Women are enemy of the women. Women do not get equal rights with their husband pertaining to properties.

For a long time, many people are demanding thirty percent seats in the temples of our democracy—the Parliament and State Assemblies. But this demand has not been fulfilled so far. Many political parties are evading this demand on certain arguments. This fact cannot be denied, that still by and large women are deprived of their due rights. As such, it is necessary that all women should be educated, so that they become self-supporting. If the women are well-educated they will be able to depend and support themselves.

Also, the ladies are not safe. There occur many cases of molestations and rapes in the society daily. Bad elements in the society try to robe ladies. In many household helpers commits crimes like murders, thefts and chain pulling etc. The administrators and police are helpless. Such unsocial, heinous and uncivilised happenings can only be stopped by proper education of women. Giving school and college education cannot be a composite education of women. There is a need to educate the women comprehensively. The complete women education has wide and varied aspects. The need and versatility of women require the study women psyche and inculcate values and attitudes in women to face their psyche problems. In this regard there is a need to innovate and motivate the girls, while they are getting school education, to be aware about their future journey. After, being young they are to be married and to go another home. They must also be made aware about familial life. For this they must know that a joint family is a composite whole in which self-centredness and greed should not have any place. They have to live in a patriarchal setup in which they will have to respect the elders and love for all youngers. As such, adjustment in new homes for the girls is must. As such, women education should also try to mould the women psyche, so that, they may prove model housewives in future. For this the girls should learn to adjust with all family members. They should be broad and open minded, tolerants, sacrificers, sociable and open hearted. Women education should also inculcate the spirit of cooperation and sharing sociability and adjustment. This can only possible when girls may learn to discard their psyche of human greed, acquisition and self-centredness. The women should also be taught some elements of sociology and philosophy. The girls should know that they would be housewives and mothers and should be made aware that 'unity in bio-diversity' is the need of family life. In their educational programme there should be a provision for such education. Also the school education should arrange such co-curricular activities programmes, which could make the girls aware about their anta-property life. Through these programmes should be encouraged to know all about their future life—as housewife, as daughter-in-law and in future also mother-in-law. In other words, it can be said that the girls during their school education should be made aware about all of their genetic roles of women in their future life. They should be made aware about importance of 'unity in bio-diversity' in their future family life. The educational programme should also prepare the girls to fight for their rights. Some criminals make the girls and aged women as their targets. They should be taught some self-defence techniques as karate and use of some techniques for their defence. There is an adage "one girl is educated whole family is educated". If the girls are educated they will educate their children in future. Proper education makes the girls stringent to face life situations bravely. In the family, the girls should be given equal rights as given to their brothers. Also when they are married their in-laws should respect and give duly care to their daughter-in-laws. They society should also pay due attention to this aspect.

Many mothers spoils their daughter as they do not inculcate in them required work habits, with the result the girls find it difficult to adjust in their real homes. Many girls become megalomaniac due to too much of love. They always think that their decisions are always good. As a result, the girls as housewives fail to create a congenial atmosphere in the family. As such, proper attitudes should be inculcated during their familial as well as school education.

2

Education

Education is a recovery, as well as, life-building process. From the times immemorial, since the inception of society, the human beings have been educating and bringing up their offsprings. Not only human beings but animals have also been doing this activity since their emergence. Mere passing of information can never be education. Shri Jaetobhai Desai said that a child can never be taught, he or she can be brought up. So education is a process of bringing up and taking out of hidden potentialities of the child. Therefore, for educating the children, both boys and girls, a process should be applied which may innovate and motivate them to think, reason, analyse and comprehend and finally learn. Educating is done through familial ways, as well as, through school education. Because of 'unity in bio-diversity' as, the girls are to be married and go with their husbands, so, it is necessary that they should be partly educated in familial ways to live a happy married life. Therefore, there should be provision in school education to inculcate proper life attitudes in them. So it is necessary that the teachers while teaching in schools should be kind hearted towards the girls and nurture life attitudes in them, so that, they may know how to adjust in their future real home. So educational process should always develop attitudes for sincerity, integrity, devotion and erudition for learning and towards life situations. It is, therefore, necessary to know about education in detail.

GENESIS OF EDUCATION

It is necessary to understand the word 'education' etymologically. The English word 'education' is a derivation of Latin words 'educe', 'educatum' and 'educare', meaning to bring out and developing. So education is an act of bringing out human innate potentialities and developing various intellectual, social, physical, behavioural, aesthetical, mental as well as manual faculties of which they are unaware. So education entails knowing, learning, analysing and comprehending. Likewise, the 'Sanskrit' word 'Vidya' has emerged from Sanskrit word 'Vidh' meaning raising (उभारना). The word 'Siksha' has come out from the Sanskrit root 'Sikhs' meaning bringing up from within. Also the Arabic Word 'Talim' = Ta + alim means self-learning from within. As such, education does not mean teaching. Teaching is a process of educating, for which specific methods of teaching are used.

From the above description it can be inferred that 'Education' is bringing out the hidden potentialities of person and leading him or her on a correct path in his/her life. But the question arises what is to be brought out, from where it is to be brought out or raised? What is truth behind it? There are mythological descriptions and interpretations about it in our Hindu and Greek mythologies. These descriptions also have been repudiated by the later empirical thinkers. Aryans believed that the human soul is immortal, as it is part of Transcendental soul or Super soul—the *Paramatma*. In *Hindu Sankhya Yoga Darshan* it is stated that every soul which is embodied in a physical person is a part of the Bigger Soul, which is termed as *Paramatma* (परमात्मा) what we equate or presume with Almighty God. Another is 'atma' or individual soul (जीवात्मा), which is embodied in every physical person's body. So it is believed that every individual soul is part of the bigger 'whole', that is *Paramatma* (परमात्मा). When the physical body of a person gets exhausted and becomes old, the 'atma' (जीवात्मा) leave the body and after sometime, it comes to another body of human being or living being. This process is termed as transmigration of the human soul, which is termed as rebirth (पुर्नजन्म). And the soul is immortal.

Atma or human soul while embodied accumulates the acquires experiences gained by it through per-se (perception), gained by the sense organs of the human body in which the soul is embodied. What we remember, we remember what was experienced and stored by the human soul. This has been stated in *Hindu Naya-Veshiska Darshan*. According to Greek thinkers the recovery of these soul accumulated experiences which were gained and stored in previous life and supplemented further through experiences, is a process of education. This recovery is done through educating or bringing out these experiences through the logical process of teaching done by the teacher.

It is also believed that the Greeks came to know about the immortality of the soul from Indians. It is believed, as described by a Russian mythologist, it may be a true or a mere hunch or a pure imagination, that during the rule of Greek king Pericles (543 B.C.), the Spartans used to create troubles for their neighbours, as many of the countries are still doing in the present days also. Ultimately war erupted between Greeks and Spartans which continued for 27 years (431-404 B.C.). This war is known as Peloponnesian War. The population of Greece was about eight thousand and population of the Sparta was three thousand. But the Spartans were a marshal race. They had proficiency in using weapons and spreading the terrorism. There was a tradition in Spartans to test the efficacy of their new born male child. They used to slip the child from a hill slop. If the child is survived till coming to the ground, the child was worth living. As such, the Spartans used to prepare their male children to fight and terrorise their neighbours. As the Spartans gave big jolt to the Greeks. As a result of it, Pericles made military service compulsory for all able bodied Greeks between the age 18 years to 40 years by imposing a law of conscription. This was a kind of an emergency.

There existed individual differences in all times. Some Greeks liked to fight the Spartans some did not. Some want to the war front unwillingly. Those who did not dare to go to war front tried to escape. There was one Greek Sophist (name not known) who escaped military duty and fled to Egypt, where he tried to know why people fight each other. Getting no satisfactory reply, he went to Mesopotamia (present Iraq), where he was advised to go to Taxila in India, via Aryana (present Iran) and Gondaspur (present Afghanistan). Both these countries were Åryan countries and had deep relations with India. He stayed at Taxila for about 8 years. At Taxila, he studied all Indian schools of philosophy—(1) Theistic schools: (*a*) Sankhya-yoga, (*b*) Naya-Visheska, (*c*) Vedant and Adit Vedant and (2) Atheistic schools: (*a*) Buddhism, (*b*) Jainism and (*c*) Carvak. He also studied all Upanishads, Puranas, Aryankas and Shruties. He also studied Indian Epics: (*a*) Ramayana and (*b*) Mahabharata. He finally read Shrimad Bhagawat Gita and came to know about the immortality of the soul as various Indian scriptures and philosophical schools adhere to.

As already mentioned, according to Indians the human soul is permanent, invisible imperishable, undestructable and is part of the permanent, transcendental soul which is called *'Paramatma'* (परमात्मा). All individual souls (जीवात्मायें) are part of the bigger 'soul' or a whole that is *Paramatma* (परमात्मा) or God. Therefore all individual souls (जीवात्मायें) are immortal. Prime or Supreme soul (परमात्मा) is present in all human bodies, as such, all human beings are true representative of God and are equal. This is why Indian society in spite of its rigid caste system rests on the foundation of equality and is a homogenous society to some extent. The individual soul takes work from the human body. It acquires experiences through the sense organs of the body. It accumulates these experiences with it. And the human soul (जीवात्मा) takes these experiences when it leaves the human body after death. Bringing out these experiences from human soul or brain is called education. As for digging out from earth instruments like spade (फावड़ा), digging chisel are required, for bringing out human old experiences some methods like teaching and use of teaching aids are required.

The Greek Sophist after staying at Taxila about eight years and knowing that human soul is immortal and never dies, this is why Arjuna after listening sermons of Shrimad Bhagwat Gita from *Bhagwan* Krishna fought and won Mahabharata war, he went back to Greece to participate in Peloponnesian war. He went to King Pericles in Athens and offered himself to go to the war front. He told the King "That human soul never dies nor is destroyed. Only human body dies. Therefore, there is no reason to be afraid of war". With this adhoration the Greeks got encouraged. They fought the war against Spartans bravely. They not only defeated the Spartans but totally eliminated them. And the terror of Spartans was eliminated forever.

This message was picked up by other Greek Sophists thinkers and philosophers. They started thinking why individual's soul (जीवात्मा) does not die and is immortal? Socrates (470-399 B.C.) was an original thinker, speculator and philosopher. He used to think, reason, speculate and analyse himself about new things. Also he used to discuss all ontological, teleological, epistemological, axiological and also all sociological problems with his disciples in the street corners. Plato, Crito, Hereclitus, Pythagoras, Theatutes, Parmenides and Isocrates and many others were his important disciples with whom he used to discuss all important matters. His wife Xentippe was very self-centred, covert, introvert and nasty lady. She did not permit Socrates to allow his disciples to enter in her house. If any outsider dared to enter in her house, she used to pour a full pot of cold water over his head. This is why Socrates had not accepted that the women are worshipped in India as was told by the Greek Sophist who had studied at Taxila staying there for eight years. But he was conscious to know about the reality of the Indian concept of immortality of human soul, so he discussed such an important ontological question in detail with his disciples in the street corner before his house.

Indians merely said that the human soul is immortal. It cannot be destroyed, burnt or buried. But no concrete proof about the immortality of soul is available in Indian scriptures. Also no concrete proof in this regard has been advanced nor given by the later seers. The Greeks were eager to know why human soul does not die along with the human body? Socrates discussed this ontological question at length with his disciples and finally came to believe that human soul is actually immortal. Later on, his disciple Plato, after the death of his teacher Socrates, compiled the dialogues of Socrates with his disciples. These dialogues covered all problems as mentioned above relating to truth, beauty, justice, ontology, epistemology and axiology. In Phaedo, the concept of immortality of soul was discussed in detail. Further, the concept of education was discussed in dialogues Menu and Republic VII and VII and Symposium at length. In Phadelo along with the concept of immortality the concept of education was also discussed. Three proofs were advanced proving the immortality of the soul. These are: (1) law of contrariness, (2) law of form and (3) law of reminiscence. In Law of Reminiscence the concept of education was also discussed.

Law of Contrariness

Everything in this world comes and goes. One who was born and brought up will positively die. Like sun arises in the morning and sets in the evening and every day is followed by a night and another day. So coming of day and night is a regular feature. Similarly the life of a person which comes, ought to go. As such, life follows death and death follows life. There is a continuous circle of coming and going. This process always entails contrariness. There is some transcendental element which keeps this coming and going process on and, continue giving life to the physical world. This transcendental element is nothing but soul (जीवात्मा), which is part of the 'Omnipresent', 'Non-visible', Undestructable 'whole', that is God which is immortal. This is *Paramatma* (परमात्मा) or super soul or God according to Hindu Philosophy. Therefore, soul (जीवात्मा) is immortal, till souls remains in the body remains alive.

Law of Form

Since everything in this world is temporary, illusionary and perishable, this temporariness has a permanent base or image or form elsewhere. This idea is analogous to the Indian idea of *Maya* (illusion) and *Stirtha* (स्थिरता) (permanence). The things or lives in this world are all temporary, illusionary and perishable. And permanent base of all these world lives or resides elsewhere, which is invisible, untouchable, and permanent. This is a transcendental form. This idea of permanent form is analogous to the Indian idea of Supreme Soul or *Paramatma* (परमात्मा) or God, which is imbibed in all individual souls. In other words, all individual souls are part of bigger 'whole' that is Almighty God. The individual soul is parmount and governs the human body.

Law of Reminiscence

We remember many things. How do we remember? What is the power that makes us to remember? It is the soul (परमात्मा). Since it does not die, it keeps the experiences stored with it, it is due to the enlightenment of the soul we remember all past experiences. Therefore, the soul is permanent, imperishable, undestroyable and immortal. The process of education is nothing but remembrance of the past experiences. Education is a recovery of past experiences which is already with the soul.

In Indian thought *Naya-Visheska Darshan* (theistic philosophy) a more advanced convincing argument is advanced in this regard. The Naya-Visheska Darshan argues that, we only remember till we are alive. A dead body cannot remember. We remember what we had experienced through our sense perception in the past. We perceive through our sense organs—ear, nose, touch, taste and smell. But the moment human body dies, and the soul leaves it, human organs become inactive and dead, neither the sense organs perceive nor the human brain or head remembers. Then what is the force behind remembering? It is nothing but human soul. Till the human soul resides in human body, the body can see, hear, smell, taste, touch and remember. When the human body dies, the soul goes along with it already acquired experiences and transmigrate to another body. Taking out all these already acquired experiences is nothing but education (शिक्षा). This is done through remembering.

Various thinkers have defined education on these lines, though they did not attribute total creditability to the soul for all of our education. Even Plato did not give direct credibility to the soul for the emergence of education. He said that education is the result of per-se (sense perception) plus comprehension. Some perception leads to comprehension, learning and knowledge. Aristotle laid stress on the analysis of the matter for acquiring education. Rene' Descartes believed in innate ideas in human beings and laid stress on thinking, reasoning and comprehending for taking out the innate ideas which are possessed by the human body at the time of birth. Rene' Descartes believed that through thinking education is possible. He said that he existed due to "Cogito Ergo Sum" that is thinking and reasoning. British Empiricist, Philosopher, John Locke, repudiated the rationalistic theory of Rene' Descartes. He believed the mind of the child at the time of his/her birth is blank like 'Tabula Rasa' that is, 'blank state'. As the child grows he/she perceives the physical things and gets primary and secondary ideas through sense perception and writes on his/her blank mental slate. As such, the individual is born without any previous knowledge or experience. As he/she grows, he/she perceives and gathers knowledge. At the time of birth an individual's mind, is like a blank slate. As such, John Locke's thinking is against the hidden knowledge stored in human mind, as believed by mythologists. For him the main source of knowledge is experience. And the teacher while teaching the students should provide experiences sincerely and strictly, and John Locke termed the process as 'hardening' in education. If a child is to be made aware about hail storming, he/she should be forced to go out while it is hail storming. This formula of education can be suitable for the modern boys and girls in the present empiricist age. A few quotations of the thinkers on education as below:

"Education is a training which leads you 'to hate what you ought to hate' and 'love what you ought to love'". —*Plato*

"Education is the creation of a sound mind in a sound body". —*Aristotle*

"Education is defined as a natural, harmonious growth and development of mans innate powers". —*Pestalozzi*

"Education is defined as a process of development which consists of passage of human beings from infancy to maturity, the process to which he adapts himself in harmonious ways to his physical, social and spiritual environment". —*T. Raymond*

"Education is the manifestations of perfection already in man". —*Swami Vivekananda*

"By education I mean an all-round drawing out of the best in child and man's body, mind and spirit. Literacy itself is no education". —*M.K. Gandhi*

"Education is the development of capacities which could enable man to control his environment". —*John Dewey*

"Education is to equip man to understand truth, beauty and goodness". —*Socrates*

"Education is to create humbleness of mind". —*Dr. Arnold*

"Education is thought that leads bodily expression". —*R.N. Tagore*

"Education is to know what one does not know and behave well". —*John Ruskin*

Education of the child should be according to nature. When the child is born he is free but after his birth he finds himself in chains. There should not be social restrictions on the child". —*J.J. Rousseau*

"Child's education should be based on play". —*Madam Montessori*

"Child's feelings should not be hurt. Education should lay stress on emotional development of the child". —*Froebel*

As such, viewing the above opinions it can assumed that education is a process of development of latent or innate, potentialities or capacities enshrined in the child or student or an individual. Mere passing of information or imposing one's knowledge upon the students can never be education. Every child or student has/her innate capacities and capabilities. The child or student is not an ignorant client. The development of the innate capacities and capabilities is education. The nature has gifted every body or girl with specific unique capabilities and capacities. In comparison to other living beings human child has been gifted with bigger brain to think, reason, comprehend and take a decision for appropriate action. He has been rewarded with moving hands for acting and flexible legs for walking. Other animals lack all these facilities. A student cannot be dictated to accept the diction of the teacher, as an ignorant client of a doctor or a lawyer accepts their advice. Therefore, it is essential to educate the students (boys or girls) in a proper or logical manner and in a congenial atmosphere while teaching, so as to develop their innate capacities.

3

General Aims of Education

Before considering what to teach, how to teach, we should know what we want to achieve? In other words, what should be the prime aim of education for which the teaching is to be done? Educational aims always are generally framed keeping in view the national requirements. National needs are always determined keeping in view the present social structure, culture and economic base of the society. Socio-economic, religious, moral, political and cultural heritage weave the social structure of any society and the country. If the economic conditions of a country, which provide job opportunities are not good the people cannot prosper. They, generally, remain jobless and poor. The first and foremost aim of the educational programme should be to provided job oriented education to the younger generation, so that they may earn for their livelihood easily and, may lead a happy sane life. As a matter of fact every society and state should try to create conditions for the economic development for its citizens. The economic conditions for the development of country's economic infrastructure should be laid on a logically equality based foundation. Along with this educational aims should look to the enculturation of the younger generation. Education should inculcate some socially desired attitudes like good work habits, simple living high thinking, cooperation, respect for elders and respect for fair sex, preparation for fighting the existing social stigmas and social crimes. Also educational aims should take into consideration the human psyche of males and females. Finally, the educational aims should concentrate on the cultural development and on checking the cultural diffusion and acculturation. And, finally the educational aims should be designed to develop a social ethics in the younger generation considering the social needs of the social millieu. Many thinkers have suggested some core aims of education briefly mentioned as under:

Dr. Arnold	:	Humble mind
Socrates	:	Understanding of truth, beauty and goodness
Aristotle	:	Magnanimous mind
Nietzsche	:	Ideal is not that of Christianity
Christ	:	One who loves
Immanuel Kant	:	No action of which love is not motive can never be virtuous
Brutus	:	Duty
Conficius	:	Family Care
Bertrand Russell	:	Neither dogmas, no scepticism but relief
M.K. Gandhi	:	To create conditions for upbringing of man
R.N. Tagore	:	Conditions for natural upbringing
Plato	:	Appropriate action
T. Raymond	:	Laying process of development
Swami Vivekananda	:	Manifestation of perfection
J. Krishnamurti	:	Creating conditions for enculturation, cultural development and love for nature

As such, divergent views and opinions about the aims of education have emerged in different societies. The different societies subscribe to different aims of education according to their philosophical thinking and social structures and related needs. The economy of an economically backward country can only be improved through appropriate educational structure and, many such countries have to frame educational aims accordingly. A fundamentalist theocratic state, as noticed in many Muslim countries, will try to impose teaching of religion as a compulsory subject. A secular state like India, where so many countries believing in different religions and faiths live, does not allow teaching of any religion in schools. A communist country, in order to perpetuate communistic ideology will not also have place for religious teaching in schools. A capitalist country always would like to adopt 'Laissez Faire' theory for the development of economy. As such, the main aim of the education in a capitalist country will be to create a cut-throat competition in economic field and, the educational aims will be framed accordingly. A terrorist state, like Sparta did in the past, and few countries are still doing, would like to train their younger generation in terrorism. The Spartan's educational aim was to promote terrorism. They had terrorised the Greeks and ultimately war between Greeks and Spartans had erupted which had continued for twenty-seven years. There are still many countries which wage a proxy war against democratic secular countries. A democratic country will always try to mould its future citizens to be true democrats and frame educational aims accordingly. Such a country always tries to perpetuate its democratic institutions through good education. As such, if we peep into the history educational aims have always been in flux from society to society as well as from country to country.

Earlier traditional education was classical in nature and conservative methods of educational aims as well as teaching were used. Men were to read religious scriptures. They were required to follow the religious codes of conduct. In India, the Brahmans were supposed to read Vedas and to tell the people about Vedas and other religious scriptures like Upanishads, Aryankas, Puranas, Brahmans Shruties, Epics—Ramayana and Mahabharata and Shrímad Bhagwat Gita. The main purpose of such education was to equip the masses with classical religious knowledge in order to educate the common people about the *Karma* (कर्मा), *Dharma* (धर्मा), *Adharma* (अधर्म) and *Kama* (कामा) so that sanety may prevail in the society. Likewise, in Greece, the Athenians were asked to learn 'Homer', the Chinese were asked to learn confucious, the Christian were asked to read the Bible and the Muslims were asked to learn 'Quran' and Hadees. Athenians paid reverence to the God. The Indians were asked to believe that good actions (कर्मा) can give *Moksha*, so the old Indians laid stress not to commit *'adharma'* (अधर्मा), that is non-religious action so that sanety and homogeneity may prevail in the society. Likewise, all old societies had subscribed certain religious codes for their citizens so that harmony may prevail. All societies had a notion to enjoy life as an aesthetical conception for which brotherhood, equality and cooperation were necessary. And educational aims were designed accordingly. Greeks were energetic and Chinese were lazy. They (Greek) devoted their energy to promote art and culture, examination of natural flora and fauna, thinking, reasoning contemplation and propitiating new knowledge. Politics and propitiating moulded educational aims to Greece. The Greek educational aims gave energy to Greeks. Whereas, when a Chinese official retired he used to go to the hills and write poems.

Chinese education produced stability and promoted arts. But it failed to develop science, so China lacked progress. Perhaps this happened due to scepticism. Passionate beliefs neither progress nor give stability. Science when attacks the traditional thinking, has its own structure and creates an atmosphere of epistemacy and analysis. Same happed to Indians as for a longer time they stuck to such beliefs which did not motivate them to progress. Indians rulers fought each other, with the result they became slaves, and remained slaves for about thousand years. Indian religious dogmatism created condition that many Indians were converted to the religions of the foreigners. The result was a long chronic national weakness. The belief of some upper castes that they are superior made them megalomaniac. They were educators also. But they never thought of appropriate educational aims. All this made the Indians self-centred and disunited which encouraged the foreigners to occupy the country and exploit the Indian human beings and natural resources. This happened due to unclear unidealogical and undesirable educational aims.

In the present materialistic pugnacious world energy is necessary for self-conservation. Energy sources are necessary for human existence, which cannot be possible without the knowledge of science. So educational aims should be so framed that science could progress. Without science economic progress is not possible. Without economic progress neither social institutions nor democracy can progress. So educational aims should give due attention to the teaching of science along with other subjects. And boys and girls both should be encouraged to study science.

In old times traditional education was confined to a small percentage of the population of the countries be it Greece, Rome, China or India. With the passage of time the countries felt the need of universal education and prepared to adopt new type of education, that is education for all. Modern Japan has a tendency to make the nation great. This motto is the supreme aim of Japanese education. Japanese educational aim is to train the manpower in such a way that the Japanese prove great before the great pioneers without sacrificing their own culture. The Japanese education produce a devoted, active, sincere and religious man and women workforce which could truly adhere to shintie religion. And due to this fact Japanese could emerge as one of the most powerful industrialised nation, even out of the debris of Hiroshima and Nagasaki. They could also explicate a national character.

Western world tried to erode the cultures cottage industries, trade, religious and social structures of many Eastern and African countries for making their own industrialisation and westernisation a success. And finally they had captured many of these countries. The western world further aimed at cultural diffusion and acculturation which they could achieve through the educational aims of their educational system they had imposed on these countries. Many of these Asian and African countries lost their social customs, traditions, cultural heritage and social structures to great extent. India became worst victim of this acculturatory feature. China had resisted the penetration of western cultural diffusion for a longer time. Finally, Chinese were also affected, but they could protect their cultural heritage to some extent. Due to this China could emerge as a big nation.

There are many organisation which are still dogmatic and follow outdated beliefs which do not permit them to come out and move forward. Such societies do not adopt new educational aims. As such, these societies remain backward.

Educational aims in all societies are framed according to their socio-economic needs. A nation having democratic form of government would like to see its citizens purely democratic and humanistic. A society having speculative bent of mind will always allow free expression and discussion on all matters. This trend will lay foundation of an ideal sane society. Some democratic ideals will be the base of the educational aims in such a society. Societies following such ideal educational aims will be ideal sane societies and their educational structures will be considered ideal educational structures. Hegel and Nietzsche were the prepounders of such educational structure and related educational aims. Nations having communist governments like to produce obedient citizens who do not voice their dissent. Such governments lay down educational aims which sent to their system. Countries having capitalist economy would like to make their future citizen competitive and acquisitive. In such a system axiological norms will go to the backyard. And in such countries there remains a wide divergence between people to people. Some remain very rich, some very poor. So capitalist governments always adopt a pragmatic approach while laying down educational aims. So educational aims are always decided according to social structures and related needs.

In the present age of science and technology and consequent industrialisation education is an instrument of change. And the school is a workshop where this instrument, that is, education, is developed. The teacher is an operator of educational instrument for bringing social change. He/she proceeds as per educational aims. A nation cannot prosper if it is lagging behind in education. And if we look to the nature of man and woman ontologically and biologically that the man and woman are best equipped by the nature to exploit the natural resources for their use. As man and woman are biologically topsy-turvy in body structure and have divergent psyche, the educationists should give some divergence in educational aims for both man and woman. Both man and woman of course are rational beings. But they are greedy also. The educational aims should also cover this aspect. And educational aims should be so framed that these may inculcate rationality in human beings for being moral, homogeneous, sane and cooperative. They should be competent to earn their livelihood honestly and may confirm to socio-axiological norms so as to keep the greedy human nature under control.

As a matter of fact every state tries to improve its economic conditions for the betterment of its citizens. But such a development should always entail some moral norms which may carry on a logically honest, corruption free economic development. The youngers should get instruction in social ethics along with training in economic activities. The younger generation should be made aware about the bad effects of greed, hedonism and xenophilism. They should be made aware about the bad effects of corruption.

In olden times the elderly men/women and grandparents used to make the younger generation aware about the menace of corruption. They used to tell the younger generation about 'dharma' (धर्म), *netikta* (नैतिकता) and *anetikta* (अनैतिकता) through action theory (कर्मा सिद्धान्त). These teachings are more or less absent in the present society because of dys-functioning of joint family system and sound community life. Present period is over ridden with activism which is done for the material gains. Both the parents go out for doing jobs leaving the children at the mercy of commercial schools like crèches and nursery schools. The parents, being parts of nuclear family, expect the schools to discharge their familial duties. How can the teachers do this tedious parental familial job while they are busy in preparing the students for annual examinations and in so many other activities.

However, when both the parents generally do jobs, the younger generation should be educated about moral values at the school which is also very very difficult due to absence of religious education due to the policy of secularism. This can be done if some knowledge of sociology and thereby axiology could be given a place in educational aims. Then only the future guardians may adopt some norms of honesty in earning their livelihood. Therefore, the prime aim of education should be to make the students aware about the honesty and sanety in social life. Nobody can live without these in a society. Providing social norms or inculcating these in the young students should be the prime of educational aim. This will make the society an ideal society.

Nobody can live without a society. Even beasts, birds, animals, insects and bees form and maintain their societies. Society is a big whole of which man and woman are parts. They should be trained to live in the society harmoniously in their homes as well as in the society. So educational aims should reflect the ways and means of social harmony and homogeneity and also the importance of social collectivity. For this all social agencies and educational institutions should strive.

While framing the educational aims social perspectives as equality, gender bias, cultural development and protection, what kind of men and women are required in the society should be kept in mind. Does the society require acquisitive or greedy men and women who run after money and exploit others? Or the society needs just, rational, sane, tolerant, cooperative men and women who will never try to exploit others. Therefore, for preparing just and honest human beings who could protect the society, logical and appropriate educational aims should be prepared and implemented. For doing this the educationists should try to know about all types of socio-political structures which exist in the world. And after visualising capitalist, democratic, autocratic, theocratic and social orders a suitable decision regarding educational aims should be taken. One of the prime aim of education should be the personal, social and cultural development of the individuals. Society is a collectively, rather a big whole, of which all individuals are parts. So the personal development of the individual, be it a man or woman should be so designed that a person should always regard the society as his/her mother. And this demands education for social cohesion, integration and cooperation for a stronger sane society. A covert corrupt and selfish person can never be useful for the society. As such, appropriate development of the individuals demands the rational educational aims. A few tips for these aims are given below:

1. To inculcate a self-introspection. An individual should know what is good or bad for him/her in the interest of social integrity, national pride. An individual must know the truth.
2. Through education good attitudes should be inculcated in the individual so as to instill social acceptability in him/her. For this inculcation of some sane values, good character, moral attitudes, spirit of active participation in social activities for a common cause in the society are necessary. Spiritual awareness, respect for elders and for fair sex and love for the weak are also necessary. Finally inculcation a spirit to treat all on equal footing is necessary.
3. Though our country is secular but often some communal riots occur in the society. Our educational aims should inculcate religious tolerance, respect for all religious faiths and various religious communities for maintaining social and religious harmony in the country.
4. An individual, be it man and woman is not a mere physical being or object which has only a form. An individual is a conscious being. A conscious being requires some concepts through which experiences are gained and used in right direction for proper use. Our educational structure through its aims should ignite consciousness of the human beings.
5. Our educational aims should develop an intentionality and capacity in the students to visualise, analyse and comprehend physical things for correct use.
6. Our educational aims should inculcate a spirit of tolerance, sharing, cooperation and commitment to goal by adhering to social values, traits and customs.

7. Our educational aims should enculturate the students and should take steps to stop the blind acculturation through cultural diffusion.
8. Our educational aims should focus on the life-building of our future guardians. Good future living should be the main aim of our educational programmes.
9. Creation of an aesthetic sense in the students should also be one of prime educational aims. A creative person is necessary for the cultural development of the country.
10. There should not be any place for discrimination in educational programmes. All students should be given equal opportunities in schools as well as in colleges.

The teachers can contribute a lot in achieving the educational aims but not alone. The administration should come forward to help the teachers in the realisation of educational aims.

BASES OF EDUCATIONAL AIMS

Before educating the children one should know what are their life requirements in the society. Because in view of social, economic, political, humanistic needs of the individuals, the individuals require different kinds of life orientations. For example, though the men and women make a 'whole' of both by creating a 'unity in bio-diversity', still their life attitudes, functions and devotions differ. Therefore, the bases or orientations of their work culture differs. So the bases of educational aims also vary. So educational aims for boys and girls should be specific. Man, since the dawn of the human society and civilisation has been living in varied and heterogeneous situations, that is, in different climate conditions, speaking different languages, adapting different cultures, believing in different faiths and adopting different life styles. So the man and woman have been trying to adjust themselves in the wide and varied life situations and, have been living accordingly. The child is born without culture. So the man and woman have been jointly moulding the behaviours of the child accordingly to social needs and accepted rules of the society. Since the man and woman have different roles to play in their lives, there should be a sort of diversity in framing educational aims for boys and girls. This has not been given a place in our educational aims. In different societies we find different educational aims, but not a clear distinction for woman education and man education is still found in educational programmes.

In early primitive societies the transmission of culture was the prime aim of education, so emphasis was laid on enculturation. The purpose of primitive education was to mould the child in the manner in which he becomes a good member of the tribal community. These good manners were clearly specified for male and female children. Obviously, because of variety of countless cultures in the primitive societies the roles of males and females used to be identified and, they used to be educated and trained in specific activities accordingly. So the educational roles were decided according to the roles of males and females. Margaret Mead has called this as empathy, identification and initiation. The tribal initiation of curriculum does not include practical subjects. Instead it consisted whole set of cultural values, tribal religion, myths, philosophy, history, tribal knowledge and other life related knowledge. The tribal women used to play a vital role in inculcating the related life values in the youngers.

As the societies become more and more complex, the scope of educating and learning more and more increased. So the educational aims also increased. In Egypt, culture and education were preserved and controlled by the priests—a powerful intellectual class in Egyptian theocracy served as political bulwark, and their guidance advances were made in many fields so the educational aims consisted training in skills, relating to areas as architecture, engineering, sculpture besides training in religious activities. Likewise, in Mesopotamia educational aims were prescribed for training of scribes for government jobs and priests for the preservation and practice of religion. But women were not given priorities for doing these jobs. In India the certain women having religious bent of mind were worshipped like Durga, Saraswati, Lakshmi and Shakti. But no specific educational aims were prescribed for women education through female psyche is more or less different than the males.

Indian culture is considered to be one of the classical cultures of the world, the main aim of which was to live in peace and harmony in the society. So main aim of education in classical India was to prepare an individual for saneful living, and educational aims were laid down accordingly. For achieving this end for suitable education, Gurukula system of education was developed accordingly. This system was good for preparing a sane person, but this system was only open to the males of the two upper castes, Brahmins and Kshatriyas. The other two castes Vaishyas and Sudras were not allowed entry in the Gurukulas. Also the women of all castes including Brahman, Kshatriyas were not allowed Gurukula education. Later on, the Buddhist and Jain schools laid down the similar educational aims. But these schools also ignored the women education. Good government was the basic aim of education in China. The family was the basic unit. Educational aims were laid down for modelling human character, participation in rituals, respect to elders, good behaviour were the basis of aims of education.

In Israel, ancient education was familial, thus moral, religious, good relations between the teachers and students and respect to the elders were the bases of educational aims. In ancient Greece the ancient Greece the education was aimed at to create good citizens who could honour truth, beauty, goodness and ethical values. But the Greek 'dialogues' do not show any specific roles of women. Only the harsh and uncivilised behaviour of Xentippe, wife of Socrates is mentioned, which shows the psyche of women needs appropriate education for women in every society. In Sparta, contrary to Greece, the educational aims were designed to prepare the individual for warfare. There is no mention of women's role. The Spartans were trained under the strict discipline to obey blindly the orders of the superiors, at the same time the Spartans were trained in dissimilation (espionage and terrorism). On the Spartan pattern many countries are running such educational camps in many countries till today. In Rome, the quality of Latin education conjunctured on rural development, dominated by landed aristocracy engaged in exploiting lands.

The characteristics of Persian Empire, due to the elements dominated by the Persian religious physical environment, activists Zoroastrian religion and ethics were of expansionist nature. These elements made the Persian adventurous aims mingled with intense national feelings which motivated them to lay down educational aims accordingly. The development of good thought, good deeds and good work were the basic aim of Persian education. Likewise, in Byzantine empire education which patronised by Greeks and Christian orthodoxy, framed educational aims with the changing times. Russian educational aims changed with the circumstances emerged with the time. Earlier it was influenced by Greek and Christian orthodoxy but, under the new Christian regime it was changed according to the communist philosophy. Though the Islamic world preserved the Greco-Byzantine combined with Russian elements of philosophy and Indians thought for a long time and based their educational aims accordingly. Later, the Muslim theocratic orthodoxy adopted its own aims of education. In Muslim world the women are not treated on the same footing as men are treated.

Above all alone the nature of man, keeping supremacy remained the main factor in deciding the educational aims almost in all different societies. In many societies rational thinkers made humanity as the prime aim of the education. In societies where individuality dominated the life educational aims have been such which make the individual competitive and challenging. So the educational aims have always been decided in different orientations. Divergence of views and opinions will always produce different types of educational aims.

Different societies ascribe to different set of aims of education according to their culture and social structures. A fundamentalist theocratic state, as we notice in some Muslim countries will make religion compulsory as a school subject. A country like India where so many communities believing in different religions will have secular notion of religions. No religious aim will entail in educational aims. A communist country would like to perpetuate the communist ideology and the school curriculum shall have a place for it. A capitalist society would like to adopt 'Laissez Faire' in the economy of its state and, aim of education shall be to generate a spirit of competition basing on democratic norms. Religious and philosophic ideals also provide basis of aims for education. As such, if we peep into history of education we shall find that the educational aims have always been in a flux from society to society. And interests of the fair sex have always been ignored by male dominated society.

So, rarely the human bio-diversity of human beings that is woman and man has been taken into consideration while making the base of educational aims. Of course, woman and man are two important parts of human whole who are joined together by the social institution of marriage and, there is a 'unity in human bio-diversity'. Woman and man live together lifelong, make the existence of society possible. But it is an utmost social necessity to give equal rights to both the partners of human bio-diversical whole which could be possible by providing equal opportunities in all fields including education. Both of them have specific body structures and mental psyche. The bodies of woman and man are topsy-turvy. The man has body to do more physical and manual work. Woman has a body to bear the child, bring up the child. As such, the woman is supposed to impart necessary familial education for the life development of the child and make him/her a sane citizen. On the other hand, the man is supposed to earn and sustain the family. But this social situation also is going to be topsy-turvy. Man wants that his life partner should also earn and contribute in the family expenses. This is why contemporary boys want to have educated girls who may become their earning partner. As such, the present woman also has to go through arduous family situations. She has to do a job, bring up her children and also to do household work. Her husband hardly contribute in the household affairs. As such, while deciding the educational aims for girls and boys these bases of educational aims should be considered. And educational aims be framed taking into consideration these situations, psyche and social equality.

4

Women Education

The men and women are two parts of a natural genetic whole. It is an 'unity in bio-diversity'. The nature made them to live together throughout their lives and produce their offsprings for the continuance of the human society. Of course, the women and men are biologically different, opposites and topsy-turvy but they are for common cause, that is, human lifelong harmonious living, and for the continuance of human race. As such, they should got an equal chance for development for lifelong living. For this they should be educated on equal footing. Since their lifelong common function is the continuance and sustenance of human society. But their functioning is bit different. The man is supposed to earn for living. The woman is supposed to perform genetic function, that is, to produce human offsprings with the help of her male life partner and, to bring them up, educate them for lifelong good social living. So, the woman has to impart all sort of necessary familial education. As such, the woman and man are two kinds of pillars of the human family, like the pillars of a building. If the one pillar of the building is weak the building will collapse. Likewise, the woman and man, being two pillars of human genetic whole, they should not be weak in any sense. Both should be healthy, socially developed and well-educated. This is in the interest of the complete whole of the human beings, that is, the human society. This will make the human beings harmonious living possible. This is also necessary for the peace and prosperity of the whole world. So, women need upbringing and education equal to men.

But, from the beginning since the dawn of the society the woman has always been considered weaker than the man and was downgraded in respect of her social, economic, cultural, political and epistemic rights. Being considered physically weak than the man, both the parents of the woman and, in-laws of the women always did not considered women fit for taking the outdoor responsibilities. So the society did not pay due attention to the socio-economic, socio-cultural, political and epistemic development rights of the woman.

As such, the women community suffered a lot and could not be educated well in comparison to the man community. From the very beginning, the community and society as a whole had made up its mind, about the young girls, the future women, that they are 'anta-property' (परायाधन या अनन्या). They are only for "unity in bio-diversity" for genetic purpose. They are to be married with their male partners, within the ethnic group having different totems (गोत्रा). They have to live lifelong with their life partners, that is, husbands, and perform their genetic duties, that is giving births to the children and to bring them up and educate them for lifelong living. They have to do other family duties as cooking, washing cloths and maintaining the household. For bringing up their children they have to impart familial education for inculcating good life attitudes in their children for morality development, character building and personality development. While living in their real homes, that is 'Sasural', the women have to observe some familial customs as doing *purdah* from family as well as community elders. In spite of the fact that the women give births to younger generation and do a lot of family work, they are the real source of human life-building. As such, the women are the moulders of the youngers who become the members of the society. But the woman has ever been considered inferior to the man. And due to this fact, women from the very beginning have not been given full opportunity for required education.

In many societies still the women are not given equal treatment as given to the men. They are harassed, maltreated and even beaten by their husbands. Also, the women are the enemy of the women. The mother-in-law (सास) and the sister-in-law (ननन्द) are on the top list of harassers of the daughter-in-laws. They forget that they are also daughter-in-laws. This kind of treatment by the women to women is nothing but mental as well as physical torture which proves a serious handicap in women education. This fact also cannot be denied that women in many societies were given treatment of divine women. As in India, many women like Saraswati, Lakshmi, Shakti, Parvati, Chandi Devi, Vaishnav Devi, Kali are given divine status and are still worshipped throughout the country. Also the virgin girls in India are still worshipped. But still, the general condition of the women in India is deplorable. The rate of crimes against the women is still increasing day by which is becoming a great hurdle for the women education. The men who commit rapes and do molestations of women are becoming beasts and barbarous day by day. They (very few) do not hesitate raping their own daughters and nieces. And the administration is becoming incompetent in handling such an awful law situation. This is happening due to delaying justice to the women by our courts. In some countries the women are not given such respect as are given in India. This happening due to the unsocial psyche about the women. The Greek did so because their women are not following the required social character. Even Xentippe wife of the renowned philosopher Socrates did not allow anybody to enter her house. Even the disciple of Socrates were not allowed to enter in her house. If anybody or any of his disciple dared to enter in Socrates house, she used to pour a full pot (an earthen pot) of water over his head. Such ladies, even they are literate, cannot be said educated as education contains a wide spectrum of social behaviour.

In the present materialistic age the women are only considered a bio-genetic necessity and nothing else. This is why boys' families want girls as the brides for the boys. The girls' (brides) parents want to get rid off their daughters thinking or considering them anta-property (पराया-धन). Once the girls are married they are thrown in others houses which become their real home. After the marriage, the girls' side keep rapport with their daughter for a short period. After this, they do not dare to know about them and treat their girls as bio-garbage. As such, the girls' parental relatives such as brothers, and nephews totally turn their backs to the married girls, and cut off their links with the married girls. They think that after marrying these girls with others and sending them to other families, these girls are *paraya dhan* (पराया-धन) and they have nothing to do. Even some women are ignored by ill of her parental kith and kins, who do not ask her or enquire how is living, whether she is healthy or not? In such a situation, when many women have lost their husbands live in a very bewildered situation having no means of livelihood. Had they would have been educated and prepared to face such awkward situation, they would have been saved from such an ugly life situation. As such, the women education is a social necessity of the day.

In India, in olden Vedic period, the main aim of education was preparation of an individual for saneful happy living. And this was supposed to be done for all. For this, it was considered necessary to inculcate religious faith and a sense of spirituality in all citizens—men and women. This was done along with general education, which contained Sanskrit language (संस्कृत भाषा), mathematics (गणित), astrology (ग्रह विज्ञान), science (विज्ञान) and handicrafts (हस्त कलायें), that is, art and crafts. The general education and religious education and inculcation a sense of spirituality was taught in Gurukula Ashramas informal way. The Gurukula Ashramas were situated in jungles on the river banks, and were run by the society. The state had no control over Gurukula Ashramas. These were residential educational institutions where all *shishyas* (students) and *Gurus* (teachers) used to live together under the roof of Gurukula Ashramas. This was considered necessary for the students to inculcate in them a spirit of simple religious living to be away from their parents, who were supposed to pour too much of love on them. Too much of love without strictness is always poisonous. In Gurukulas only the male children of two upper castes—Brahmans and Kshatriyas were admitted. The women of any castes and the male children of Vaishyas and Sudras were not at all admitted in Gurukulas. Since the women were considered as part of the male-female whole, it was believed that their husbands will educate them. The artisan castes taught their male children non-formally involving them in their hereditary vocations. A carpenter used to train his son in carpentry. Likewise, all tradesmen like blacksmith, tinsmith, coppersmith and mason used to train their male children in their family trades. But usually the girls were supposed to be trained in the household works by their mothers, aunts and grand mothers. There was no provision for formal educations for the girls in *Pathshalas* (schools). Neither the women were permitted to join the Gurukulas nor they were allowed to work with their father in their family trades. Their training was only limited to household affairs. That too, was affected if any girl had a step-mother. The girls of rich upper castes were usually taught at home some subjects like language, religious spirituality and arithmetic by the home teachers. However, some of rich castes girls were allowed to attend the religious discourses in the Ashrama of Rishis and Munis along with the elderly persons, where they used to take part in debate and discussions. As such, the women education was totally ignored in ancient India. Main reason for this ignorance of women education was considering them anta-property (पराया-धन) or anothers' properly (अनन्या). The girls were to be married and sent with their husbands forever. This is why the parents of the girls generally evaded girls' education. Another reason was 'captive' marriage. A strong Raja if liked or loved a particular girl, he used to force the girls' parents to marry the girl with him. If his request was not accepted he used to manage to capture the girls through kidnapping or snatching her per force. He used to marry the captured girl in spite of the unwillingness of the girl. Many such cases happened in Ramayana, Mahabharata period. Gandhari was a captured wife of blind emperor Dhritrashtra. Maharaj Prithviraj Chauhan of Indraprastha (Delhi) had captured the daughter of Raja of Kannauj. This kind of unsocial happenings of kidnappings had affected girls' education very badly in the past in India.

During the Muslim the situation more worsened, because according to Muslim Hadees, the Muslim women are required to do *purdah* and restrict their movements outside their homes. Many Muslim rulers like old Hindu Rajas tried to marry the Hindu girls of their choice. Akbar had married a Hindu Rajput girl. Such incidents made many Hindus cautious, about their girls. They kept their girls in a hidden atmosphere. The married Hindu girls started to do *purdah*. Under Muslim 'Shariat' a Muslim can have four wives. Recently a newspaper report that a Muslim ruler age 36 years has eleven wives and 24 children. All this affected the girls' education in all communities. The Hindus restricted their girls going out of their homes. So the girls stopped going to Kanya Pathshalas. The Muslim like Hindus had special Madarsas like Darul-Ulem, Deoband in which the girls entry was restricted.

After grabbing the power and making the Indian slaves, the English Administrators' main aim was to perpetuate their rule on Indians. They thought to make the Indians loyal to them. For this end they thought to acculturate the Indians. For this purpose they thought to introduce their educational structure in India. Lord Macaulay, the then Member law in Viceroys' council had suggested that Western type of formal education be introduced so as to prepare a white collared work force for the government offices run by East India Company. To bring such force from England was not viable and economical. For the perpetuation of the English rule it was necessary to make three Indian subjects loyal to them. The loyalty of Indians could only be possible through their acculturation from Indian culture to Western culture. They wanted to make the Indian men and women loyal to them. Therefore, they opened equal avenues of education for men and women. Another reason for the imposition of formal education on Indians was to exploit both Indian human as well as national resources for the promotion of their industrial infrastructure. For which they thought woman can be equally useful. So they encouraged women education in India.

In the beginning the British type of alien foreign education was started from primary education. The primary schools were first opened in cities, towns and villages in rural areas. In rural areas the primary schools were managed by the District Boards. In towns, by the Town Areas Committees and in cities by the Municipal Committees. There was no restriction on the girls to seek admission in these primary schools. But hardly the girls were admitted in the village primary schools. The number of primary schools in rural areas was not high. Sixty or seventy years ago there was hardly one primary school for five or six villages located near a village having a population approximately of two thousand people. The village from which the writer hails had such primary school. Not a single girl had sought admission in this primary school. In spite of the fact that the village trio-leaders of the independence movement: (1) Late Shri Maharshi Harishchandra ji, (2) Late Shri Babu Malkhan Singh ji and (3) Late Shri Pt. Babu Ram Munde had girls' education on their top most political agenda. They had opened: (1) One adult education centre and (2) One girls separate primary school. But people had opposed the opening of girls primary school and not a single girl was allowed to enter in this school. Later on, this school was converted into a co-educational middle school. With the passage of time this middle school progressed. It is now Rashtriya Intermediate Co-educational College, Bhalswa Gaj, Distt. Haridwar, Uttaranchal in which more than one thousand girls are students. This Intermediate college has a polytechnic in it. It has a full-fledged library and well-qualified lady teachers. One of the girls who had done Intermediate from this college is a now doctor (MBBS). As such, where there is will there is a way. But still many parents do not send their girls to this college.

Child marriage is one of the hindrance in girls education. Child marriage may have been banned in India some more years ago, but one in every 17 girls in the 10-17 age group is already in a wedlock. And generally most of the villagers want to see their girls in wedlock early. This is why they do not want to see their daughters fully educated. The prevalence of child marriage is much higher in the north, Rajasthan, Madhya Pradesh, Bihar, U.P., Jharkhand and Haryana, it accounts for 63 per cent of all under-age married people. This is why the girls of these northern areas of India could not get good education and many of the girls remain illiterates.

The latest census held on marital status reveals that 49 million women under age of 18 are already married. It shows that one out of 17 girls in the country in the age group of 10-17 is married. Child marriages contribute to many social problems including lack of women education. The other problems which can be checked by women education are: (1) demographic explosion due to increasing birth rates. It is observed that mostly illiterate and uneducated women gave birth to more children, (2) higher illiteracy, (3) infant mortality, (4) mortality of mothers at the time of delivery of child and (5) low life expectancy. All these can be controlled by proper women education.

Ancient scriptures and customs sanctioned early marriage for the girls—preferably before puberty and certainly immediate after her first mensuration. Sociologists also trace it back to foreign invasion in the northern parts of the country, that began more than 100 years ago. The invaders were said to have carried away young girls as war booty. This had promoted the local communities to marry their daughters at a very early ages.

The 1976 amendment to the Child Marriage Restraint Act raised the minimum legal age for marriage from 15 to 18 for women and from 18 to 21 for men. And, yet not holy or legal but wholly illegal matrimony continue to flourish in Indian society. A noted demographer Ashish Bose points out "The act was a legal construct, not a social or anthropological one. In rural areas particularly a boy is deemed a man when he develops facial hair. And a girl is considered old enough for marriage once she attains puberty". This helped the people neglecting their girls for school education.

Of course, the prevalence of child marriage is much higher in northern India which affected women education very badly. But in southern states the child marriages are hardly found. In Andhra

Pradesh, there is only one child marriage out of forty marriages. In Kerala, there is one child marriage out of 135 marriages. While in Chennai, there is only one child marriage out of forty-three marriages. But in the rest of Tamil Nadu the ratio is 1:66. In Kolkata, there is one child marriage out of forty-seven, and in the rest of West Bengal ratio is 1:49. Also in northern India in Rajasthan, child marriages are arranged even before the boys and girls start speaking. On the other hand, ratio of child marriage is very low in Himachal Pradesh. There is one child marriage out of hundred marriage. Also the ratio child marriage is also low in Punjab. As per census report 1921, there were 600 baby brides in India who were in the age group of 12 months. It means, that 85 years age there was a practice to settle the marriage just after their births. This used to happen generally in Rajasthan. The child marriage practice is not limited up to India. In Nepal 7 percent girls are married before the age of 10 years and 40 per cent up to the age of 15 years. In Africa's Democratic Republic of Congo 74 percent girls are married before the age of 18 years. In Afghanistan 54 percent girls are married before the age of 18 years and Bangladesh 51 percent girls are married before the age of 18 years. All these figures show that child marriage is an universal phenomenon and it affects women education wherever this matrimonial practice takes place.

It is a recognised fact that the child marriage practice causes high rate of mismatching due to which the woman suffer throughout their lives. It creates high rate of illiteracy. It snatches the educational opportunities from the girls, which ultimately brings the women education to the lowest ebb. It decreases women work—participation also towards the lowest ebb. The women are deprived of skill formation. This also brings the women empowerment to the lowest ebb. As such, there is a need to increase the marriage age limit for the girls further. This cannot be done through the enforcement of law. There is a need for social will. Until and unless the parents of the girls make up their mind to marry their daughters only after full education there cannot be improvement. The practice of child marriage is a major hindrance in women education. Improving the educational standard does not mean increasing the literacy rates through more years of schooling. It is much more. It is socio-economic, cultural and general epistemic awareness. Education is much more. It is inculcation of appropriate human attitudes for the development of desirable cultural traits, sociability, good character and good work habits. Education increases the awareness about the socio-economic conditions, demographic explosion and desired birth control. If the women are well-educated, they can contribute in the family economy. They can contribute in the life-building process of the future guardians of the nation. So, women education is necessary for the national development. All measure should be adopted for the women education and stoppage of child marriages is one of the important measures in this regard.

After opening some primary and middle schools for elementary education, the British Government in forties of the nineteenth century had opened at least one High School (up to 10th Class) or Intermediate College (up to 12th) in every district. Main purpose of the establishment of these schools was teaching some subject content, which could prepare the Indian youths to work as clerks in British East India Company Government offices. The boys availed this opportunity in the beginning because they were to be employed as clerks in offices. The subject contexts were like English, mother-tongue, arithmetic, accountancy, economics, civics etc., etc. The teaching was done formally. The students were examined after 4th class, 8th class, 10th class and 12th class by the State Examination Boards, like Board of High School and Intermediate Education, Uttar Pradesh. After passing the examination, the students were certified and employed as clerks in offices. In the beginning this facility was availed by the boys only because they were to be employed in government offices. With the passage of time, it was felt that the girls should also be given this opportunity for education. As a matter of fact this type of formal education was not true education, it was only a preparation of the Indian youths for availing their services in offices. Some private organisations first came forward and opened separate schools for girls. Later on, these schools were aided by the government. At the time of independence there was hardly any girl school in Delhi. Now, there are many girls schools not only in Delhi but in all States. After completing the school education the girls also do higher education in colleges. In comparison to boys, the girls are very dedicated, hardworking, sincere in their studies and they always shine and come in flying colours in their annual examinations. Many of the girls do jobs and, later on help in family economy.

The industries also require trained workforce for doing technical works. As such, industrial training institutes, wood working institutes, polytechnics were opened by the government. These institutes prepare the skilled workers for doing various types of fabrication work. The girls can prove to be very useful for discharging official duties in industrial establishments. But hardly, they are permitted to undergo training in industrial institutes. For fabrication they can contribute in designing and making orthographic drawings. Now every organisation has been computerised. The girls can contribute a lot in handling the softwares. The women can do a commendable contribution in teaching. So the girls should be highly educated for becoming teachers. As a teacher, a woman can contribute a lot. She can do teaching by establishing good rapport with the students. After doing graduation or post-graduation the women should be trained as a teacher in a teacher training institute. There are many women polytechnics in the country, the women who are interested can do creative work, should be allowed to join any of these polytechnics and to learn the related technical work and do it later on.

One of the greatest lacunae in the field of education—be it men's education or women's education, is that education is only considered teaching some subject content only and nothing else. The education contains a wide spectrum of knowledge building inculcation of appropriate attitudes in a person both in man and woman. The knowledge building occurs when a person learns himself or herself. But this does not happen in the present system of formal education. Teaching is considered education which is not real education. Real education is that which gained by the individual himself or herself through thinking, reasoning and comprehending. The present system of examination is totally examination oriented and the teacher is supposed to pour information on students as much as possible. The present system of formal education does not innovate and motivate the students to introspect in himself or herself. This is why the present education, be it women education or men education is not suitable to inculcate good attitudes in the future guardians. And the society is going to be barbarous day by day. The crimes like, rapes, molestations, exploitations of females by males are increasing day by day. The society, parents, community and educational institutions are mad after annual examinations. Due to lack of proper education of the youngsters we are loosing our culture. We have been totally accultured to western culture. And crimes like burglaries, loots, chain snatching, corruption are increasing day by day. If women are to be properly educated and made aware about all these unsocial happenings; all these undesirable social happenings can be checked by women as they are life-builders.

Women education should not be limited up to teaching alone. As education is much more and has a wide spectrum, the women education should include many life aspects of the women. Their psyche, sociability, adjustment with the members of their new homes, national culture and related ways of enculturation, to be prepared to fight for their social and economic rights, to learn hospitability and behaving well with members of the family, relatives and community members. They should be educated to know to introspect themselves, analyse all social milieu, social and political infrastructures correctly.

VERSATILITY OF WOMEN EDUCATION

The concept of versatility has emerged out of the word versatile. The word 'versatile' is a derivation of Latin word 'Versatiles', meaning 'to turn or turning with ease from one state to another', 'readily applying one thing to another', 'applying oneself to a task or taping capacities of one living being by moving or turning around'. Versatileness or versatility means a facility of easily turning one's tasks to new good tasks or subjects, a facility of utilising various intellectual pursuits. As such, in ordinary sense, it also means importance of any pursuit. Since the women have to play so many familial and other life roles in their lives, they are also laden with wide educational spectrum for which they need to be educated.

In the present modern scientific industrial age the role of education has been restricted up to only knowing few subjects which may help an individual to earn money and nothing else. So the teachers are supposed to teach only few subjects relating to languages, humanities as civics, economics, history, science subjects like mathematics, physics, chemistry, biology, botany and orthographic drawing, in school under formal system of education, which side-tracks other aspects of education. The school teaching is also examination oriented which has nothing to do with life-building. As a matter of fact, only teaching can never be said education. The word 'teaching' is a derivation of Greek word 'Taccon', which means passing of information by a knowledgeable person to an ignorant person. Education is not only passing of information, it is much more. It is a process of self-learning. The word 'education' has emerged out of the Greek word 'educare' which means to take out what is already there. These are hidden potentialities of a person as already explained earlier. Education should be used for moulding the life of a person to meet the life challenges. These life challenges are so many. Every man and woman has to pass through life stages. So the education of every person, man and woman, should be based on a moulding procedure for life-building of ones life to face all life situations.

In olden days, the old Indian educational system aimed at to mould the individual's life. Such education was imparted in Gurukula Ashramas only to the youngers of the two upper castes—Brahmans and Kshatriyas, who used this type of education to mould other two castes Vaishyas and Sudras through religious discourses. Taxila (now in Pakistan) an institution of moulding human life was named on this assumption. The life of *Shishyas* (disciples) were moulded by *Gurus* (auspicious teachers) for living a sane life. Likewise, all Gurukulas in India were aimed at moulding the life of the youngers, that is, *Shishyas*. But like two castes Vaishyas and Sudras the girls or ladies of upper castes were not admitted in Gurukulas due to their genders. The girls, the future women, were educated in families through familial education by the joint family members to perform their life roles. Some ladies were educated in Rishi Ashramas about their life role. The Indian women used to be sane, honest, hospitable, sociable and religious. This was because the whole Indian society believed in simple living, high thinking, common good and religiosity. As such, the Indian education was life moulding oriented.

Nowadays, the socio-economic scenario of all countries including India has totally changed due to social change occurred because of industrialisation and commercialisation which made the Indian society totally hedonistic, consumeristic and xenophilic. Due to this, like men, the women community also has been affected. They also became accultured and they adopted the western ways of hiring and, forgotten the national culture of large extent. The girls, would be women, are also admitted in girls schools, where they get the formal education like the boys get formal education in like girls' schools. The girls' schools, like boys' schools, have no place for religiosity and spirituality due to the national policy of secularism. Also there is no place in girls' schools to educate the girls in their future household roles. Mostly the girls are educated in this regard by their peer group girls in informal way and they get little knowledge of faminity. Being anta-property (पराया-धन), when they attain young age, they are married with the boys and are sent to their husbands' families due to patriarchal social structure. As such, being uneducated about their familial roles they face many arduous life problems and difficulties in their married lives. This affects their psyche, which affect their family relations, and also on many cases their children also. As such, the society as a whole, the family, the community and educational institutions should realise the versatility of comprehensive education of women in the society, and should educate girls accordingly. Then only the society will prosper.

As already explained in 'Epistemic requirements of the women' all educational aspects of women education should be taken into consideration while planning women education. The girls' families and the girls' schools have to play a vital role in girls' (would be women) education. The girls' families should not discriminate against the girls. They should not be side-tracked in their education, familial as well as school education, being anta-property (पराया-धन). The girls' parents should realise that the girls are the utmost necessity and requirement for the existence of the society. They also need girls as their daughter-in-laws. As such, there should not be gender bias against the girls. The ladies of the family should give due care to the girls. The familial education of the girls covering all aspects of girls should start very early when the girls are young. Crumbling of the joint family is the major cause of drawback of girls' familial education. The crumbling of joint family, system usually occur due to women's greed. Greed takes place due to the influence of western cultural diffusion and acculturation. The ladies of the family should inculcate religiosity in girls in order to save them from the craze of greed. This can only be possible when the families become religious and spiritualists for avoiding greed. The joint family system, if revived and regenerated the familial education could also be revived for making the girls as future sane women. The following aspects as explained earlier should be covered under the girls' education:

Knowledge of 3 Rs.

Every human being man and woman, and even all living beings—animals, beasts, insects, birds have an urge to know about their surroundings. As such, all men and women want to gain knowledge. Knowledge can be gained through perception (per-se), thinking, reasoning and analysing. Practical experience leads to comprehending. Also reading, writing and remembering or storing of gained knowledge help in the acquisition of knowledge. Knowledge acquired by the elders can be utilised by the youngers through reading writing and remembering. Our present form of education is based on this pattern of education, and this is imparted through formal education. For this end the state has established many boys and girls schools. When the Constitution of Indian Republic was promulgated and adopted in 1950, it was aimed all boys and girls should at least get primary education within ten years after the adoption of the Indian Constitution. Fifty-five years have elapsed this constitutionally prescribed educational aim has not yet been achieved. And the girls are most affected. Social orthodoxy that the girls are anta-property (पराया-धन) may be one of the main reason for the negligence of girls' education. Another reason may be the barbarous nature of some male members who commit inhuman crimes of rape and molesting on girls. In rural areas approximately ten percent of the girls population do not enter into the gates of even primary schools. The parents, the community, the society and the government should realise that the girls are the soul of the society. They should not be denied their education rights and should be given equal educational opportunities. Then only the socio-economic and socio-cultural conditions of the nation can be improved.

Versatility of Women Social Roles

The women's social roles are many and are very versatile. The woman is supposed to be the mother. She gives birth to the children and bring them up. But many mothers, in spite of their being educated, play such dirty motherly roles that they spoil the future of their children. They shower too much love on their children and spoil them. Too much of love is always poisonous. The love should always entail strictness, directing the children for their life-building. Like that, enculturation of the children is one of the most important roles, which is done always through inculcation good habits, aestheticity and religiosity. If a mother herself is deprived good habits, how can she inculcate good habits in her children. Generally the T.V. programmes are very harmful for the school-going children. If a mother is fond of seeing T.V. programmes how can she stop her children seeing T.V. programmes? The T.V. programmes generally diverts the attention of the children and become epistemically dangerous to them. Also, many mothers are fond of cooking junky fast foods. They cannot stop their children eating junky fast foods. Similarly if a women believes in fashion and its Xenophility how can she stop her children to do so? The girls should be made aware about their future life social roles through familial education. But this is not possible in the present hedonistic period when both the father and mother are living in a nuclear family and are in the rat-race of money-earning. The girls should also be made aware about the bad effects of materialism and consequent hedonism and their effects on familial roles. This is not possible in the present nuclear family. It could have been possible in a joint family. The joint family social structure has been totally crumbled due to human greed. The present society also expects that the 'girls school' should also perform the role of familial education. The 'girls schools' are mostly very busy. They have to teach and prepare girls for annual examinations. They (teachers) have to do all family duties. Their husbands hardly contribute and help their wives in household affairs. They want that everything should be done by their wives. In such a odd situation, for the sake of social upliftment, the girls schools should educate the girls about their future social roles, so as to save the nation, from the social degradation. Versality of women's social roles cannot ignored and denied. The girls schools can achieve this goal through organising some related co-curricular activities either once a week or one a fortnight. The school can also organise some seminars on women's social roles. The women's organisations like 'Strisakti' (स्त्री शक्ति) can also educate the girls as well as housewives by organising some 'Stri Sammelan' (स्त्री सम्मेलन) either at community centres, Panchayat Bhawans or at a religious places like *Arya Samaj Mandirs, Gurudwaras, Churches* and in other temples through lectures and discourses.

Versatility of Social Education

Social education is necessary to maintain social unity, harmony, compositeness and integrity and also living peacefully. This can be achieved by inculcating good life attitudes from the beginning by the family members and later on by the educational institutions. Sociability requires good rapport with the children by the family members and later on by the teachers in the schools. Sociability is most essential for all and for educational system sociability is necessary.

Motherly Roles' Education

The genesis of human beings existence and the society lies in the mother. And young woman aspires to be a mother and also becomes a mother ultimately. So every woman needs to be educated about motherly roles as these are most versatile in a woman's life. As such, every woman must be educated about all aspects of motherly roles. Such education initially could be imparted through familial education and through informal education through the peer group and later on through school education. The girls school can educate the girls, who would be women and mothers, through seminars, small group discussions, etc., etc. Through such programmes the girls could be educated about the youngers' care.

Broad Mindedness Education

One of the most important epistemic requirement of the women is to be broadminded so that they may not be greedy and self-centred. This is necessary to revive the joint family system. This can be done by making the girls aware about the socio-philosophical aspects of the human society. For this some important aspects of sociology and philosophy should be taught in the school. The school curriculum cannot have these subjects permanently, but these can be taught under general information.

Creativity Education

Creativity is very essential. The girls should be taught and encouraged to be creative. This can also be done at two levels—at family level and school level. At family level the parents should encourage the youngers to create new things. Mothers can encourage to do creative cooking and to do another things like stitching, embroidery and cutting and tailoring.

In the school the girls can learn doing creative things like making greeting cards, doing display like hangouts and doing creative decoration by doing alpana and rangoli. The art teachers should play a vital role in this regard.

IDEAL WOMEN EDUCATION

For an ideal woman ideal education is essential because the life roles of a woman are many, varied and specific. She is the life-builder of the future citizens of the society and future citizens and guardians of the country. For this a woman is required to do balanced parenting of her children—not too much of love and not too much of harshness. Showering of too much of love over the children is poisonous. Also, too much of harshness over the children make them emotionally disturbed. The mothers who love their children too much and try to fulfil their every demand always spoil them. A woman has to run a household. She has to maintain the unity and integrity of the family. She is supposed to boost the unity of the community. For doing this she has to be social, cooperative, sacrificer and coordinator. To be hospitable is one of the prime quality for being an ideal woman. She has to look after the unity of the joint family. As such, the women should be educated to gain all these qualities. Then only they can perform their family roles sincerely.

In the present industrial and hedonistic age all these ideal life roles are very very difficult to inculcate or develop in the girls who are our future mothers. All persons are generally involved in the rat-race of money-earning. So also the girls visualise that their future will also require money-earning. So they generally devote mostly on school and college education and not show any interest in learning their life roles. Both, the mothers and fathers generally keep themselves busy in earning-money. This materialistic shadow also fall on the girls and they generally devote all of their time to secure highest marks and desire to come out in flying colours in their final examinations. Our present formal system of education has nothing to do with the ideal life-building. The present formal system of education only prepare the students for passing the examination. This can never be said an ideal education. It is only a track to walk on for employment which cannot be said on ideal real aim of education. Ideal life education is different from the present system of formal education. One present system of formal education is an alien system of education imposed by Lord Macaulay for acculturating the Indians. Lord Macaulay has been so successful that we all Indians have been totally acculturated. Of course, the dream of Lord Macaulay keeping Indians slave for every could not be achieved, but his dream of acculturating Indians has been so fulfilled that we Indian have lost our culture totally. He might be enjoying in his grave and eating Indian milk cakes. Our formal system of education, though gave a chance to our girls for adequate school and college education, has side-tracked them of their life roles. For this a lot of reformation in girls' education is required.

Of course, Indian old Gurukula system of education did not have any place for girls ideal life role education, but the women were educated, for doing their life roles, through religious discourse at religious places like temples and Satsang Bhawans and sometime in Rishi Ashramas. For achieving aim of ideal role women education, which is necessary for the good health of the society and also of the nation, it is necessary to reform our school and college education. This can only be done if there is will to do so. If there is a will there can be a way to achieve the desired ends. Our present system of education if reformed can be helpful to achieve the ideal roles of women education. Some women educational institutions are trying to achieves these aims of ideal roles of women education. Banasthali Women Vidyapeeth, Banasthali Rajasthan is proceeding in this direction. It has prescribed special ideal women educational aims which are called 'Panchmukhi Stri Shiksha Udesha' (five direction educations for women). The S N.D.T. Women University, Mumbai has also prescribed similar aims for women education. Both of these women universities lay stress on women empowerment (स्त्री शशक्तिकरण) and life-building process of women. In these educational institutions, very few women get chance to get such education.

As such, for moulding the women to do or perform their desirable life roles, there is a need to educate the girls, the would be women, about the desirable ideal women life roles. For achieving this end, there is a need to inculcate certain life habits and qualities in the girls in the initial stages first at home and later on in the school. Self-learning by the girls (would be women) through observation, thinking, reasoning analysing, comprehending and by driving influences is very necessary. Reading, writing and remembering which is done through teaching in schools and other educational institutions can be helpful in learning ideal roles of the lives of girls. Following five faced girls education (पंचमुखी शिक्षा) is necessary.

Educating to Adjust

Educating the girls, the future housewives, to adjust with the family members of their future homes, that is, in-laws (ससुराल) should be one of the top most aim of girls education. This is the utmost necessity of the girls being anta-property (पराया-धन). The girls should be educated right from their childhood through familial education. First the girls should learn to adjust with their siblings in their parental homes. They should be educated to have patience. They should also learn to respect elderly ladies and elderly members of the family and of the community. The girls should be made aware that under social law 'unity in bio-diversity' they will have to marry with boys and go with them to their houses, that is Sasural (ससुराल). This is necessary according to patriarchal structure of the society. For the adjustment in their Sasurals, the girls need to be tolerant. Without a spirit of tolerance the girls can never adjust in the new real homes. After the familial education of the girls, they have to go school for formal education. The girls' schools should also try to teach the girls to adjust with the family members. This can be done through some co-curricular activities. The girls should also be taught to be tolerant and speak less when some family member is adopting an aggressive posture. If the husband is aggressive the wife should remain silent. If the husband and wife both are aggressive it will affect their children. They will also become aggressive and intolerant.

The girls should also be taught to adopt some self-defence postures in the event some trouble created by some social bad elements. In the present hedonistic time incidents like molesting, raping and kidnapping have become a common social feature. Not only young girls but the elderly women also become the victims of such criminals. So, teaching of self-defence techniques should be one of the top most priority of the school curriculum for girls self-adjustment and safety.

Educating for Self-Introspection

Generally the present generation, in the present materialistic and hedonistic age do not try to know how the money is earned, how it should be spent. The present generation also do not try to know their past, present and future. Their parents provide them all opportunities to eat, drink and be merry. The present children generally want to lead a consumeristic and Xenophilic life. And both the boys and girls want to compete each other in their consumeristic life. So the idea of self-assessment and introspection does not emerge in them. Until and unless a man or woman or a boy or girl knows about the reality of life a person cannot progress in life. Many parents, especially the mothers deter their children to know about the reality of human life and the physical world. Such children become megalomaniac and atheist. They generally remain unaware about their psyche. For knowing once psyche self-introspection is very necessary. Such children, both boys and girls, generally remain in darkness and cannot do anything new in their lives. Many times, the parents, specially the mothers create such an awkward familiar situations which make their children inactive and megalomaniac. Such situation make the children unepistemic. They do not do anything themselves. They become rubbish. They never succeed in their lives. It is, therefore, very necessary to make the children, specially the girls self-introspective.

Educating About Motherly Roles

The mother is the second form of the Almighty God. As the God is the creator of all universe and flora and fauna, the mother is the creation of living beings. All mothers, be it an animal mother or human being mother comes under this category. The mother gives birth to a child and bring up the child. And this process comes under the motherly roles. So it is very necessary to educate would be mothers, the girls, about their future motherly roles. Many mothers due to lack of knowledge of proper motherly roles either mothers shower too much motherly love or do not care and give proper protection to their children. Due to this their children either are spoiled or remain neglected children. So it is very necessary that the girls, who are future mothers, should be properly educated prior to their marital life about their motherly roles. At the initial stage, it can be done through the familial education and later on by school education through co-curricular activities.

Educating about Sociability and Cooperation

Society is a whole of biological wholes, that is, of human beings. In other words, society is a collectivity of men and women who have individual difference and variance in their ways of living and behaviour. So for keeping the members of the society united, it is necessary to adopt some social traits. Sociability is one of the social trait which keeps the members of the society united. As such, sociability and cooperation are most important for living in the society. Without these social norms or traits a man or woman remains isolated. For a woman to be social is most essential. If a woman is sociable and cooperative she will behave with her children well. And she will be able to inculcate other life qualities like speaking true, helping others, doing their own work themselves, to be moral etc., etc. So, it is very necessary to inculcate sociability in girls in their initial stage through familial education, when the girls join the schools, the school teachers should inculcate the sociability and a spirit of cooperation in the girls, who are going to be women.

Avoidance of Meglomaniaty

The meglomaniaty is the individuals' egoistic quality in the area of epistemacy. Many individuals—men and women start believing that they know everything, and there is no need to know further from others. Such thinking stops a person to know further in his or her area of working. And it puts a halt on further learning and gaining knowledge. This trend of believing that one knows everything makes a man or woman ignorant about many things. There is no limit to knowledge. Therefore, the girls, who are going to be women and mothers should be educated that there is no end in the field of knowledge. Knowing is a continuous process. This will save the girls from being egoistic in their marital life. And they will make their children non-egoistic and epistemic.

Aestheticity and Epistemacy

For knowing doing new things is necessary. Necessity is the mother of invention. When a person needs a new thing, either he tries to acquire it or buy it or make that thing himself or herself. Creating a thing always involves thinking, reasoning, analysing, comprehending and learning. It is an artistic process. It entails both aesthetics and epistemics which finally enriches knowledge of human beings. As such, doing and knowing, both go in hand and glove. Every action requires aestheticity and epistemacy. These lead to creativity. The things which are created for the first time are called 'art'. Creativity leads the promotion of new knowledge. Creativity and knowledge are necessary for cultural development. Without these enculturation of the youngers cannot be possible. All world cultures and civilisations could be possible due to aestheticity and epistemacy. Aesthiticity and epistemacy add new lives in the human life, as men and women both can create new things and lead a happy life.

As such, it is necessary that the girls should be educated in aestheticity and epistemacy. This process of education should start from the family. From the early age, the girls should be encouraged to learn to do new things. In the home there is a vast field of learning and doing new things, as doing alpana, rangoli, embroidery, cutting and tailoring and cooking. This can only be possible when their mothers are involved in doing new things. Cooking is also an area of aestheticity. In cooking girls can learn preparing new food stuffs. But many mothers do not encourage their daughters to do all these. They argue that they will have to do a lot in their married life so they should not be forced to do anything. Such thinking is very harmful for future life of the girls. So the girls always should be involved in creativity.

This process should be continued in school education. The school should involve all girls in creative work as doing alpana, rangoli, decoration on various occasions as foundation and parents day, etc. etc.

5

Aims of Women Education

When there are general aims of education prescribed for all human beings, that is for men and women, should there be any specific educational aim for women alone or not, is a very controversial question. Majority of the people will oppose and reject such proposal on the ground that women are also human beings. They are also members of the society. They are of the same race. They speak, eat, behave and work like men. They live with their husbands lifelong and share the same culture. Why should there be some specific educational aims for women. Even many women will oppose such a proposal and will argue that this will create a barrier between males and females. Of course, this proposal is new and looks awkward. But all aspects of this proposal should be considered logically and examined.

Man and Woman are genetically different in many respects. They are biologically topsy-turvy. If we look to the bodies of man and woman, man's body and lady's (women) body are totally opposite to each other. Man's head, shoulders, breast, muscles, body texture are totally opposite to woman. Man's head is flat. He is supposed to put up some weight on his head. Woman's head is bulging in a curve shape. The nature has made woman's head bulging because she has to cover her head with her hairs. The bulging head is the crown of woman. Man's shoulders are broader than that of woman. The nature has provided broader shoulder to man because he has to do a lot of manual work. Whereas, the woman's shoulder are not so broad. The woman's hips are broader. These are not so broad as the shoulder of man are. The nature has done so because the woman is to bear a child in her womb, and for holding the weight of the child woman's hips are made stronger by the nature. The man's face has hairs, whereas woman's face do not have hairs. It is because she may look beautiful to her male partner. Woman's body is slanting whereas male's body is not. Male's muscles are overlapping. Through this males body is strong. Woman look beautiful whereas man does not look so. The voice of man is not sweet as that of woman. The man is supposed to go out of his house for earning-money for running household. Whereas the woman is supposed to live in the house, bear and bring up the children. The woman is supposed to impart a lot of familial education so as prepare the youngers for lifelong living. In other words, the women are the life givers and builders of youngers who are the future guardians.

The nature has made woman and man two biological opposites for human beings' collective living. This collective living becomes possible through "unity in bio-diversity". This 'unity in bio-diversity' makes the social existence of the human beings, that is, of man and woman possible. Due to this unity human being are born, brought up and go. But the existence of the society remains in tact. As man and woman play different roles in the society, they should be prepared for different social roles. As education play a positive role in bringing up the men and women, the educational aims should be framed accordingly.

For framing specific educational aims for women there are many sociological, psychological, epistemical, cultural and axiological aspects which should be taken into consideration while framing educational aims for women education. And for doing so the educationists who decide the educational aims should be aware about all these aspects. These aspects are many:

1. Though the woman is the producer of human beings that is, men and women, but generally the birth of a girl child in family is not considered good and auspicious as the birth of a boy is considered. In other words, the family members do not take it good for their family. The reason is that in the patriarchal social structure the girl child when becomes young will have to go to another family after her marriage where she has to live lifelong. As such, the girl till she remains with her parents is not given a fair treatment as is given to her male siblings. In other words, the girl child is considered as an anta-property. She is not given full care also. She is not given full freedom. As such, mostly the girl develops an alienistic psyches. And from the beginning they start thinking that her real home is elsewhere. So the girls develop a sort of alienatory mental set up which they continue in their new real homes. They

start behaving with the members of the in-laws family in alienatory manner. This develop greed and self-centredness in them. They only treat their own who came out from their wombs. This kind of mental set up generally breaks up joint family system. And the joint family system is the soul of Indian culture. Such women like to live in nuclear families. As such, educational aims for girls' education should be to apprise about these aspects. Generally, the girls are educated in girls school, the teachers and administrators of the girl school should pay due attention to this aspect.

2. Another sociological aspect which hampers the girls education is dowry system. The greed of the dowry has so much increased that, majority of the girls parents cannot afford, to give the dowry as desired by the bridegroom side. Many tragedies occur. Woman becomes woman's enemy, mother–in-laws of the brides forget that sometime back they were also daughter–in-laws. They continuously harass their daughter-in-laws for not bringing sufficient dowry. Sometime, the mother-in-laws do not hesitate in getting their daughter-in-laws murdered and eliminated. In many cases, the daughters-in-law commit suicide themselves. Also there are many cases, when the bridegrooms side do not take dowry at all, but in due course of time their daughter-in-laws forget their generosity and start misbehaving their husbands and also in-laws. It happens due to lack of rationality in the daughter-in-laws. As such, one of the educational aims should be to make them aware about the mother-in-laws irrational behaviour and to inculcate an attitude in the girls to appreciate those who do not demand and take dowry. This can be done by girls' school teacher through good rapport with their girl students.

3. Another sociological bad aspect is that the girls are not safe. Some bad elements in the society target the girls. They molest and rape these girls. Generally some already known or related persons try to do these anti-social crimes. So one of the important educational aims should be to prepare the girls save from such crimes. They should be made aware about such crimes at school level. The girls should be trained to use some defensive technique as *karate* and *boxing* etc. This should be utmost important aim of girls' education as the Indian society is facing such crimes daily.

4. One of the psychological aim of the girls' education should be to make the girls aware about 'female psyche' which is good for desirable social life. Majority of the women, especially uneducated,

are conflict ridden from the very beginning due to undesirable socials happenings, lack of their proper care, sociability due to lack of proper social living in childhood. Because of this many girls become introvert. Many of the girls do not get due care in their childhood being girls. In the Indian society due to some social reasons in some families the girls are eliminated even before their birth. Such foeticide generally takes place as mostly the people like male child. These may be reasons for female foeticide. The reason number one is that the girls are anta-property (पराया-धन). They, due to patriarchal social structure, have to be married with a boy and live with him throughout life. The parents of boy (bridegroom) demand a substantial dowry which becomes very difficult to give by many parents of the girls. This is the reason many parents elude girls' education. It is estimated that about 10 crores girls do not peep into the doors of the schools. When the girls are young it is also feared that they may be molested or raped by some unsocial elements. So, the parents keep a watch over their daughter and impose some restrictions over them. Such awkward happenings which the girls face and experience in their childhood change their psyche right from the childhood. They hardly forget such illogical, unethical, immoral and unsocial treatment given to the fair sex. This sort of social treatment to the girls changes the psyche of the girls right from the childhood. They do not forget such treatment to the fair sex throughout their lives. This develops a sense of alienation towards their parental family. They become self-centred, non-cooperative, irrational and non-accommodative, which they generally follow in their real homes, that is, husbands' homes. They always think that their's is only are those who are born from their wombs. No rationality for joint family is maintained by them. Such ladies are generally killers of the joint family system. Since the prime aim of education is life-building and not passing out examinations, the women education should be to reform the psyche of self-centredness of the girls. This can be easily done by the teachers and school administrations through suitable rapport and discussion. But now-a-days what generally happens is that the teachers do not want to move beyond teaching school subjects. The women constitute half of country's population. They are all life givers until and unless they are not rational and harmonious, the sanety cannot prevail in the society. Therefore, it is necessary that all life-building measures may be included in educational aims of the women education.

5. Epistemologically, it has been observed, that the girls are not only equally intelligent rather are more intelligent than boys. Their performance in normal examination is better than the boys. This is because, the girls are generally hardworking, diligent and sincere than the boys. Generally girls always leave behind the boys in academic work. Due to epistemic achievements many girls become megalomaniac. Many of them even start treating their life partners as inferior to them. Such attitude creates disharmony in their family life. The school education should also aim at it and should also check this tendency. This can also be done through educating the girls at school.

6. Enculturation should be one of the prime aim of school education. Nowadays, the Indian social milieu is badly hit by the cultural diffusion and consequent acculturation, which has killed the Indian culture to large extent. We eat, drink, wear clothes and talk in western style. Preservation of culture is very necessary for every country. From the early olden days the women always have been the preserver and builder of culture. Women have faith in religious practices. In case girls are educated about national culture, its preservation and enculturation it can be a boon for the health of the nation. Therefore, it is very necessary that enculturation should be the prime aim of women education.

7. Lastly one of the most important aim of women education should be axiological development in them. Our girls, who are our future women should be made aware about morality, sanety and kindness. These qualities were found in the Indian ladies in the past and are still found. This is why women were respected in the past. The women who had axiological qualities were respected and worshipped by the people. Devi Durga, Vaishnav Devi, Shakti, Saraswati and Lakshmi were such women who are still worshipped in India. The women worship in India was an astonishing feature for the people of the world. Even Socrates got surprised when one of his discipline who had studied in Taxila and stayed there for eight years informed him that women are worshipped in India. One reason for his surprise might be that his wife Xentippe was a harsh, unsocial and unaxiological lady. Such ladies are also found in Indian society. Therefore, it is very necessary that inculcation of axiology in girls should be one of the prime aim of Indian women education. This can be done through continued rapport between the teacher and taughts in girls' educational institutions. Appropriate co-curriculum activities may also be very helpful.

6

Epistemic Requirement of Women

For the survival of all human beings—men and women need many things, such as, food, water, energy, air, sunshine, rain, oxygen etc., and a social whole, that is, society are necessary. If an individual is ignorant about all these, or any of them or about other things found in the vicinity of his/her residence, he or she cannot utilise or enjoy them. Therefore, it is very necessary that an individual men or women always must be eager to know all things available in his/her surroundings. In others words, an individual must be epistemic then only his/her survival can be possible. The word epistemic is offshoot of the term epistemology. The word epistemology is a derivation or development of Greek word 'Epistemic', meaning 'knowledge' or 'logos' or 'discourse'. As such, a process of knowing or theory of knowledge is called 'epistemology'. And one who is eager to know new things, and tries to know new things is called 'epistemic'. As a matter of fact all living beings are generally epistemic, but human beings—men and women are more epistemic. They have been endowed by the nature with bigger brains to think, reason, analyse and comprehend all natural phenomena, cosmos and their own physical being. But epistemacy in human beings can only be developed through proper education and required training. Many human beings—men and women do not get this opportunity. Specially all of the women do not get the educational as well as instructional opportunities due to social stigma against women that they are considered anta-property (पराया-धन). With the result such women remain backward in the society. As the women constitute nearly half of the population of the country they should be properly educated and trained in their life activities. So the epistemic requirements of the women should be given proper attention in the society. Such epistemic requirements of the women may be as under:

ACADEMIC KNOWLEDGE

In the present materialistic age the concept of education is limited up to academic knowledge, that is, subjects knowledge—knowledge of mother-tongue, knowledge of one another language, that too English, knowledge of some humanities like, civics, history, economics, commerce and accountancy and some science subjects like physics, chemistry, biology and botany etc., whereas, the arena of education is much wider. Education should cover self-learning, inculcating of ideal life roles in both men and women, good life attitudes for the development of morality, sociability, hospitability and spirituality. For women these roles are much more important than the men. They must know self-learning in all of their family roles. They must know how to bring up their children. They must know the credentials of familial education, through which they can create right attitudes in their children. They must know to care and respect their in-laws. And they also must know about their rights. But under the present system of formal education, which is alien and was imposed by the then British Government on the advice of Lord Macaulay in 1833 A.D., the formal system of education is limited to imparting instructions about reading, writing and remembering, that is only 3 Rs. Of course, these are necessary to gain knowledge through reading and conserve such knowledge by writing and remembering. As such, under the present system of formal school education mother-tongue, one other language, that too, foreign English language and some subject of humanities and science subjects are taught only. Other life-building measures are totally ignored. The formal system of education is totally examination oriented. So the school education lays emphasis on teaching of school subjects only ignoring all life-building aspccts of education which are very necessary for the life-building. The demographic picture of the country shows that the women constitute the half of country population, but all women do not get chance of even school education. In rural areas due to anta-property stigma, at least ten percent of the girls do not get chance to enter the primary school. Getting higher academic education is not at all possible for them. In cities the majority of the girls get chance for higher academic education, but most of them could not avail due to restrictions imposed by their in-laws. Most of the graduate and post-graduate women only remain satisfied being sincere and obedient housewives. They should be allowed to utilise their academic knowledge for their own economic as well as national interest by their husbands and in-laws.

KNOWLEDGE ABOUT WOMEN'S IDEAL ROLES

Every individual, man and women, has to play some specific role in his/her life. Since a woman is physically topsy-turvy to a man, her life roles are specific, very important and different to man. A man is supposed to be an earner of livelihood, whereas a woman is supposed to be life giver, life builder and life protector. She gives birth to the children, brings them up and inculcate life attitude through familiar education in them. In addition to these, she has to maintain her household. As such, for a woman's life role are many, auspicious and ideal ones. A woman has to mould the life of her child, the future guardian of the nation. She has to enculturate the children. She has to develop the work habits in the children. A woman can developed spiritually in the children by observing spirituality herself.

But in the present scientific and industrial age many women spoil their children because they do not want to sacrifice their comfort and enjoyment. When a woman would see and enjoy T.V. programmes and serials, how can she stop her children doing so. The woman doing so spoil their children. Many women believe in hedonism. They prepare fast and junky foods, eat themselves and also motivate their children to eat junky fast foods. They make their children 'carvac'. Such women should be educated by family elders and community's elder ladies. The women should be educated in the childhood about such bad habits through familial and school education. Rather they should be encouraged to develop morality, simplicity, diligency, epistemacy and aestheticity in the children.

KNOWLEDGE ABOUT SOCIABILITY

All human beings—men and women live in a society which is a collectively, a composite whole of living beings, living together in spite of their bio-diversity. Living of human beings together is necessary for their safety, existence and sustinance The word society is a derivations of Latin and French words 'Societes' and 'Societus', meaning good relationship between men and men and, men and women to one another when associated and united for common good; objects or aims as liberty, safety, religious benevolent, carnival, the life sustenance, usefulness, for which development of manners, attitudes, common behaviour traits and character. A sociable person is one who follows and goes on to social trends and attains viable sociability for becoming sociable. French thinker, Auguste Comte in his books (*i*) 'Cours De Politique Positive' (*ii*) 'System De Politique Positive' conceived the word Sociology in 1839 in which he discussed the term 'Society'. Auguste Comte had thought of 'Social physics'. Later on he dropped it as it was already adapted by Adolf Quetlet, a Belgian sociologist. Comte's main concern was the reorganisation of political and practical recognition of the society concerning the totality of humanity at the time of industrialisation and commercialisation. He was concerned about the humanity and sociability of the members of the society. Later on many thinkers as Karl Marx, Emile Durkheim, Etzioni Amati, I.P. Desai, Andre Beteille, Raymond Aron, Talcott Parson and M.N. Srinivas contributed in the field of sociability in society.

As such, it can be said that sociability of the members of the society is most essential. Sociability of human beings can be done by familial education, socialisation by the community and by the educational institutions, schools and colleges during teaching through co-curricular activities. Many women are not sociable at all. They do not behave with other human beings in the human manner. Many women used to behave with other human beings in a very rude manner. And this was not limited only one country it was a universal social phenomenon. Socrates wife Xentippe did not to talk to anybody. If any of the Socrates disciple used to enter in her house she used to pour one full water jug over his head. There are many ladies who are sitting on big administrative positions but they are not sociable. As such, the society should give due attention to the sociability. Women's unsociability may be due to some frustrations. The family members and community should look do this aspect also. Some women organisations like *Strishakti* can contribute a lot in this regard. Such organisation should establish a variable rapport with all women.

HOSPITABILITY

Every woman should be hospitability. Majority of the Indian women are hospitable. This is why many foreigners always admired Indian hospitability. As women can only be hospitable, if she is expert in cooking. Cooking can be taught by mother and by other ladies of the family. This can also be taught in school.

FAMILIAL EDUCATION

Every women desires to be a mother. A mother has to bring up her children and mould their life for being a sane person. For this, the mother has to inculcate good life attitudes in the children as simple living, speaking true, to be punctual, to do hard work and own work as washing of *kachha, baniyan* and *towel*, to do school work regularly, early to bed and early to rise, to respect elders and ladies, to know about the national culture and to be spiritual. This can be done if the mother knows all about these and believes in religiosity. Above all these, the child be guided to love the youngers and the siblings.

BRINGING UP OF YOUNGERS

One of the most epistemic requirements of the women is bringing up of her young children, which is also a difficult procedure. After the birth of a child, the mother is to feed her milk. After few minutes the child is to be fed. The feeding procedure is also a longer one. Thereafter, the procedure of inculcation of good life attitudes and begins. All this can only be taught to the girls in the family through familial education. The mother, grandmother and after the marriage, the mother-in law should do this job. Too much love is poison should be taken into consideration by the mothers.

COMMON GOOD

The woman should never be self-centred and greedy. But these are main drawbacks in the life of women these days. The woman in the present materialistic and hedonistic age, are found self-centred and greedy. They only think of their own who are born out of their wombs. Others are alien to them. This is why, nowadays joint families are conflict ridden and, finally these are crumbled. This situation can only be tackled if the women are made aware about the reality of human existence. The human existence is totally temporary. Nobody takes anythings with him or her. Only religiosity can make the women and men aware about this fact. Ours is a secular country. Our school education cannot inculcate religiosity in school students. Only the mothers should award religious fruit. They should involve their children in religious prayers daily.

AESTHETICITY

Aestheticity is the science of soul of creativity. And creativity develops work habits and diligency in an individual. Doing work diligency and regularly is necessary for any human being. Therefore, the girls should be motivated to do creative works. Of course, the girls, the would be women, cannot do hard manual work, but they are more creative than man. A creative work is that which has been done for first time without any inclination. Such creative works are called art work. There is a wide field and spectrum for girls for doing creative work. First of all cooking is the finest creative work. The girls (would be women) should be trained in cooking by their mothers and aunts. They should also be encouraged to do experiments in cooking. They should also be advised not to prepare junky fast foods and depends on simple vegetarian food. The mothers who encourage their children to eat junky fast foods generally spoil their own children. If the children are not provided such foods in their adolescent age, they become violent. There are many works as embroidery, knitting, batik work, cutting and tailoring, making decorative collages and mobiles which can generate aesthiticity in girls. The parents and the school teachers should make the girls aware about the national culture. All these creative activities will lead the girls to enculturation. On some religious days as Diwali, Basant Panchami and Holi the girls should be encouraged to do alpana and rangoli. The mothers and school teachers should guide the girls who are would be women.

SELF-INTROSPECTION

Every individual has physical mental limits, so every individual must know about his or her capacities. He or she must try to know about his or her epistemic limits. He or she must know her working capacities and capability. Without this nobody cannot proceed in life. As a women has to play different vital life roles in her life, she must be aware about her mental as well as physical capabilities, then only she can be successful in her life. So a women first introspect into herself than do any work.

KNOWLEDGE ABOUT SOCIAL STRUCTURE

A society is a composite whole of all human beings that is, men and women and also is an aggregation of different social institutions like family, community, caste and creeds, marriage, religious institutions and educational institutions like schools and colleges etc. A social structure is a composition of all these. An individual has to follow the rules and regulations of the social structure, then only social harmony can only be possible. The woman is to be mother. She is to bring her offsprings. She has to educate her children through a familial education. If the woman knows the pros and cons of the social structure in which she is living, she can make her children aware about the social requirements. The school education should educate the future women about the forms of social structures, so that they may educate their children about the society and its structure.

AWARENESS ABOUT WOMEN'S RIGHTS

The woman is an important member of the society. She is a logical part of 'Unity in Bio-Diversity'. Their number is nearly half of the total population of the country. But due to patriarchal social structure, the women are considered inferior to men and they are not given their due social rights. They are not given educational rights as given to boys. In rural areas nearly ten percent girls cannot seen the gates of the primary schools. As they have to go to another homes leaving their parental homes. In their new homes, they are tortured by their husbands and in-laws. The women are considered as anta-property (पराया-धन). The women are ignored inferior on many fronts and are denied of their due rights. The women should be aware about their due rights.

7

Sources of Women Education

The spectrum of the sources of the educational processes of youngers, both boys and girls is wide and varied. As a matter of fact the child starts learning since his birth, the moment the child is born, he or she feels hungry and learn sucking of milk from his or her mother's breasts. As the child grows he or she start observing and perceiving things available in the surroundings. The child starts responding through his/her gestures. And in due course of time he or she starts speaking and, the interaction between the child and the parents starts. As such, the family has been a prime source of initial education which is called 'familial education'. Through familial education the life-building process of the youngers starts. Parents and other family members try to inculcate some life habits as, taking food, behaving well with all family members as well as community members, development of good life attitudes as going to bed early and rise early, development of work habits and to be epistemic. As such, the familial education has been the foundation stone of life-building and enculturation of the youngers from the beginning. Familial education had contributed in the development of various world cultures and civilisations in the world. Greek culture and civilisation, Hebrew civilisation, Indian Mohan-jo-daro and Harappa civilisations and Chinese civilisation were the result of familial education. Still in India, many tribal sects. try to educate their youngers through familial education. Indian all artisan castes still educate their children through non-formal education which is a sort of familial education. And generally most of the women education is done through familial education.

With the passage of time the man learned to utilise the natural resources to meet his needs and requirements. He conceived many new things for human use and fabricated these things out of natural resources. As such, a viable human social structure came into being and some social changes have also taken place. Human needs and requirements have continuously increased. So the need for better sources of education of human beings—men and women, was also felt. Some educated persons started teaching youngers in their houses. And these teaching spots were called 'Pathshalas' and the persons who used to teach the youngers were called 'Padhas' (upadhyas). Some rich persons and aristocratic families of Rajas and Maharajas also used to engage these 'padhas' as tutors of their young. These teachers (Padhan) used to go to the houses of such children—boys and girls both. So the girls of the rich families also were taught. All girls of the poor families did not get chance to get this type of tutorial education. So the girls of the poor families used to remain illiterate and devoid of the knowledge of 3 Rs. As education is not limited to teaching 3 Rs, it is much more. It is a process of self-learning and life-building. The families of the girls used to educate them inculcating in them good habits like sociability, honesty, morality, cooperation, punctuality and doing work for living a happy future married life. Many of them were better than the present so-called educated women. Still many illiterate women are better educated than the highly educated women. They are sociable, hospitable, care-takers of the children. It is because their good familial education imparted by their parents and other family members. Such women live a happy family life. They play a very positive role in bringing up their children and enculturating them better than the present educated women.

With the development of science and technology and consequent industrialisation increased more chances of exploitation of natural resources, which required more human resources. New industries required many technical experts for managing these industries intelligently, many skilled technical workers, clerical staff and semi-skilled workforce. Earlier, when there were no mechanised industries, every kind of fabrication of usable things was done through the manual work. After the development of industries a trained workforce was required. So, for this the industrialists thought of some schools established some schools for boys which were used to train them formally in particular areas. Such schools prepared the youngers to work in the industries, teaching them required subjects as needed by the industries. Such schools took the shape of formal schools in future.

The present formal system of education is the legacy of the schools established by the industrialists. In the beginning no such schools were not established for the girls as they were supposed to do household work and not any skilled manual work. Also in Gurukula system the girls did not find any place. Only the women of well to do family due to their religiosity, could attend some Rishis-Munis discourses in their Ashramas. As such, the women education was neglected in India from the beginning.

After the occupation of India by the Britishers, the then British East India Company Government thought of changing the Indian Gurukulas and Madarsa system of education which were aimed at enculturation of the youngs. The then Viceroy convened the Viceroy Council meeting to consider this issue in 1832 A.D. Some members of the Council were of the view that the Indian indigenous Gurukula education system of Hindus and Madarsa education system of Muslim were best suited to India as these were aimed at enculturation of Indians. The then Law Member of the Viceroy's Council Lord Macaulay was of the view that for keeping India under their control forever it was necessary to kill the Indian culture first, for which western cultural diffusion was necessary. So he suggested to introduce the western type of formal education in India. The formal system of school education was to be introduced for moulding the life patterns of Indians on western style. He suggested that the British type of formal education would be helpful to produce a clerical workforce which was not economical for the Britishers to bring from England. They would be employed in British Government offices and would be loyal to the Britishers. As such, with this aim of British imposed formal education which was to acculturate the Indians totally. So the British type of formal education was imposed on Indians in 1833 A.D. The then British Governor of Punjab, Lahore (now-in-Pakistan) had also openly opposed the imposition of British type of formal school education on Indians. He argued that the British type of formal education in India will kill the Indian non-formal system of education in India. In his view the non-formal system of education in India was one of the best systems of training the artizans in the world. But his arguments were also ignored and the formal system of education was imposed on Indians. In the beginning boys schools were opened at the capital and big cities like Calcutta, Madras, Bombay, Kanpur, Lucknow and Lahore etc.

Main purpose of the establishment of the formal education was to produce clerks. After sometime, some persons thought for opening the girls schools. The illustrious person like Shri Ammembal Subba Rao Pai (1852-1909) founder of the Canara Bank had opened Canara High School (for boys) and Canara Girls High School in Karnataka. Like him, many eminent philanthropists had opened girls schools throughout India in big cities. But due to gender bias the girls education remained ignored in the Indian society. Main reason for such gender bias against the girls was their being anta-property (पराया-धन). After the independence the Indian Government looked to the girl education, and at least one girl school in each district was opened by the government. Society as a whole realised the versatility of the girls education and opened girls schools even in villages. Many people still objected to the girls education. In the writers' village the trio freedom fighters, late Shri Maharsi Harishchandra, late Babu Shri Malkhan Singh and late Pt. Shri Babu Ram Sharma 'Munde' had opened a girls primary school. Many orthodox people had objected to it, but this is new famous Rashtriya Intermediate Co-educational College, Bhalswa Gaj, District Haridwar (U.A.) in which more than one thousand girls and approximately two thousand boys are studying.

Now, the main source of girls education, where 3Rs are taught through some subjects. Real educational aspects are totally ignored. The girls are educated so that suitable grooms may be found for them. The prime source of girls' education is the family. The family used to educate the girls about their life roles. Now due to hedonism and xenophilism the familial education does not educate the would be women, the girls cooking and doing household works due to undue load of school examinations. Now, the girls desire to be educated for earning in their married life. They want to be self-supporters. Also, the grooms want their wives should be so educated that they may also earn. As such, the educated women are also in rat-race of earning. For earning they join some vocational courses like cutting and tailoring, computer operation, typing, fashion designing, drawing and painting, textile designing etc., etc. Many vocational training shops are also functioning in every nook and corner of the cities.

Girls are not behind in gaining higher education in colleges, engineering institutes and polytechnics. They are very sincere, intelligent, diligent in comparison to boy. Their performance in examinations is always better than the boys. They also try to compete the boys in every field. In teacher education their performance is always commendable. They are always ahead in taking part in creative activities. But they, being educated always lag them behind in their house activities. It is because in their young age they remain busy in their academic studies and they do not find time to learn household roles fully and they face many ordeals in their married life.

Now the main source of women education are educational institutions. So it is necessary that the women should also be taught about their life roles first in girls schools and later on by the other educational institutes like, colleges, polytechnics and engineering colleges. This can only be done if the teachers of all these institutions are also educated about the women's life-building roles. The teacher education should look to this important women educational aspect. Only a few teacher's training college are equipped to impart such education to teacher trainees So first the teaching staff should be trained about the women life roles, then only other sources of teacher training can be helpful in this regard.

8

Human Social Stigmas

As every system of working or operation or process of fabrication may have some weaknesses or loopholes or drawbacks, so every living being or human beings also may have some behavioural problems or drawbacks in their ways of living. Such shortcomings in human social behaviour are called social stigmas. The men and women though form a 'unity in bio-diversity' are biologically topsy-turvy. They have to play different specific roles. Their psyches are also different to each other. They may have varieties of social stigmas. The men have some specific social stigmas. The women also have some specific social stigmas. In spite of all this they are ought to be united through the institution of marriage. They live together lifelong after marriage. Due to patriarchal social structure the women leave their parental homes and go permanently to their new real homes, the homes of their husbands. They, men and women jointly produce the future members and guardians of the society. But in spite of all this they adopt the divergent ways of living, due to which their ways of thinking and acting take the form of some social stigmas, which prove to be harmful for sane harmonious social living. Social stigmas also creates social conflicts in family as well as social life. In order to live harmoniously and peacefully in the society, there is a need to know about the genesis of social stigmas and find out ways and means to check the emergence of social stigmas in the social life. For this, the familial education, social interruption and awareness in school education to the girls and boys are necessary.

The men and women develop different kinds of social stigmas. And for both—the men and women social change, which occurs with the passage of time, plays a positive role. Hereclitus, a Greek Philosopher, said that every physical as well as social phenomena is in continuous flux. So the behaviour of the human beings—men and women continuously change. Women and men continuously change as their hearts beat at every movement. Physical atmosphere change at every moment due to sunshine and flow of air. Social change occur due to human nature. Human beings—men and women are considered rational beings, because they have been rewarded with bigger brains, to think and moving hands and legs to act and walk. But the nature has made the human beings very greedy too. They exploit the natural resources to the maximum for their benefits. Human beings are exploited by human beings for their material ends. Majority of the human beings became hedonistic. They adopted the acculturation blindly. Originally the Indian society was a monotheistic, spiritualistic society. But due to western cultural diffusion the Indians become totally accultured. Originally the Indians believed in simple living and high thinking. Now they believe in *hi-fi* living. This has brought many social evils and social stigmas. In the olden days also the Indian society had become stigmatic due to rigid caste system based on purity and pollution. In the present age, materialistic temper which emerged in the society due to acculturation which made the Indian society more stigmatic, due to which many people suffer. Many social stigmas followed by men who make the women victims. Likewise, many social stigmas followed by women make men victims. Therefore, it is very necessary to check the stigmatic behaviour of both men and women. For doing so the men and women need to go in the depth of this social problem of which women are victims.

The genesis of human social stigmas lies in human greed, unfairness, irrationality, arrogance and ego (अहंकार). The origin of the ego (अहंकार) or proud (*Abhiman* अभिमान) does not lie in the chemistry of the human body. It is the result of misguided morality for materialistic desires which generate hedonistic temper in the human beings. This social change has occurred in human beings due to copying blindly those who believe blindly in material gains for their comfort and luxurious life. The process of copying the cultural traits of those who are living at distant places can be said acculturation.

The Vedas and other old Indian religious scriptures tell us that the human mind is also the source of ignorance (*agyan* अज्ञान) or bondage which is the source or fountain head of worldly social stigmas which lead to human miseries. The arrogance or ignorance (अज्ञान) is traced into a profound and pervasive sense of duality of human self with other worldly objects. Undue desire for worldly objects becomes a source of human miseries and social stigmas. The Indian old culture used to check the duality of self and worldly objects in the past. Our religious scriptures used to guide the men and women for observing restraints on the desires for the worldly object, surrendering human ego and believing in the spirit of sacrifice (त्याग). Sacrifice leads to the ultimate victory over the human self and greed. The faith in sacrifice can be inculcated through 'familial education' and 'sanskaras'. For this the family members are required to follow an idle character which can influence the youngers. Nowadays, the familial Sanskaras have gone totally topsy-turvy due to acculturation to western culture, which has made majority of the Indians greedy, hedonistic, consumeristic and xenophilic. All these made men and women totally stigmatic. Social stigmas has created many social evils, which affected not only the education of the women but their peaceful living.

In the present materialistic age the man and woman both have been greedy, self-centred and unsocial due to which the society has become more or less stigmatic. If this trend is not checked the days are not far off the society as a whole will become barbarous. Having sex by the men with the unwilling women by force is called 'rape'. Rape is one of the worst social stigma of the present age. Rapes of the innocent women by men has become a common social feature, not only in India but also throughout the world. There is no need to give exact figures of rape cases. We daily read cases of rapes of women by men in newspapers. Such news are shameful slap on the face of humanity.

Recently, under the column 'Teacher to Tormentor', the *Times of India* dated 22.6.2005 reported that a teacher in Xingi in China is likely to face death sentence for debasing for molesting and raping 26 girls studying in 4th and 5th grades in a girls primary school in Xingi, China. The school was located in rural area. One of the fourteen-year old girl reported about her rape to her mother. The mother reported the matter to higher authorities and the teacher who taught her was arrested. The school is considered a safest place for the girls, but if the teacher is rapist and stigmatic criminal who will protect the girls. Then the school becomes a hell for the girls. Also in Delhi a few months back a Principal and a teacher of a Government school were arrested for raping a school girl in a guest house in Samepur Badli. In Delhi and also in other cities raping the innocent girls has become a common practice, which is nothing but a social stigma which is hurting the community.

This kind of social criminal stigma is hurting the women community which is a genesis of social existence. This cannot be stopped by school education. The schools can only train the girls in some self-defence methods. This can be rooted out from the society by adopting some strict steps. In the neighbourhood of the Village Bhalswa Gaj, District Haridwar, U.A., there is a Gurjar Village 'Bindu'. A boy guest of a Gurjar family was staying there with his relatives fifty years back. The period was winter season. The village young girls used to go out in the field for morning ease. The guest boy also used to go in the fields in the morning for molesting the girls. Since the girls used to go in a group of four or five, the boy failed to molest and rape them. The parents of the girls complained this to the family with which the boy was staying but nothing concrete happened. Finally, the Gurjars approached to the Writer's village respected elder man late Baba Man Singh who directed a man to find out the truth and in case there was something wrong to take some action. A group of three persons went early in the morning and sat behind the bushes. The boy and the girls came as usual. The boy tried to molest a girl. He was caught. First the group of three persons cut his nose and asked him to follow with them towards railway station. He followed. After few minutes they cut his penis. Thereafter, they cut his hands and finally murdered him and cremated him in an empty sugarcane field. After this nobody dared to molest or rape any girl in the area. In a co-educational intermediate college in the village nearly one thousand girls come to study without any fear. Such a harsh treatment is needed to stop such crimes and save the innocent women.

Another social stigma which is prevalent in the society is considering the women another's properties, that is, anta-property (पराया-धन). Due to this the girls are not equally treated with the boys. They are not well-equated. People do not realise that the women are auspicious beings which make the human social existence possible. People after the marriages of their girls forget them totally. In another words, generally the women are treated as bio-garbage by their parental family members. Only the parents of the girls till are alive remembers them. After this, their parental near ones as the brothers, the nephews do not remember them at all. In many cases, the many women become widows. But, neither they are remembered by their parental siblings or kith and kins nor by other relatives. Such widows pass their time in agony. They do not have any capacity to earn as they are not educated being anta-property. Main reason for this kind of treatment to the women is human greed due to hedonism. As such, there are many social stigmas which harm the women community. For all such social stigmas the youngers—the boys and girls should be educated at home and at the school.

Another social anti-women stigma in the society is that, is that, the women being weaker than the men are always considered weaker than the men. Media reported on 23.6.2005 that on 22.6.2005 a father-in-law ordered his daughter-in-law to bring a glass of cold water. The daughter-in-law being in advanced stage of pregnancy (8 months) requested her father-in-law to take water himself from the fridge. The father-in-law started abusing her. Listening the dialogue between them, the husband of the woman came and started beating her and thrashed her. Listening the cries of the woman the neighbours came and took her to nearby nursing home where the women (26 years) died. Also many women misbehave with their husbands and spoil their children.

So there are many women and also men who become the victims such social stigmas. Therefore, there is a need for proper education of women as well as women which may help in the life-building of the youngers and save the women from social stigmas.

9

Socio-Stigmatic Effects on Women Education

In the present empiricist industrial society the man has become hedonistic, consumeristic and xenophilic. And for achieving these ends, the man has become mad for gaining materialistic gains, which always entail many stigmatic happenings, those affect human social life badly. The stigmatic concept has emerged out of he concept of stigma. The world 'stigma' is a Greek word, included in English language, which means 'a brand of life like a 'red hot iron' used on slaves to suppress them', 'an infamy behaviour', 'a sort of social disgrace, which applied to a person', 'an extremity of life'. In the present social life when the human beings have become too much greedy, due to social change occurred due to continuous cultural diffusion and acculturation, there emerged many social stigmas of which poor class or castes and women have become prey.

Though the human beings are considered rational living beings, they have been gifted by the divinity with bigger brains to think, reason and analyse. They have been endorsed with moving hands to act and make creative objects for the use of human beings. They have also been rewarded with flexible legs to walk and perceive the natural phenomena. But the nature has made human beings very greedy acquisitive and exploitative. As such, the human beings always think of their own interests. And for materialising their own interests, the human beings generally ignore others' interest. This tendency always entails many social stigmas and evils. This human tendency has made the human beings, that is, men and women very greedy, self-centred, uncivilised and unsocial. They always think of their own interests for their hedonistic and xenophilic needs. This is happening due to human beings' greedy nature which has come into spate due to undue acculturation. These days men and women have totally forgotten their old socio-cultural values and largely adopted the values of the foreigners who have always been involved in material gains and values. Now, due to social stigmas crimes in the society have increased. And fair sex that is, women have been badly affected due to certain social stigmas.

It is also true that the social situation always continuously change and affect a large section of the society. Greek philosopher, Hereclitus said that everything is in flux and every physical and social phenomena continuously change. So, change in the status of women was sure to occur. The women who were worshipped in India in the past are now continuously tortured, molested and raped in the society. Also bad treatment to the woman by the men is now a social stigma. Dowry is the cause of this social stigma which is affecting the women in the present materialistic age. Not only dowry there are so many other stigmas which have changed our socio-economic, socio-cultural and moral conditions of the Indian society. What conditions have affected the health of the women and education need to be studied in detail. A few of these are as under:

1. *Topsy-Turvy physical condition*: Woman being physically topsy-turvy to man is one of the bio-stigma, due to which a woman is considered weaker than man. And the man is always dominant up on a woman. As such, no innovation and initiations emerge in the society for the epistemic development of the fair sex. A woman is always considered to give birth to the children, to bring them up and to inculcate some attitudes in them for saneful living. As such, the women are considered to look after the household, to bring up the children, to cook food and do all other household activities. On the other hand, her male partner is always supposed to earn and to sustain the family. Of course, many women do jobs and earn but due to their physical topsy-turvy conditions they always have to do all household work. Their husbands do not contribute or help in the household work of ladies. As such, working ladies remain very busy and cannot add to their epistemacy though they are as intelligent, as their male partners are.

2. *Patriarchal social structure*: Families all over the world are patriarchal. Male members have always upper hand in family

management or all family affairs. Female members come from their parental families are not given equal rights real families. All property including the offsprings are recorded under the name of the father. Since the girls ought to go with their husbands, the parents of the girls do not give much importance to women education. Though the girls generally are intelligent and diligent as the boys are. But in very small section of the society, that too in some tribal communities which follow the matriarchal pattern of social structure give importance to girls. The mother is the head of the family. She looks after the family management or all family affairs. Her husband is to obey her orders. All family property and offsprings of the family are recorded after the name of the mother. As in patriarchal family bridegroom takes his marriage party (Barat) to the house of the brides' parents, in matriarchal society, the bride takes her marriage party to bridegrooms' parent's house, and after the marriage bridegroom goes permanently to bride's house. The matriarchal family system is found in some tribal belts in Kerala and in Jaunsar Baber in Uttaranchal. In matriarchal families the women education is given more importance than the men education as the boys are anta-property in matriarchal families.

3. *Anta-property feeling*: When parents start thinking that their children of particular gender are another's property and it is a social obligation for them to send their particular child to another family, their interest towards that particular child subsides. In patriarchal families the girls' education is ignored. Parents start saying that if the girl does not shine in school education they will marry her soon. Similar is the condition in matriarchal family of the boys. Parents do not pay much attention to the education of the boy, as they after their marriage will have to go to their brides home, where they will have to obey their brides and mother and other senior lady family members. As such, the patriarchal and matriarchal patterns of family affect the women education.

4. *Family disregard*: Generally the girl children do not get that much attention from the parents as much is given to the boys. This is because the girls are considered anta-property. At the time of the birth of a baby girl an atmosphere of sadness prevails. The ladies do not sing songs. Neither the family members perform rituals as are done at the time of birth of a boy child. Parents generally pray to gods and goddesses to give them a boy child. Though boy and girl are two bio-diverse living beings, whose 'unity

in bio-diversity' makes the social existence. Without a woman life is not possible. Then why human beings—women and men always do not want to have girl child? And for a boy they become henotheistic also. This is because the girl is always considered another's property. And this anta-property (पराया-धन) thinking hampers the women education in the country. In school education—in both in girls and boys school, this kind of thinking can be removed by making the future guardian aware about its reality.

5. *Social alienation*: The another reason of hampering women education in the society is the alienist attitude of the society towards their girl wards. The girls are generally alienated by the elders in all kinds of social interaction. So the girls do not get real education for their lives. When they go to their real homes they do not get a chance of full interaction with all family members. If any girl want to study further after her marriage, she is hardly allowed to continue her studies.

6. *Marital life*: Married life also becomes a great hurdle for the women to continue their studies. After marriage when a woman becomes mother she has to devote her all energy to bring up her child. After attending to her child she will have to attend her household duties also. As such, the married life also hampers women education. But it is also true that married life, which is a 'unity in bio-diversity' amongst the human beings, is utmost essential. So, through the education the boys and girls should be apprised about the 'unity in bio-diversity' that is, married life. This does not happen in the present system of formal education, which lay emphasis only on the teaching of subjects. Education should also emphasis on life-building measures also.

6. *Crimes against fair sex*: Crimes against women have increased so much that it has become very difficult for the young girls and young ladies to walk alone. The media reports indicate that many girls and young ladies are molested and raped. The men commit such heinous crimes are barbarous. Even beasts and animals have sex with female beasts and animals after their consent. But the men do not hesitate to rape their own daughters, nieces. And in cities like Delhi, committing of rapes with the innocent girls and even with aged ladies has become a common feature. The people and the police are helpless. In many cases, the rapists walk scot-free. The society and the rulers are also helpless. Rape criminology

in the society has badly affected the women education. In the past in monocratic rules, the monarchs, used to apply very harsh rules for such heinous crimes. And most of the rapists were to face the death sentence. In the village of the writer, once a guest Rajput boy had tried to rape a beautiful sweeper girl. The girl fought the criminal bravely and saved her. The matter was brought to the notice of the village's oldest man late Shri Baba Man Singhji, who ordered to punish the guest Rajput boy. The face of the boy was blackened, he was adorned with old shoes' mala and put on the back of a donkey in topsy-turvy condition. A drum-beater was called and the criminal was taken into all of the four Mohallas of the village. Criminal boys' relative did not object to such a harsh punishment, rather they thanked to late Shri Baba Man Singhji. Due to fear of such harsh punishment no rape case occurred in the village. The administration should also think of such harsh treatment for the rapists. Then only the heinous crime of rape, which affects the girl education can be stopped. During their school education at school the girls should be trained in self-defence activities. The society as a whole should punish the rapists in the way late Shri Baba Man Singhji had punished the rapist who had tried to rape an innocent sweeper girl. Then only the women education can get a boost in the society.

7. *Women v/s women*: Generally it is seen that all living beings including human beings cooperate amongst themselves as well work against each other also. If we look to the animals we find that they also cooperate amongst themselves also, sometimes work against each other. Sometimes animals fight with their fellow, beings. But the animals are not greedy as human beings are. In in spite of this some animals like dogs, do not see their own fellow dogs. They try to push them out. This tendency is also seen in human beings. Human beings also sometimes do not like to talk to their own fellow-beings. In human beings it is seen that women sometimes work against women. Generally the mother-in-laws behave like this against their daughter-in-laws. They generally forget that they were also daughters sometime back. Some daughter-in-laws, sometimes are continuously misbehaved and tortured by their mother-in-laws. Some daughter-in-laws are sometimes murdered by their mother-in-laws. Some daughter-in-laws are forced to take suicide. In such a situation, when the daughter-in-laws are not fairly treated in their real homes, they

remain depressed. They do not dare to educate themselves further after their marriage. Such a situation is very bad for women education, as well for the social life.

For overall women education, there is a need to visualise all these situations which generally hampers women education in the country. The school authorities, especially managing the girl schools, should look to this chronic social problem. Society, social institutions like women empowerment bodies should look to this problem very seriously.

10

Women Psyche

Psyches of all living beings differ. There can be many reasons for the divergent psyches of all living beings, such as gender difference, biological diversity, different genetics and bringing up conditions, living conditions and standards, socio-economic and cultural conditions. All living beings are biologically divergent wholes having different psychological mental set ups which show different psyches. If we observe and the study the body structures of all livings, we find some difference in their body structures, skin texture, colour and size. The bodies of all living are different. In all human beings, the bodies of males and females are topsy-turvy. The body of the males are broader near the shoulders, under their heads. This is so, because the males are supposed to do hard work, pick up the load and weight of things. On the contrary, the body of a female is different. Her shoulders are slanting so as she may look beautiful. The head of a man is always flat so that he may keep some load on it when required. On the other hand, the head of a woman is always slanting and bulging. It is so because they keep on their heads hairs. Woman's head hairs are their crowns. Their hairs look beautiful on a curved or bulging head. The woman is broader at her hips. This is because she has to bear the child in her womb. The body of the woman is slanting whereas the man's body is overlapping. The man's and woman's bodies texture are different and topsy-turvy. If we look the bodies of a male and a female, these will be like this (p. 78):

In all livings there is a gender variation and there are males and females. They live together which is an "unity in bio-diversity". Without this unity there cannot be a genesis of living beings. These variations are the base of psyches of all living beings. Some analyst analyse human psyche by observing some human body parts. Take for example, the human face or faces of some animals, beasts or

Female Male

birds. Their faces depict their psyche. Human face and its parts—eyes, nose, ears, mouth and lips always portray human psyche. For example, if the nose of a person is like the nose of a parrot, the man is supposed to be self-centred. If the ears of a person are big he will be considered a rationalist, and well-wisher of all, like Mahatma Buddha. If the neck of a person is small and dumpy the person may be irrational and cunning. This is why a painter or a sculptor while making a portrait through painting or stone carving or bronze casting will always try to portray the correct form of the face of the person of whom he is making a portrait. Likewise, many psychologists try to analyse the human psyche of the human beings through their body parts.

There are many other features which are taken into consideration while analysing the human psyche. These features occur with the life journey of a person from child to old age. These occurrences especially build the human psyche of a woman. When a girl child is born in a family, it does not bring an atmosphere of joy and happiness in the human family. In other words, generally people do not like a girl child. Because a girl child is for 'social unity in bio-diversity' and is to be married with an outsider boy and sent to another family, thus a girl is always considered an 'anta-property' (परायाधन) and is not given due attention by many parents, if not all. As such, from the very beginning a girl child has not been treated on equal footings with the male siblings of the girls. And the girl child has also been feeling herself ignored and alienated to some extent. This kind of treatment has been generating a specific psyche of the girls. Further stigmatic conditions added fuel to this fire and created a specific woman psyche in the society. And mostly girls, the future would be women after their marriage, depict that alienistic psyche in their real homes that is, *Sasurals*. The main aim of the women education should be to reform and improve this kind of woman psyche. The woman education should make the girls aware about this kind of psyche. For doing this, the school education should generate a spirit of self-introspection.

Elders' behaviour towards youngers generally evoke emotions in the youngers. If the elders' behaviour is good and balanced, so to say equal to all children, it would evoke good emotions in the children, and the childrens' psyche in future life will be balanced. If the elders do not behave with the children well, it would evoke wrong emotions in the children. According to Sigmund Fraud, human emotions are multiplied. Some emotions are very deep rooted, some emotion stay in the middle and some emotions remain on upper edge of human mind. All these three kinds of emotions remains in the human mind like a piece of ice remains in water in a pot. Only a small portion of it is visible in the water. If these depressed emotions are not taken out through some psychological treatment, these emotions may be very dangerous for human life. These may spoil the psyche of the concerned human being. If these are properly handled the person may become intelligent, diligent, sociable and sane person. Sigmund Fraud had suggested that the artistic creative activities can reduce the repressed emotion of a person. This is why he had suggested teaching of art and art related activities in school education. But the elders should also introspect in their behaviour. They should treat all youngers, be it a girl or boy nicely on equal footing. It does not happen. Many women misbehaves with the young girls. They cannot be educated when they are leading a family life. It should be done when they are being taught in schools and colleges.

Not all, but many women, especially step-mothers treat their step-children including girls as bio-garbage. Generally the psyche of such women is, that they always think their own children who have come out of their own wombs. So the step-children for step-mothers are always like alien children. They do not treat such children nicely. Many of such ladies even do not provide good food to such children. It would not be wrong to say that the step-mothers always treat step-children as an unnecessary burden on them when their husbands, the father of the children, remain out for doing jobs, they generally beat their step-children. Such an uncivilised, unsane, undesirable, unsocial and inhumanistic behaviour of step-mothers toward step-children can be said barbarous. It evokes very bad emotion in such children. Such emotions always distort the psyche of the children who are our future guardians and builders and protectors of the national culture and the nation. Such children, especially girls who are would be women, always try to do with the youngers like this, in their future life. First of all parents, family members, step-mothers, aunts, grand mothers, community members should behave with the girl children very nicely and kindly. Thereafter, when the girls go to school for school education, the school teachers and school authorities should try to mould the psyche of the girls. The school education through some co-curricular activities should apprise the girls that they are the real builders of the future guardians as they are going to be mothers. The school teachers should generate a spirit of self-introspection in the girls. If the girls are properly educated our future guardians will be automatically rightly educated.

11

Life Journey of Woman

Life journey of a woman is very hard and tedious, a courage of life of her life span. It is like a transplantation of an emerging plant from one earthen pot or filled pot to another earthen filled pot, because a woman is born in one family and after becoming young she is transferred to another family through the social institution of marriage. But, like a botanical plant when transplanted from one earthen pot to another pot is given full care, such as watering, manuring and digging and, due to this the plant gives sufficient flowers and fruits. A women, when she is transferred to another house after marriage should be given due care at her all life stages. But generally it hardly happens at both of her life stages of a woman, that is, at her parental house and at real permanent house. And woman education can play a prominent role in this regard.

Life journey is a combination of two words—life and journey. The word life is a derivation from the Anglo-Saxon word 'lif' meaning 'a period from birth to death', 'a period of performing life function', 'a period of distinguished outward manifestations', 'a period in which a living being concentrates on certain activities like morality, sociality, sacrificiability', 'a period of happiness in favour of Almighty God through perfect living. The word 'journey' is a derivation from the French word 'journie' meaning travelling from one space to another. As such, every living being be it an animal, beast, insect, bee, human being and flora and fauna travels from stage to another, passing through various stages. And it ends. In human beings, the life journey of women is very astonishing, difficult, surprising and sometimes painful. Therefore, it is very necessary to educate the emerging women, that is, young girls about the stages of women life. This can be easily done while they are being educated at school stage.

Generally, patriarchal social structures of majority of the societies is the vehicle in which a woman completes her life journey. There are only very few matriarchal societies in the world which also do this job. A patriarchal society is a male dominated society in which the males always have a say. They always manage all of the human family affairs. Though the woman lives with her life partner. She also contributes a lot in the family affairs. She gives birth to the new society members and brings them up. Since woman is biologically weak than the man, so male, that is, man, always dominates over her. This tendency affects the woman's journey. Because the woman is an anta-property (पराया-धन) or an alienated individuality (अनन्या) she is always considered inferior to man and is side-tracked in her bringing up, so woman's life journey becomes very difficult from the beginning.

Before the birth of a child, the parents and the family members start praying Almighty God to reward them with a male child. Also, for this they become purely polytheistic and henotheistic and pray many gods and goddesses. After the mother conceives a child, many parents try to know about the gender of the child, whether the child is a boy or a girl. Knowing that the would be child is a girl, they want to get rid off of the girl child through foeticide. As such, the birth of a girl child in many families, not in all families, is not considered a good happening. This is why the first face of girl child's (would be woman) journey is not considered auspicious. It is followed with grief, sorrow and distress in the family. On the contrary on the occasion of the birth of a male child, a *hi-fi* celebrity is arranged in the boy child's family. The women of the family and of neighbourhood sing songs and dance. And also some feasts are arranged after performing some rituals. Whereas, on the occasion of the birth of a girl child who is going to be a woman and a generator of the neo-members of the society, no such celebraty is arranged. The main reason for this kind of sorrowful dump-atmosphere on the first face woman's life journey is that due to 'unity in bio-diversity'. When the girl becomes young she is to be married with a male partner and has to go to another's house. She is considered anta-property (पराया-धन). And for sending her to another's home, which becomes her real home, the girls' parents have to proceed through a difficult path. First of all they search a suitable boy groom for the girl which is a difficult job. They have to walk on different tracks for this. Knowing some boys the girl's family members and some relatives try to reach to the boys' parents with a proposal of the tying the knot of their daughter with their son. The grooms' parents have some different matrimonial inclinations. They forget that they have also daughters. First of all they try to know about the psychology and abilities of the girls. The girl's parents tell them about these. After this groom's parents insist to see and examine the girl. Then priorities generally remain that the girl should be beautiful, intelligent and diligent. She should be so educated that she may earn money in her married life. She should also bring huge things and heavy dowry. So the girl's parents always remain in state suspense and financial difficulties. Because they have to part off their beloved child for living in another's home for lifelong living they have to sufficient dowry. Besides this, they will have to entertain Baratis. They always remain bowing position before the bridegroom's parents and relatives. This is why the woman's first journey is considered very difficult and inauspicious for the parents of the girl. And due to this reason generally the girls are given second grade treatment in their parental houses in comparison to their brothers. And due to this reason bad emotions are formed in them due to which they remain frustrated throughout their lives, and an undesirable psyche is developed in the girls which becomes a social stigma for them.

It is also true that in India virgin girls are not only respected but are worshipped on many occasions and festivals like *Navratras*. Also many goddesses like Saraswati, Shakti, Lakshmi, Durga, Chandi, Kali and Vaishnav Devi are worshipped in India. Till the girls are married and are sent to their real homes, that is, *Sasurals*, they are duly cared and protected by their parents and other family members. They are educated on equal footings, equal to the boys. But for the girls, who have lost their mothers and are looked after by other ladies, either by step-mothers or by any another lady of the extended family, generally are not well-treated. In many cases such girls are badly ill treated and even tortured by such ladies. Such ladies treat such children as a burden, as they have not come out from their own stomach. They do not allow such girls to meet with their peer group girls. They force such girls either to read or to do household work as cooking, cleaning the utensils, washing of clothes and doing other household work. Of course, it is true that the development of work habits in the children is also necessary, but this should not be inculcated through torturing and punishment. The girls who face such a situation in their childhood experience a bitterness experience. Their early life journey becomes very bitter which is not forgotten by them throughout their lives. So it is necessary to educate the women in their early age about all these eventualities and to make them human for building the same personalities of the youngers who are our future guardian. This is necessary for building a sane society.

The second face of woman's life journey, which is very arduous, starts after her marriage with a man. Before marriage the woman was a virgin girl, an auspicious human living being. She was loved, respected and often worshipped in her parental family. The process of human life is a long living continuous process. The man and woman are born and brought up and pass through many life stages, as an infant, child, adolescent young, youth and a matured human being. In all these human life, the process of education plays a vital role. The man and women are joined by a process of 'unity in bio-diversity', which is called marriage. After the marriage the man and woman live together. During this second face of life journey they produce children, bring them up and mould their life. The 'unity in bio-diversity' is for the human existence. As such, they should live together harmoniously. But in some cases, this does not happen. The girl who was leading a harmonious life in her parental home, now supposed to lead a bowing life. As she enters in her new life she bows and touches the feet of her mother-in-law and other elderly ladies. She has to observe and follow strict family discipline. She will have to touch the feet of her mother-in-law and other elderly ladies in the morning daily, every day. She will have to obey her mother-in-law at every step. Many mother-in-law do not treat their daughter-in-laws on equal footing as they treat their daughters. They desire that their daughter-in-laws should bring sufficient dowry. If this does not happen, such mother-in-laws start torturing their daughter-in-laws, which becomes an apex harassment to the new member of the family, that is, daughter-in-laws. Sometimes, the situation becomes so bad that the daughter-in-laws, gets deeply depressed and commits suicide. Such inhuman mother-in-laws forget that they were also in the same condition. And many got the daughter-in-laws murdered for not bringing sufficient dowry. Such cases of daughter-in-laws torture, harassment, suicides and murders have become a common feature in the society these days. The girl's parents who had given births to such unfortunate daughter-in-laws, lament for the loss of their precious daughters. Such unfortunate happening occurs because of ignorance of the reality in this regard by the mother-in-laws. Had they would have been educated in their early age, such nasty tragedies would have been avoided. It is, therefore very necessary to make the fair sex educated about their life situations and roles as a women while they are being educated in schools. Reading only subjects and knowing about physical things cannot be said education, education is much more. Since the women are life-builders and sustainers of the society, they should be made aware about all such life situations.

After becoming daughter-in-law, every woman wants to become a mother. Being a mother, a woman has to perform certain duties herself alone. Because after giving birth to a child, the child is to be brought up. Earlier in joint families all family members used to contribute in brining up the child. Now the joint families have nearly crumbled and nuclear families have come into being. As such, bringing up of the younger child is the responsibility of the mother, which is a tedious job, because she has to do all household work also. As such, it is very necessary that the girls while studying in school should be made aware about the maternity and its related responsibilities. But this is not done under our present formal system of education. Our formal system of education is only examination oriented and not life oriented.

Another factor which makes the life of a woman hazardous is that groom's side wants that the brides for their sons should be well-educated and so proficient that they may also do some jobs and contribute in the family economy. This is why the girl's parents want that their daughters should also be highly educated. Due to this reason the frequency of women education has considerably increased. This is also true that the girls are equally intelligent as the boys are. The girls are diligent and sincere in their studies. They also shine in education and leave the boys behind in examination results. They also are employed. But when after their marriage they shift from their parental homes to in-laws homes that is, 'Sasural', they will have to do all homework, to look after their children and to do jobs in government organisations. Doing all the three jobs together as a housewife becomes very difficult for a working woman. Because the working housewives do not get a support neither from the father-in-laws and mother-in-laws nor from their husbands. These days both the father-in-laws and mother-in-laws generally do not want to sacrifice their independence. They generally want to live separately from their sons and daughter-in-laws. Also, the husbands generally do not cooperate with their wives. They expect that their wives should do every kind of household work. Even they are not happy to wash their *kachha* and *baniyan*. To help their wives in kitchen work is an unthinkable activity. But this fact is also true that if the women are self-supporting they can meet any life challenge bravely. So, making the women self-supporting is logical and correct. But for sustaining the self-supporting capacity of the women all related persons should cooperate with the working women. Specially the husbands should realise that their wives are doing hard work, so they should cooperate with their wives in all household work. So also, the in-laws should cooperate with the working women. All of them should be educated for discharging this responsibility.

The women's life processes is also affected by many other factors, such as, biological, social, economical, political and sometimes theological. The process of life is a biological continuum of woman and man. It is not certain that both of them will remain healthy lifelong. If any of them becomes biologically weak they should cooperate each other. For being healthy both wife and husband should develop good health care habits, such as doing exercises daily. While the girls are studying in schools such health care habits may be developed in schools. These may be going on morning walk daily, doing jogging, yoga and meditation. For doing all health habits women have to follow a set of life routine, as going to bed early and wake up early, to adopt a simple way of life and to avoid fast and junk food. These methods will pave the way for happy and harmonious living. Another most important aspect in the journey of women's life is sociability. It is necessary that a woman should be sociable. She should know how to behave with others. Sometimes the women do not behave well with others. Such habit damages the harmony and homogeneity in the family and community. So, for social harmony, the girls should be educated in the family as well as at the school to behave well with others. Economy is also an important factor in woman's life. Earlier, the husband was supposed to earn and sustain the economy of the family. Now in the present hedonistic period women and men have become consumeristic and xenophilic. This attitude has also made their children hedonistic and consumeristic which is very dangerous for their future life. The school education should also have provision to make the future wives aware about the implications of hedonism and xenophism. The school education should also make them aware about simple living and high thinking. The ladies should be made aware about their political rights. And finally the ladies should also follow theological tolerance and harmony. This can also be done if the school education have a provision for religious tolerance and secularism.

Many women become victims of natural calamities, such as becoming widows at a very early age, loosing their dear ones and ignorance of them by their parental family members. Many ladies become physically handicapped in their childhood and even loose their parents. Their lives become hell. In the village of the writer there was a saying that anybody who would change his or her religion will surely die. One Rajput and his wife had converted themselves to Islam in Aurangzeb's time. Both of them had died. After this, one hundred and fifty years ago (approximately) a Bhatt Brahman and his wife got converted to Islam on the advice of a tantric Maulvi, they had also died after few days of conversion. They had left a four years' old blind girl. Though there were four or five other Bhatt Brahman families, but they had declined to look after the blind girl as she was the daughter of Bhatts who had converted to Islam. This situation for the girl was very tragic. But the villagers decided to look after the blind girl one by one by all irrespective castes. The name of the girl was 'Shivbi'. The villagers supported the girl till she survived up to the age of eighty-eight years. Though the people of the village looked after supported 'Shivbi' throughout her life but it was a tragic journey of her life.

In Hindus in many upper castes do not allow re-marriage of the widows. Many widows do not find a place to live after the death of their husbands. Some of them are accommodated in their parental homes, where they pass their time. But there are many widows who are not supported by anybody. Neither they are self-supporting, nor they are supported by their in-laws, nor they are looked after by their parental nephews, who consider such widows as dead biological garbage. Such widows are generally supported by the general public as 'Shivbi' was supported. To avoid such an awkward situation the girls should be educated so that they many face any awkward situations in their lives. Such situations generally happen due to the social anta-property mindset of the people in the society.

In the life journey, the women find women as their killers. Generally it is observed that women are murdered by women due to obsession of taking too much dowry, treating the daughter-in-laws as their obedient servants and getting them harassed by their husbands. In order to mitigate this maltreatment of innocent daughter-in-laws, it is necessary to educate all women about this unsocial, illegal, unethical and undesirable behaviour of the women against women. Out of one thousand father-in-laws only one or two father-in-laws will be found unethical and unkind to their daughter-in-laws. But majority of the mother-in-laws, and sister-in-laws are very unkind to the newly married daughter-in-laws and they cut of their life journeys.

On the whole, it can be assumed that the life journeys of the woman is a very tedious and difficult job. There comes many stages in which the women find it difficult to proceed further in their life journey. To avoid this arduous life journey situation of the women, versatility of complete women education is unavoidable. Any girl should not be deprived of complete life education. They should be completely made aware about their alienistic life situations. They are born and brought up in one home and transferred to lifelong in other home, wherein they face many life situations. They should be educated about all these.

UNITY IN BIO-DIVERSITY

Unity in diversity is essential for peaceful living of different people believing in different religions and faiths, hailing from different ethnic and racial groups and backgrounds, speaking different languages and following different cultural traits. Similarly, the 'unity in bio-diversity' is must for the existence of all living beings, that is, animals, beasts, birds, insects, bees and all human beings. Not only the living beings, but also the flora and fauna and earth have a sort of unity in bio-diversity. The nature has created two kinds of living beings—males and females. The union of these two kinds of living beings, that is, males and females make the life and existence of the living beings possible. These two kinds of living beings—males and females are made topsy-turvy by the nature.

Due to this opposition, the males and females in all living beings come together and unite. The animals, beasts, birds and insects unite temporarily for having sex which results in giving births to new ones. But in human beings in spite of their biological diversity, the men and women are united together through the social institution of marriage. They, when bound together through marriage, live together throughout their lives and contribute to the social development, as they produce the future members of the society. As such, it is necessary that both the man and woman after their marriage should live together throughout their lives harmoniously. And for their harmonious living, the parents, society and social institutions like educational institutions should adopt a viable process of their life development. The man and woman should be given equal chance for their life development. Education can play an important role in this regard. But nowadays due to hedonistic and xenophilic mindset of human beings, due to materialism, the role of education has also been confined up to passing examinations in flying colours, and, life-building role of education has been totally side-tracked under formal system of education.

Unity in bio-diversity opens the gates for the human social development. Men and women learn to adjust and live together lifelong. For the betterment and security of all human beings, the men and women develop perennial social institutions like marriage, family, community and religious and educational institutions. The human beings have developed various forms of marriages as—arranged marriages, love marriages, capture marriages, monogamy, polygamy, heterogamy, intercaste marriages for unity in bio-diversity. In India, in all castes and religions, arranged marriages are done. Such marriages prove permanent and these continue lifelong and no divorce or disunity in bio-diversity is generally seen. The marriages of young boys and girls are arranged by the parents of both, young girls and boys. They settle the marriages of their wards, keeping in view the suitability and prospects of sound joyful lifelong living. Generally in Hindus the marriages are not held in near relations. So marriages are held between the families of different *totems* (गोत्रा). The *totems* of the parents of the boy and girl should be different. The Indian society is patriarchal, so the girls are sent to the houses of boys (bridegrooms).

During the childhood the girls witness the marriages of many boys and girls and see the girls going from their parental houses to their in-laws home (*Sasurals*). So they also set their minds to be ready for going to another homes after their marriages. The parents of the girls are also convinced to send their daughters to the houses of their husbands after their marriages. They treat their daughters as anta-property (पराया-धन). This kind of thinking in girl's parents changes the psyche of the girls. The girls becomes alientistic and start thinking for their future living. To some extent they become self-centred. Many girls start thinking in advance to live separately from their in-laws and establish a nuclear family. Generally this happens due to hedonistic and xenophilic changes in the society occurred due to acculturation. Due to this many women think their own, who have born from them. Other family members are alien to them. Due to such drastic social change many social evils like corruption, greed, self-centredness, loot, dacoities, harassment of ladies takes place in the society. Many women also involved in corruption. They try to earn money by unfair means. In many cases, though very very few, involved themselves in unfair sex relations and for that they do not hesitate even in getting their husbands murdered. Many women becomes so greedy that they do not hesitate in occupying public land or property through encroachments.

One of the main reason of self-centred psyche of the present women is drastic social change which has occurred due to economic development. The modern economic development has entailed hedonism, consumerism and xenophilism which have become a common social feature. Every women wants to become hedonistic and consumeristic and wants that her own children should avail all such benefits. Other children of the joint family are not her own. All children are neither equally intelligent nor diligent. Some are intelligent. Some are diligent. Some have both these qualities, so such children do progress in life. The women who are only interested in their own children pour too much love on them. Too much of love poured by the parents generally prove poisonous. As such, children who are too much loved neither develop necessary work habits nor they read. So they do not acquire good education. On the other hand, children who are sincere in their studies and do hard work progress in life. But the women who love their own children too much and spoil them, do not feel happy to see the progressive children. They rather grudge and hate such children. Due to their frustration they generally want to live separately from the other family members. Such ladies generally break the joint families. They establish nuclear families. They motivate their children to break the relations with their kith and kins. Now the situation has gone so bad that the original family members do not see each other. They do not regard their elders. They do not find time to ask their elders how they are living? The children also walk on the same track their parents have adopted. And this has happened due to the negligence of illiterate women in the society. So women education is a vital issue in the present Indian society. But the women education should not be limited up to 3Rs. It should cover all aspects of familial education which a women is supposed to do, then only the 'unity in bio-diversity' can be successful for harmonious social living.

Earlier, the wider common aspect of 'unity in bio-diversity' was aimed at to unify the all members of ethnic group through the social institution of family. Due to the human greed and self-centredness the institution of family became diversified in small joint families, extended families, and, original families of olden days also. Also, it was very difficult to manage a big joint family. So the families like expanded family, extended family etc., etc., had emerged. But there are no nuclear families of the western type in olden days in India. Now, the nuclear families which is mostly the gift of acculturation has become a common feature in our country. Now the 'unity-in-bio diversity' is not for the development of a 'bio-whole', that is, for an integrated human social living. It is now limited to a nuclear family which is a 'solo-unity in bio-diversity'. In the earlier days, the 'unity in bio-diversity' was not for the living of husband and wife children only. Unity in bio-diversity was aimed at to bring unity in a 'bio-whole'. This 'bio-whole' used to entail or contain all members of the family of an ethnic group. And this 'bio-whole' was called a joint family. In a joint family there used to be a head of the family who used to look after all members of the family equally in all fields. All women of the joint family used to look after all members of the family equally.

The Indian joint family system used to be an institute of familial education. The elders of the joint family used to enculturate the youngers by inculcating good life habits as to respect the elders, to love the youngers, to speak true, to develop good habits like 'early to bed early to rise'. All these were to make the youngers future sane citizens. The youngers were asked to respect ladies and elders not only of their own family, but of all entire society. As such, the joint family, which used to be product of 'unity in bio-diversity', that is, of living male and female together. Though, in olden days, there used to be some incidents of joint families breaking, but incidents were few and the women used to be the breakers.

The old joint family system which was the result of spiritual 'unity in bio-diversity' was applauded throughout the world. In 1964, the writer was attached to a USAID team to learn preparing audio-visual aids to be used in teaching, by Late Prof. P.K. Roy, former Principal, Central Institute of Education, University of Delhi. The writer worked with Prof. (Dr.) Arthur William Earl for six months. After completing the training, the writer had invited Prof. (Dr.) Arthur to his house for tea. Prof. (Dr.) Arthur William Earl reciprocated and invited him to his house on tea. The writer went to his house for tea. His wife asked "why Indian marriages are permanent". The writer counter questioned "why she was interested to know this? Madam Arthur William Earl replied that Dr. Arthur William Earl was her fourth husband, earlier she was divorced by her earlier three husbands. She praised the Indian arranged marriage system. In her view 'unity in bio-diversity', is a true reality in Indian society. Mrs. Hillary Clinton wife of Mr. Bill Clinton, former President of United State of America not only had praised the 'unity in bio-diversity' in Indian social system but had advised the Americans to adopt Indian marriage and joint family system. In 1954, one Mr. Albert Coommer, student of late Prof S. Radhakrishnan, former President of India, who was Vice-President of India in 1954, decided to visit India and meet his (*guru*) teacher in Delhi. He had done B.A. (Hons.) Philosophy under Dr. Radhakrishnan from Cambridge University, London. After crossing the British Channel he decided to travel up to India on foot through some European and Arabian countries. He was looted eight times up to Kheber and Bollan Pass on the west of Pakistan. When he entered in Pakistan he was fully entertained and was given food and shelter. After entering in India, he stayed for sometime in Swarna Mandir at Amritsar. He found Indian families and also Pakistan families most hospitable. In Delhi, he stayed for a fortnight with his *Guru* (teacher) Dr. Radhakrishnan. Finally, he decided to visit Haridwar and *Swargashram* in Rishikesh (U.A). He started his journey on foot from Delhi to Haridwar and Rishikesh. After staying one night in the mid-way up to Govindpuri, Modinagar he entered the Government Training-Cum-Production Centre, Govindpuri run by the U.P. Government in which the writer was working as Carpentry Instructor. This centre used train the refugee students in four disciplines: (1) Television and Radio, (2) Electricity, (3) Sheet metal and (4) Carpentry. After seeing all the three classes (1 to 3) in the last he entered in carpentry class. The writer asked him, whether he would like to eat something? He replied anything be offered to him because he was hungry. The writer sent him to his house along with his attendant Kothari with an instruction to cook food and give him. Mr. Albert Coommer stayed with the writer and his fellow instructor Shri Lohani for three days. Both the writer and Lohani used to leave him alone during the day while they were on duty. While going to Haridwar on fourth day he highly praised the Indian hospitality due to Indian joint family system. Likewise, many people used to praise the Indian joint family system due to 'Indian spiritual unity in bio-diversity'. In the past the Indian pairs, that is, husbands and wives were not so greedy and self-centred as are now-a-days.

As such, in the present materialistic hedonistic age it has become necessary to look into the all aspects of humanity covered by the 'unity in bio-diversity'. This long unity of man and woman should be for the betterment and prosperity of human beings. The word human is a derivation from the words: (*i*) French word 'humanide' and (*ii*) Latin word 'Humanus', meaning belonging to mankind which posses the qualities of a man or human being. A man means a male or adult or husband. And a female means a 'wife'. Both are supplementary to each other. Then unity is an 'unity in bio-diversity' which is necessary for the existence of human society. The human beings, that is, men and women are called rational beings. They have been gifted by the nature with bigger brains, erect posture, moving hands, and foots to work and walk. They can think, rationalise and generalise about their actions. In spite of all this nature has made the human beings very greedy. Due to this the psyche of men and women has become hedonistic, consumeristic and xenophilic in the present empiricist industrial age. And they are going to be irrationalistic like animals and beasts.

The women do not lag behind in this respect. It is, therefore, necessary to educate properly both of them, to make them aware about their psyche, natural resources, socio-economic conditions cultural aspects of the society. In other words, both men and women should be properly educated for saneful living. Only teaching of humanities, science and mathematics can never be real education. Real education is a process of life-building. And women are lagging behind in this regard. So women education should contain life-building process.

12

Life Roles of Woman

All living beings—animals, beasts, birds, insects, bees, men and women and flora and fauna have a life circle. They are born and brought up and after their life journey death terminates their life circle. During the tenure of their lives they have to play certain specific life roles. There are some stages in one's life as childhood, adolescence, young age, adulthood and old age. In all of these stages a living being has to play specific life roles. The life of all living beings is the result of 'unity in bio-diversity'. A female is married with a male and she gives birth to the children. The children are of opposite genders. In human beings these are girls and boys, who in the long run are termed as women and men. In human beings the women and men are of specific genders, who have to travel in their lives on different tracks. As such, they have different roles in their lives. A women comes in this world as a girl child having topsy-turvy body structure and sex organs than a boy child. A girl is brought up, and when become young is married with a distant man (boy) and sent to another house, so she is considered anta-property (पराया-धन). During the childhood girls see many girls going to another houses. So the girls' psyche becomes alienestic in childhood.

In the first stage of her life, the woman as a child plays different roles than the boys. Girls are generally shy than the boys. Generally, they remain introvert with the elders—males and females both. But a girl is generally extrovert with her age group girls. So a girl generally mix up with her age group girls and not with her age group boys. As such, the girls always try to learn roles of the women. A girl always tries to work with her mother and with other ladies of the family. A girl will always try to help her mother, aunt or grandmother in their household work. When a girl becomes young she tries to mix up with her peer group girls of her age. As all of the girl notice all girls going to their in-laws, which makes their psyche alienistic. So the girls always try to know and learn the roles they have to play in new real home that is, *Sasural* (in-laws). Also the girls being anta-property are not equally treated with the boys which affects their roles in their parents house. The girls roles in their childhood are limited up to kitchen work just as cooking and serving food to the elders. In Hindu Indian society there is a custom that elders do not accept the food even water served by the virgin girls. This tradition limits the roles of the girls in their parents' home. However, the girls learn all sort of familial work in their parental house.

When the girls become young and attain puberty they have to become brides and are to be married with suitable bridegrooms. After their marriage the girls become bride and to go their real houses which is called their 'Sasurals', real homes. They have to live their lifelong. In their new homes 'Sasurals' the roles of the bride becomes more vivid and difficult. She has to perform many family roles. She has to obey her-in-laws, especially the mother-in-law at every step in doing household work. She has to cook food, keep the house clean, clean utensils. After sometime the daughter-in-law, that is, bride, become mother. She has to do all motherly roles. She has to look after and bring up her child doing all household work. Mostly all women want to become mother. In other words, a women after becoming mother has to perform double roles. She has to look after her child and do all household work. She has to perform motherly role as well as role of a housewife. In addition to these roles a daughter-in-law has to perform the roles of hospitability also. As such, life roles of a wife are many. She has to play a role of a housewife, a mother, a caretaker of elders and upbringer of the young children. Majority of the married women have to do *purdah* from the elders. In some villages the daughter-in-law are required to do *purdah* before elderly ladies also. *Purdah* system is the gift of Muslim rule. The mothers of the girls can do a wonderful job. They can educate about future roles of their daughters in the Sasurals.

Eating is necessary for the survival of the living beings. But unbalanced and undesirable eating can be dangerous for living beings. As such, one of the pious role the women is to provide the suitable edible items to all family members and to young children. The women should have the sufficient knowledge of edible things. Then only they can decide about the essential food items or menu of their kitchens which may help the family members keeping them healthy and fit. Many women ignore this fact. They are also fond of eating tasty food items. In the beginning they cook tasty items for themselves. They eat such items and enjoy. In the long they give such tasty food items to their children. Their children enjoy such fast food junky items and they become fond of such junky food items. They always demand such fond junky food items from their mothers. Such children become mad for such junky food items. And in the long run they become a problem for their parents and other family members. Such bad food habits inculcate other bad habits as to see T.V. up to late night, delay in going to bed in the night and late rising in the morning, discarding reading habits and not doing any other house work. In other words, such children become spoiled children. Not only that if they are not provided food items of their choice, the become violent, atheistic, unsocial kids in the society. They even do not hesitate to punish their parents for not meeting their food item demand. Therefore, it is very essential to make the girls aware, while they are living with their parents, about their future parental roles. The girls' parents should not make their girls fond of junky and fast foods. This can be done by the elderly women through familial education. It is very necessary for the life-building of the future guardians. Girls schools can also educate the girls about their motherly roles. This can be done through periodical seminars and familial discussions.

The women are said to be the life-builders of the youngers. One of the important role of the woman is to inculcate the desirable sane life attitudes in the future guardians. For this all women should be made aware about the original national culture, so that they can enculcate desirable life attitudes which can be useful in enculturation of the youths. Our national culture is based on simple living high thinking. Due to the hedonistic and consumeristic temper in the society our present women generally first themselves become hedonistic. They try to enjoy life themselves believing in 'eat, drink and be merry'. Thereafter, they make their children 'carvac' (चटौरे). First of all the women should inculcate a spirit of simple living and high thinking. They should inculcate habits like: (1) early to bed and early to rise makes a man healthy and wise, (2) to make the children aware about their life circle. One who has come will surely go, therefore, the children should make their life sane, (3) all human beings are creations of the Almighty God, therefore, they should respect and treat all human beings well, (4) all should lead a spiritualistic life and should pray Almighty God, (5) the mother is their creator and is like the Almighty God, therefore all children should not only respect but pray their mothers. They should respect all other ladies also, (6) children speak true, (7) the women should inculcate work habits in the children. The children should be asked to do their work themselves. Now-a-days, the mothers due to examination phobia do not allow their children to do any of the house work or their own work, (8) the women should generate a spirit of sociability in the children, (9) the mothers should make their children humane and finally (10) create an epistemic attitude in the children.

The women are said to be the enemy of the women. This role of the women is unjust, unsocial, unethical and condemnable on all counts. First, the step-mothers torture the children of man's early wife behave in such a way that such children never forget such a bad inhuman treatment. Specially the girls do not forget such treatment throughout their lives. Such treatment affects the psyche of the girls. Some girls get relief from such nasty women treatment when they are married, as some mother-in-laws treat such daughter-in-law very kindly. Their role is appreciated by all. But some mother-in-laws treat their daughter-in-laws very badly on many pretexts as not bringing sufficient dowry, not doing the expected household work. This happens because many mothers do not inculcate work habits in their daughter, who find it difficult to adjust in their new homes that is, in-laws (ससुराल). Many mother-in-laws harass their daughter-in-laws up to such an extent that the daughter-in-laws are forced to commit suicides. Many mother-in-law got their daughter-in-law murdered on false pretexts as catching fire in the kitchen. As such, generally, women act against women. Such women perform inhuman roles in their lives. For unjust, inhuman and illogical women roles some steps are very necessary. The women should be educated just in their parents homes. After, they should be educated in schools. And finally, the society should have a vigilant eye on such women. In society there are few gentlemen who try to stop such crimes. In the writers' village there were two or three Thakurs who used to sit on *dharna* at the door steps of such unkind ladies. Their 'satyagrah' used to continue till the concerned lady promised not to harass her daughter-in-law. Such unethical treatment of women by women should be stopped. This can only be done by the elders of the society.

Lastly, it is pointed out that in the present materialistic age 'unity in bio-diversity', that is, marriage, of the girls is becoming an arduous difficult job day-by-day in Indian society. The girls' side has made the boys' side more greedy as they give more dowry. Boys side want that the girls should be beautiful, educated and suitable for earning in her married life. In addition they want dowry also. As such, the girls' parents generally try to provide to girls full educational facilities. Of course, this help them to find out suitable bridegrooms. The boys' parents do not stick to a fixed dowry amount. But after the marriage of their son they want that their daughter-in-law should do a job and earn. Ultimately the daughter-in-law have to do a job. Doing job adds many complications and hardships for such working girls. They have to do full household work and do jobs also. This makes their life very difficult. They have to do full household work, to look after their children, they have to look their husbands and mother-in-laws. Their husbands do not contribute in any of the household work. Neither they help in the kitchen work, nor they wash their 'kachha baniyan' after taking bath. The working women have to do all household duties like cooking, washing of clothes, cleaning of kitchen utensils etc., etc. Above all, they have to look after their children. As such, the household roles of working women become very difficult and tiresome.

On the whole it can be said that the life roles of all woman are many and are tiresome. Their husbands should cooperate with their wives. They should also be educated to do so. The women should be guided by their parents at the initial stage. After that when the girls go to school, the school education should have a place in school curriculum for educating the girls for their family roles. This aspect cannot be taught as a school subject. The girls can be made aware through services of lectures, discussions, debates, seminars and the girls can be enlightened further through related co-curricular activities. The woman organisations should also come forward and should help the schools in organising such co-curricular activities.

SOCIAL ROLES OF WOMAN

Social roles of woman are many and multifaceted. A few of social roles of women are mentioned below:

Genetic Role

The genetic role of a woman is one of the most important social roles. A woman is like mother earth. The seeds are sown in the garb of the mother earth. The mother earth conceives these seeds and plants are grown. The crops of the plants are harvested which are used by the human beings for their sustenance and living. Like this a woman first is bound with a man through 'unity in bio-diversity', she receives the seed of her life partner, her husband. She conceives, becomes pregnant and the child develops in her womb. The woman gives birth to a baby child who grows slowly and becomes an adult in due course of time. He/she becomes the member of the society and the guardian of the youngers and elders. The genetic role of a woman is one of the difficult roles. She has to go through difficult faces from the conceivement till she gives birth to a child. After facing many difficulties the woman becomes a mother, a producer, a builder and sustainer of human beings. This is why a mother is considered a mother God. And she is respected in the society. The future women, the virgin girls (कन्यायें) are always respected and worshipped in the Indian society. The society should not ignore the important genetic role of women. The members of the society should always respect the women and should give them due attention and protection to them. The women should also give due care to all youngers, adults and elders. In the present materialistic society the woman are not given due attention by the mankind. A few men have become like animals they try to rape and molest the women. The media daily reports such cases. It is also true that many women also ignore their motherly roles. They never try to shower motherly affection to all youngers. Those are born from them are only deer to them. Due to this the society as a whole suffers. The old joint family system has been crumbled due to self-centredness and unmotherly treatment of the women. It has, therefore, become very essential that life-building should be given a place in women education, that is, the girls who are future mothers, should be educated about their future motherly duties while they are getting school education. For this the school authorities should organise related co-curricular educational programmes.

Educational Roles

Home is the epicentre of education of the young children. The mother and the other family members play a vital role in educating their young children at home. And this type of family education is called familial education. Since the inception of human society, the parents, especially mothers, and other ladies of the family have been educating their children through familial education. The familial education is imparted in two ways, that is, through informal way and non-formal way, by inculcating life good attitudes such as—to speak true, to follow punctuality, early to go to bed and early to rise, to be simple, to develop work habits and to motivate the children to be epistemic. Through this process of familial education the mother and other family members used to do life-building of the youngers. The youngers used to be encouraged for self-learning. All this was done through educating the youngers in-formal and non-formal ways. Through familial education the youngers used to learn good habits, sane behaviour. The character building morality and personality development of the youngers used to be by observing their parents and elders. The main emphasis was laid on cultural development of the youngers through enculturation. All of such familial education was imparted by the women in the olden days. All old cultures and civilisation used to be developed through familial education. Old civilisations like Greek Civilisation, Hebrew Civilisation, Mohan-jo-daro and Harappa Civilisation of India and later Aryan Civilisation and Chinese Civilisations were the outputs of familial education. In all of these civilisations the women were respected and were given due authority to mould the early life of the youngers. All this was done to lead to the life-building process of the youngers. Still in many tribal areas the familial education is given due importance in which the tribal woman play a prominent role. The prime aim of the present tribal education is to enculturate the youngers and to perpetuate the tribal culture. But now in tribal areas, as well as in plan field areas the parental familial educational roles have been subsided due to hedonistic mindset of the people.

The people generally keep themselves in the rat-race of money earning, and mothers also do not lag behind in this pursuit.

Life-Builder of Youngs

Since the genesis of human life lies in women. The woman after giving birth to the children looks after them brings them up. She devotes herself for bringing up the children continuously sacrificing her comfort. The woman is the epitome of love. She loves her children. Many illiterate women love only their own children and consider the other children of the family as aliens. So it is necessary to educate the women in their young age that all children are the form of God. They should love all children equally. This can be done while the girls are being educated at school. This can be taught by the school lady teachers. So in life-building school education should compulsory for all girls. It can be taught through, rapport, seminars, discussions debates and co-curricular activities.

Manager of the Household

A married woman generally manages her household alone as her husband remains out for earning. For managing her house, the woman should know about the family budget. She know about the implications of the social change occurred due to acculturation. Thereafter, the girls, would be housewives, should be made aware about the household management. This can be done by arranging related co-curricular activities at the school level.

Social Role

The woman should be social. For this there is a need to inculcate sociability in the girls. Generally, it is observed that mostly the girls are extrovert with their fellow girls. For others they remain introvert. Sociability is necessary for good behaviour, morality and good character. The girls should be made aware about the benefits of sane sociability during the school education. And sociability should be inculcated through co-curricular activities at schools. There should not be any gender bias against the girls. Because of gender bias the women become not only unsociable but also unhospitable. Socrates' wife Xentippe was such a lady. If, any of Socrates disciple dared to enter in Socrates house she used to pour a full cold-water pot over his head. To be hospitable for a woman is a best quality. So every woman should be educated to be hospitable.

A woman has to play multifaceted roles. Until and unless a woman does not play these multifaceted roles, it becomes difficult for her to adjust in her new home. A woman should always be tolerant. She should maintain restraints if anybody in the family does not behave well with her nicely. She should respect her in-laws and other elders in the family. She should shower love and affection to all youngers. Her love should not remain limited up to her own children. For making the girls sane future women they should be educated about their future roles.

MOTHERLY ROLES

One of the most important prime role of woman is to do balanced parenting. Of course, all women do parenting but they misbalanced parenting. Balance parenting can only possible when the mother adopts a balanced behaviour towards her children. Balanced behaviour require balancing of love and strictness. Many mothers shower too much of love over their children and do not show strictness. Their children are generally spoiled. They only become hedonistic, self-centred and unsociable. They do not develop work habits. Such children generally face a dark future. Therefore, it is necessary that every mother should try to acquire parenting pride. She should give her children a strong foundation of traditional values. Traditional values are to a child what is soil to a plant. But in the modern materialistic and hedonistic age people say goodbye to traditional values. This happening due acute acculturation in the country. The woman as a mother can revive the original culture by doing balanced parenting. A child develops strong roots when nurtured in the rich soul of culture and traditional values. From there he/she can grow and flourish without fear of looming direction. The mother should take the following steps for balance parenting:

1. *Respect for grand parents and elders*: The prime role of the mother should be to make her child follow this age-old tradition of respecting grand parents and all elders by being a role model. It will bring out a quality of humanity in the child.
2. *Love for the youngers*: The mother should tell her children that the showing love and taking care of youngers—brothers, sisters or cousins will earn them respect and love.

3. *Family values*: The mother should teach her children, while parenting to discard ego and adopt love. She should inculcate in her children to follow the family values. The mother should instil in her children a spirit of tolerance, which will be a source of happiness and success in life.
4. *Inculcation the spirit of religiosity*: Of course due to materialistic and hedonistic attitudes religious rituals have now become outdated but not their spirit. The mother should make her children aware of the importance of religious rituals, relevance of festivals, so that legacy of rich culture and social traditions, cultural traits could be maintained and enculturation of children be done. And, also morality be generated.
5. *Finally*, the mother should inculcate a desire for the love of the country.

All these steps can help the mother in balanced parenting.

It also cannot be denied that the woman, that is, mother is the auspicious teacher a life moulder, builder and the nation builder. Therefore, a mother should also possess the attributes of a good teacher. These attributes should be as following:

1. A mother should believe that her children are her students. She should allow them to realise their potentials and, utilise their potentials.
2. A mother should realise that each child is an individual. No two children are the same. They will not have the same interests. They have individual differences so that they cannot learn and do the same work.
3. A mother should shower unconditional love over her children. She should try to build a relationship where the child can trust the mother. When the child has a problem that should be addressed by listening the child patiently.
4. The mother should encourage the children to learn. Learning-process is important than learning.
5. The mother should be patient and kind. The children should be encouraged to repeat a process in order to understand a thing.
6. And finally, the mother should win the hearts of children by love. But she should not always bow to demands of the children.

13

Woman's Ideal Motherly Roles

Nature has created bio-opposite living beings, males and females. They reproduce living beings. And for this end 'unity in bio-diversity' is very essential. And for this a female ties a knot with a male. In all living beings like animals, beasts, birds, insects, it is found that they establish sexual relations within their creeds, but without any stipulated rules. As human beings are rational living beings, they do so under socially prescribed set rules. A woman ties her knot with an outsider man under the institution of marriage. Same blood contexts are saved. A girl of one particular totam (*gotra* गोत्रा) is married with a boy of different totam (gotra गोत्रा). They both live together lifelong. After marriage their sexual relations are socially recognised. After marriage every woman wants to become a mother. She conceives, becomes pregnant and, gives birth to a child who is going to become a future member of the society. As such, a woman becomes a mother.

The genesis of the society lies in mother and, she does the motherly roles lifelong. A mother has to face many arduous difficulties lifelong situation in motherly genetic process. She has to bear the weight of the child in her stomach. At the time of birth of the child she has to face the unbearable birth pangs. After the birth of the child, while lying on the bed she starts feeding the child through her breasts. As the child grows she starts the life-building process of the child. As such, the mother is the life giver, life protector, life- builder and enculturator. For all this, there is a need of balanced parenting. Since, the girls, before their marriage, remained unaware about all these motherly roles, because neither the parents nor family members nor the school-teachers do educate them, when they are married and become mothers, they face many problems. And many of them do unbalanced parenting.

Unbalanced parenting is neither in the interest of the children nor in the interest of society. It is, therefore necessary to know what is unbalanced parenting? For knowing the unbalanced parenting, it is necessary to know what is parenting? What is unbalanced parenting and how can it be balanced parenting?

PARENTING

The mother and the father of the child are the parents of the child. Because their 'unity in bio-diversity' the birth of a child becomes possible. Mother gives birth to the child and largely contribute in bringing up the child. Mother is the life giver, sustainer, life moulder, enculturator and inculcator of life habits. Father of the child also helps in parenting. Parenting of the child requires his sustinance, love and affection. This should be done in a balanced way. Both the parents, mother and father should contribute in balanced parenting of the child. The child should be given desirable food items. Junky and fast food items should not be given. Desirable clothing, love affection and proper direction for leading a saneful life should be given to the children. Generally the family is the epicentre of inculcation of good life attitudes as, sane character good behaviour, spirit of cooperation, respect of elders and ladies and also love to youngers are generated in the family during the course of parenting.

UNBALANCED PARENTING

The term balancing has emerged out of the word 'balance'. The word balance is the derivation of French word 'balanxlis' developed out of the similar Latin word—meaning an instrument for ascertaining the weight of a body or a thing. But in due course of time, the term 'balancing' began to be used for bringing an equilibrium in wider areas like painting, sculpture, architecture, social milieu and also in human personality. The face of human personality covers many human aspects, as life attitudes, work habits, diligency, way of living, sharing, respect for elders and ladies and love for youngers. The development of man starts from the family. So appropriate familial education is a dire necessity. If the parents skip this responsibility the future guardians generally become unsane and uncultured.

Now-a-days due to materialism and consequent hedonism the parents are unable to do the required parenting and generally do unbalanced parenting. All of their actions in bringing up their children go topsy-turvy. As such, balanced life development of the children is not done. Due to hedonism irrationality has so much increased that human livings have become too greedy and self-centred. They always remain busy in the rat-race of money earning. They do not find time to look after their children. Both the parents go out for doing jobs for earning money. They leave their children at the mercy of crèches and day care schools. The parents now-a-days are living in nuclear families. The joint family system has been totally crumbled. So familial system of education, which used to help in balanced parenting, has also gone. So also balanced parenting is also fractured. Present mothers used to cook fast and junky foods. They also eat this and give to their children. They shower too much of love to their children which is always poisonous. The audio-media like T.V. etc., has added fuel to the unbalanced parenting. The mothers see T.V. late in the night along with their children. The modern alien system of formal education contributed to the unbalanced parenting. The parents always want that their children should come in flying colours in their annual examination. So the parents also force their children to read more and more the school subjects. So the balanced parenting is no more, only unbalanced parenting is there, which degrades the women of their ideal motherly roles. Also, most of the women in the country are illiterates. They are so self-centred that for them their own blood is only their own. They are the killers of the Indian joint family system. The joint family used to be ideal parenting agency.

BALANCED PARENTING

Balanced parenting can only be possible if the parents are eager to do so. They have to be motivated to do so by their elders and the community members. The parents of the children should always keep in mind, that they were also brought up by balanced parenting and, it is their reciprocal duty to do balanced parenting of their children. Of course, they should love their children nicely, but should also adopt hardening attitude towards their children. They should always provide all necessary facilities. But it should be kept in mind that their children are not spoiled due to excessive facilities, which may make them lazy, lethargic and non-diligent. It is seen that many mothers shower too much love on their children which spoil them. They do not inculcate any work habits in their children. Even they do not teach them to do their own life jobs as boot polishing and washing of 'kachha', 'baniyan' and 'towel'. They allow them to watch T.V. as much as possible and, sleep late in the night and get up very late in the morning. Many children skip attending the school due to this. The mothers should inculcate a spirit of simple living and high thinking. No fast and junky foods should be provided to the children. Fast and junky foods make the children 'curvac' or 'charu' which make them atheist. Mothers should also inculcate some necessary life attitudes like good behaviour, nice character, simplicity, sociability, sharing cooperation, spirit of epistemacy, aestheticity, spirituality which may lead to theism, respect to elders ladies and love to siblings. And an ideal mother can do all this.

ROLE OF EDUCATION IN BALANCED PARENTING

Proper education of the girls who are future mothers can help in balanced parenting of the young children. Mostly, many of the women are illiterates. And those who are literates are also not educated for balanced parenting. Generally all women, in their early age are not educated about balanced parenting through familial education. Girls being anta-property are devoid of this type of education. However, the girls get some sort of information about the balanced parenting and female roles from their peer groups. The parents of the girls hesitate to tell them anything about their future marital life. As such, there is no place for making the girls aware about their future married life roles and consequent balanced parenting of the children. When the girls are married and are forced to shift to their new homes, that is, in-laws house or *Sasural* (ससुराल), and in due course of time they become mothers and are forced to do parenting, they learn themselves by observing other mothers. As such, educating, balanced parenting is almost missing in women's life. Whereas, it should start in early age of the girls at their homes through familial education by their parents, family members and ladies of community. The girls should be encouraged to mix-up with the girls of their age groups or their peer groups. As the girls are very conscious to know about their roles in their future life, they learn a lot from their peer group. Some elderly extrovert ladies can also play a vital role in educating the girls about their future balanced parenting. Some women groups, like women empowerment bodies, should come forward for educating the young women about balanced parenting. These women organisations can make the girls aware about their future life roles and balanced parenting. These women organisations can also make the girls and women aware about socio-economic and cultural aspects of the society which create hurdle in doing balanced parenting. Such aspects are unsociability, hedonism and effects of modernisation. Such groups should organise some seminars on balanced parenting periodically. When the girls start going to girls schools they should develop good rapport with their class fellows. The teachers should encourage this. They should also develop good rapport with the girl students and should not hesitate educating the girls about their future life roles including balanced parenting. They should make the girls aware about the national culture, effects of hedonism and xenophilism on the culture. And how acculturation has taken place in the country. Therefore, it is very necessary that all schools and other educational institutes should adopt an enculturation programme through some co-curricular activities. Then only ideal life attitudes can be developed in girls who are future women. This will help in adoption of balanced parenting by the future mothers. Only ideal motherly roles can be helpful in adopting ideal 'balanced parenting'.

14

Religiosity of Women

Mostly, majority of the women of all sects, races and ethnic groups are religious in comparison to men. Religion is a French word, a derivation of Latin word 'religio' meaning 'to care for', 'to respect', 'feelings about the supreme being' who is supposed to be creator of the universe, who is called 'God', 'the Divine being', 'recognition of Almighty God through regular prayers', 'a way of worship'. There are many religions in the world as 'Hinduism', 'Taoism', 'Zoraism', 'Christianity' and 'Islam'. Religiosity can be said a natural way of binding of one's mind towards a particular religion. And 'religiosity' means doing things or worship piously fearing the Almighty God.

Men and women though both are rational beings but they both desire many things for their livelihood such as children, material things, shelter for living and ways for earning money to meet their needs. For these, they both pray the 'Supreme Being' for rewarding them for all what they desire. And on getting these the human beings, that is, men and women get thrilled. Consequently they pray the Almighty God. When a man or a woman believes in one 'Supreme Being' and pray Him, such a belief or religiosity is called 'monotheism'. And believer in monotheism is called 'theistic'. In olden days mostly people were theistic. They used to be thrilled by seeing Divine creations like huge landscapes, seascapes, rivers, mountains and flora and fauna. Also the human beings used to be very thankful to the Supreme Being for being rewarded with the future guardians. As such, in the beginning the men and women used to be pure theistic. Since, the men used to remain busy in earning their livelihood, the women used to perform regular prayers to the Supreme Being, that is, the Almighty God. So the women used to pray God religiously regularly.

With the passage of time, the socio-economic situations in the society used to be changed which existed in olden days. Due to human greed, the men searched new ways for exploiting the natural phenomena for their use. The men developed new tools and developed new ways of exploiting natural resources. And when the men succeeded they used to pray many other deities also for rewarding them. As such, the monotheism got changed to henotheism and polytheism. Many gods and goddesses were started to be worshipped. The women played a vital role in developing the henotheism and polytheism.

About a century ago the religio-social atmosphere in India was spiritualistic. People were not mad after materialistic ends. They had sufficient time to mix up with the social milieu and pray the 'Supreme Being' that is God. As such, they were largely monotheistic and used to pray daily the Almighty God. And the ladies were ahead of men in this regard. Now due to materialism, hedomism, consumerism and xenophilism the socio-economic scenario has changed. The men and women have totally become hedonistic. Their main aim of life is now "eat drink and be merry". So they are in the rat-race of acquisition of money. For this end they can do anything. They also pray Gods and Goddesses for the money acquisition. So they have become henotheistic and polytheistic, if not 'curvac' (चारवाक) for the acquisition of money. Now they are no more monotheistics. The tantrik elements of the society added fuel fire to this trend of henotheism and polytheism. This social change has happened due to cultural diffusion which has brought nasty and poisonous acculturation in the Indian society. We Indians have largely accultured ourselves to western culture and adopted hedonistic ways of life. In the west people believe in Calvinistic ethics, "earn more throughout the week, enjoy and, go to church only once a week on Sunday". This etho is more or less like the etho of Indian 'carvak darshan' (चारवाक), which believes in "Eat, drink and be merry". Carvac philosophy existed in India in Mahabharata period. Though 'carvaks' were atheists, they never suggested any kind of polytheism or henotheism or weekly prayers. Now, we Indians, expecting few have renounced monotheism and adopted polytheism and henotheism, thereby people pray for material gains. After getting the desired things they do *bhajans* and *kirtans* after a gap of time. On this occasion the *kirtan* and *poojans*, *bhandaras* are also arranged. After doing so people believe they have been relieved of evils.

As such, religiosity of women which was totally monotheistic in the past, has now become totally henotheistic and polytheistic. For material and other gains the women pray gods and goddesses and do many tantrik activities. They observe fasts, do *kirtans, bhajans* and distribute *prasadas*. Of course, the ways of their religiosity have now changed but their faith and dedication are the same which were in the past when the women were also monotheistic. Still the women are more religious than the men.

Now-a-days the women are badly affected by the shadow of acculturation which has been passed on them by the men. The acculturation made both the men and women totally hedonistic, consumeristic and xenophilic. The women have been badly affected by these in their socio-economic trends. If a woman has ten saris of different colours and textures, she would like to have matching *chappals* and *bindis* of the same colours and textures. This trend is called xenophilism. This mindset of the women's mind also affects their children. They also want to be hedonistic, consumeristic and xenophilic. They start ignoring religion and finally become atheists. They want to link with a particular class which are interested in junk and fast foods. In the past the ladies were generally religions and they used to make their children religious through familial education and prayers.

In other words, the concept of magic religion is being adopted by women in their religiosity. In olden times, the concept of magic was only applied in western countries. Now in the modern times, henotheistic and polytheistic religion is supposed to do magic in bringing material gains in the society. Whereas, the main aim of the religion should be to make the men and women humane. A humane man or woman is one who also thinks for the betterment of all ignoring his/her personal interests. The Indians are all religious and like Hinduism, Sikkhism, Islam, Jainism and Buddhism always religious adhered for the betterment of all. These religions believed in helping others renouncing their own interests. Therefore, giving or donating (दान दक्षिणा) was the prime activity in the Indian society in all communities. And the women used to play a prominent role in this regard. Now many women have become so egoistic, materialistic and self-centred that their main life aim remains to grab money in any way. They even do not hesitate to steal public utility things like electricity and water. If any beggar comes to their door steps they do not unlock the door. Such women are unsocial, hedonistic, consumeristic. As such, the proper education of would be women and mothers, that is, girls, is a dire necessity. Education should make or mould the future women, the girls, to be humane. They should be made aware about the roots of national culture. The roots of national culture is our theistic and atheistic schools of philosophy which make the men and women religious. Only religiosity and a spirit of sane sociability can enculturate our younger generation. The women can revive our Indian national culture as they are the real educators, upbringers and moulders of our future guardians.

For making the Indian society a sane society our women should be rightly educated. Efforts should be made to change women psyche. This can only be done if women are given rights equal to their male partners. For this our politicians should do real efforts. For the last so many years Indian politicians are advocating thirty-three percent reservation for women in our temples of democracy. But they have been evading this demand on different assumptions or arguments. We talk of women empowerment but we are still enable to stop rapes and molestations of women. Something should be done to stop such inhuman crimes against the women in the society. The woman should also know the true meaning of women religiosity. Only our hope lies with the institution of girls schools. If these school desire they can change the fate of the girls who are our future women. This aim can be achieved through congenial rapport between the teachers and taughts and through co-curricular activities.

True religiosity does not permit partial behaviour towards human beings. Neither a person should harm anybody nor ignore the interests anybody, nor a person should be self-centred and greedy. A religious person should always be considerate, social sympathetic to all. Many educated and uneducated women do regular prayers of gods and goddesses continuously. They also believe in some tantrik performances. Sometimes they do tantrik activities to harm others. They observe fasts, donate and arrange *bhojs* and *langers*. They also do *kirtans* periodically. But it is observed that they never behave well with the family members, even with their husbands and with other family members, and also with outsiders. Their such behaviour can be said tantamount to

Mrs. Xentippe wife of the renowned philosopher Socrates, who was very harsh, unkind and unsocial towards the outsiders. If anybody used to enter her house by mistake, she used to pour a full pot of cold water over his head. There we many educated ladies in our society also who do not know-how to behave well with the outsiders, though, they claim to be religious. As such, their religiosity is fake religiosity. It is a dirty spot on Indian hospitability. Indian hospitability was praised. There are many religious women who are always interested in grabbing either states property or property of the neighbours. They do not treat all children of the family equally. If any children of the family do progress such ladies have a grudge against such children. Religiosity of such women is fake religiosity. All religions teach to love all. The religion do not teach to hate anybody. Such kind of religiosity is useless. For a religious person—man and women it is necessary to be kind, considerate and sympathetic to all. A greedy or self-centred person can never be called a religious person. The religiosity of such person will always be a show. So it is necessary to educate the women in their childhood when they are girls.

15

Girls' Education Curriculum

Teaching in schools is done according to curriculum prepared subject-wise. As such, the role of the teacher in schools is tagged with the school curriculum, pertaining to subject contents to be taught to the students. The teachers have to proceed according to the curriculum. So the school curriculum should be prepared keeping in view the aims of education. The aims of education should include the life-building process of the students. As the girls have to play specific roles in their lives, the girls' education should include all of these specific roles in the school curriculum.

ETYMOLOGICAL INTERPRETATION AND DEFINITION

The word curriculum is a derivation from the Latin word 'curricula', meaning a 'running', a 'race'. In educational context the term 'curriculum' refers to a specified course of study at a school, college, university or at a technical institute like polytechnic or industrial technical institute or at a higher technical institutes like engineering colleges or Indian Institutes of Technology, etc. Theoretically and, in practical sense, the term 'curriculum' is used to mean to plan and execute students' total systemic learning activities at the school or at an institute of higher learning. These learning activities always entail some artistic and cultural activities which may infuse in the youngers an urge for creativity and epistemacy for infusing in them general awareness about the things available in the society. Such activities also enculturate the students. As such, the schools, specially the girls schools have arduous responsibility of inculcating the good life attitudes as the girls have to travel an arduous life journey and perform difficult life roles. They will have to give birth to new generation and bring them up for saneful living in a rational way.

In modern sense of the term 'curriculum' may refer to the total structure of ideas, epistemacies, aesthetic activities to be carried on by the educational institute to meet the learning needs of the students and to achieve the desired stipulated educational aims. The curriculum consists the means and ways of instructions, which also include co-curricular activities required for the life-building processes, to be used by the school teachers for providing learning opportunities to the students. And for these ends to provide classroom teaching or instructions which include the class studies pertaining to the psyche of the students, guidance and counselling programme is necessary. Community services and co-curricular activities are necessary in order to prepare the students for their life roles. Such activities are very important for girls' education as they have to perform specific life roles. In addition to these activities the school curriculum should include health care services, like jogging, yoga, self-defence techniques and self-introspection (आत्मंथन) activities.

Curriculum as defined in Spens' report 1938 (England) is a statement or programme of study in strict sense or teaching programme for the students which include experiences which a pupil acquires under the guidance of a teacher in the school. So the curriculum is a planned scheme of directed learning, under the formal education scheme at the school, which occurs in the four walls of the school, and the group of students irrespective of their individual differences share it. Directed learning is a training whereby a pupil has to learn which is considered desirable for him or her. Such learning is given by the teacher in a planned way.

WIDE AND VARIED VIEW OF CURRICULUM

Some people use the term 'curriculum' to refer to the content what is to taught by the teacher to the students in the school. Other say that teaching and learning methods comprise curriculum, while others include students' achievements and these achievements are to be assessed. While some say that the curriculum is the moulder of values and understandings that are passed on the students in an educational institution not through formal education or teaching but unconsciously through institutions total—teaching and other programmes that is, curricular and co-curricular and also extra-curricular programmes and, social climate that inculcates punctuality, brotherhood, commonality, honesty, diligence, tolerance, we feeling, feeling to share, motivation and deference to the authority. All these create good life conditions in the students.

As such, curriculum is a path or a way through which a student covers his or her life journey to reach a desirable destination. Curriculum is a deliberate programme of education for attaining the desirable aims and objectives. Particular experts after considering all eventualities select particular subject content of courses of study, suggest appropriate teaching methods, communication media for elicitations and self-learning by the students. The schools implement the curriculum in order to achieve the desired educational aims.

GENESIS OF THE CURRICULUM

Looking to the genesis of the term 'curriculum' in school education one has to trace the steps which led to the emergence of familial education. Before the industrialisation, education of the child was the responsibility of the parents, family and of the society. The state had no control over the education. Now the educational institutes are the instruments of the state. In the past the well to do families used to employ tutors or teachers to teach their children. The teacher used to come to other houses of the child and teach him or her al subjects. The artisan castes and working class used to train their children in their trades and occupations. In India the higher castes—the Brahmans and Kshatriyas used to send their male children to Gurukula Ashramas. The girls were not allowed Gurukula education. In Gurukulas, the education was aimed at life-building. It was done by inculcating good life habits of responsibility as competency, spirituality, simplicity, working habits and morality. With the emergence of industrialisation such traditional life-building system of education became redundant now as, it could not provide required sufficient trained manpower to handle the industries. So the responsibility of educating the youngers, specially males, was shifted to the institution of school designed specially for teaching the required subject-matter to a group pupils collectively. This also relieved the parents from imparting familial education to children and also working in industries or factories by doing some jobs. Intensive industrialisation which entailed modernisation and urbanisation necessitated skilled specialisation in technical trades. So one teacher school concept was also found redundant and ineffective. The school become a necessity as a permanent agency for teaching required subject content and preparing for examinations. At one school many teachers could teach many subjects which was not possible with one teacher. After passing out examination and consequent certification the candidate could get jobs in industries according to their qualifications. As such, to cope up the demands of the industrialists, different courses as mathematics, physics, chemistry, orthographic drawing and languages were planned to be taught to the students. A planned structure for teaching these subjects in schools was designed which was named as 'curriculum'.

CURRICULUM BUILDING

Auguste Comte anticipated, when he gave the new term of 'Sociology', "Old society is dying and new society is emerging". As such, he had anticipated and suggested new science of society to deal with the new emerging social problems. As industrialisation has brought many urging social problems about which the youngers are to be made aware of. Since this awareness is to be given by the school, the school has to chalk out a programme of instructions accordingly. Because industrialisation entailed hedonism and consumerism and the members of the society generally are in the rat-race of money-earning. Both the parents, husband and wife also keep busy themselves in money earning. As such, the school is supposed to teach the students all subject content and make them aware about the new social problems emerged due to industrialisation and its other effects. And for this curriculum building for school came into being. Now the school is supposed to discharge all of educative functions of family which used to come under familial education. It has to make the students aware about all epistemological, ontological, social and axiological problems and educate them about all these. Earlier, such knowledge was transmitted by the family through familial education. The earlier school (*Pathshala*) was one teacher school. The teacher was supposed to teach all subject content and, pupils were supposed to accept what was taught by the teacher. The modern school has different roles to play. There are many specialist teachers who try to specialise the pupils indifferent fields. Now the people (man and woman) is living in a world where he or she gets information from many sources. In such a situation the curriculum construction is a difficult job. By 1900 A.D. the making of curriculum for primary education and even for secondary education was not a difficult job. The change in curriculum construction came slowly. Thinkers like Froebel, Pestalozzi, J.J. Rousseau, Madam Montessori and Margaret Macmillan influenced the pedagogic thinkers. In England, until Hadow Report (1726) school education only meant for only grammar schools education which was purely academic theoretical and was dominated by external examination. Only intelligent and rich children could avail it.

The broadened term of curriculum has emerged due to many aspects of industrialisation. The educationists felt that the child is a total process and not only a mental process, which implies that the school should have an instructional or educational programme for the whole child rather than mere classroom teaching. People learn more through participation rather than passive assimilation of the subject content. As long as, assign-study—receive was an accepted formula for the greater part of child's development, the curriculum could be conceived as of those courses or subjects, that were lined up for the students to take up. But as soon as the theory of mental discipline was conceived and belief in 'whole child' began to be realised in practice. The curriculum as broad based on total programme of related activities was conceived. These activities were to be carried on, under the guidance of the school administration, by the teachers. To provide the wide and varied activities outside the classroom and school, which till recently are generally called extra-curricular activities have become necessary for educating the 'whole' child. These activities though are considered secondary, are provided to ward off the academic boredom. But, still the emphasis is laid on teaching the academic subjects. The extra-curricular and co-curricular activities are provided only if these do not hamper the scholastic studies of the students and hamper the examination results.

So the subject approach in curriculum construction is still dominant in school studies. As such, the school curriculum is still planned and executed mechanically to prepare the students as mono-moulds only for passing the examinations, killing their initiatives and interests and keeping them away continuously from nature, social milieu and also from their parents. Only master strategists plan curriculum at the instance of those who are in power. No flexibility or shifting approaches are seen in our curriculum building.

The curriculum should not only be a framework of courses and subject contents. Other activities which are going to unfold many useful experiences to the students and enrich their personalities should be included in curriculum. These activities are to be decided in advance before the school reopens and the teachers and students start interacting. Such activities may be very useful for girl's (women)education. Everything is in flux, so social phenomena is also changing continuously, so why not the school curriculum should also be changed and modified accordingly.

One of the most glaring fallacy in the curriculum construction is that the education are prone to statistical goals. They ignore the students psyche and interests. They plan curriculum for common life, for common good, for general training and for general citizenship, for which the scale of success is success in examination. But individual differences among the students, their socialisation for saneful living and enculturation are always ignored.

While planning the school or college curriculum, the teachers, prominent intellectuals and even some prominent citizens from the society should not only be consulted but should be involved. The curriculum should not be prepared in camera. There should be a provision for continuous research in this regard as suggested by Prof. Stephen M. Corey in his book 'Action Research'. Curriculum is generally planned for general group. It should reflect a programme for life-building focussing life roles. This is very necessary for the women education (girls). The educationists should examine that the educational goals based on life roles, very carefully. General subjects should be distinguished very carefully which could help in life-building and life roles of the girls.

Various committees and commissions on curriculum construction in United Kingdom, of which educational pattern we are still following, have cautioned about the curriculum construction.

Hadow and Spans Reports and Education Act, 1944 (UK) established education as an activity for all but with a monotonous curriculum. But Newson Report (1963) UK, on the features of the curriculum, said that the present form of curriculum does not create interest in the students. Headmasters' Report 1961 (UK) suggested that the school headmasters of the schools should also be involved in curriculum construction. There should be a provision for creative arts in school curriculum. So, there should be sufficient provision of curriculum enrichment. This can be done if new innovation in teaching arena and teaching methods, introduction of new teaching aids and fresh content covering life-building and life roles are introduced.

CURRICULUM PLANNING FOR WOMEN EDUCATION

Edward A. King has rightly said that:

(*i*) Curriculum is an instrumentality for translating our hopes for materialising child education into concrete reality.
(*ii*) Curriculum is necessary for eliminating a lag between mechanical and social progress.
(*iii*) The curriculum is necessary for helping an individual to achieve greater success for living in society.
(*iv*) The curriculum construction is necessary for creating a democratic society.
(*v*) Curriculum should be so framed that the pupils should be able to understand the social problems and social roles.
(*vi*) Curriculum should reflect measures necessary for establishing permanent peace in the society.
(*vii*) The curriculum for girls schools should have a provision to educate the girls of their future roles as motherly role, balanced parenting, sociability, hospitability and integrity of the family. Home science should be a compulsory subject to all girls in girls schools. As such, for curriculum planning there should be a continuous permanent study and research so as to achieve the long-term viable social goals.

IDENTIFIABLE ASPECTS OF CURRICULUM

(*i*) Identification of social objectives as well as national objectives and suggestions for desirable roles for both men and women. Since women are anta-property in the patriarchal society, they should be a provision in the school curriculum to educate them to discharge their life roles in their married life.

(*ii*) Developing the school programmes according to these objectives.
(*iii*) Identifying teaching and learning situation.
(*iv*) Identifying the aspects which would unfold the students personality and enrich these.

PARTICIPANTS IN CURRICULUM PLANNING

Following should participate in planning curriculum for boys and girls schools:

(*i*) State-wise leadership groups.
(*ii*) Local leadership groups.
(*iii*) Women empowerment leadership groups.
(*iv*) Classroom teachers both from boys and girls.
(*v*) Representatives of general public whose wards are studying in schools.
(*vi*) Some alumnus from the boys and girls schools. These old students should apprise the curriculum committee about the difficulties they faced while they were in schools.

Following should be the bases of curriculum construction:

(*i*) Social milieu, social, philosophical, axiological and cultural perspectives.
(*ii*) Effects of cultural diffusion and acculturation and required necessary steps for enculturation.
(*iii*) National economy, chances of employment and thereby social mobility.
(*iv*) National educational objectives.
(*v*) Psychological learning about psyche, mental health, work culture, and attitudes of the students towards present social conditions.
(*vi*) Sociological bearings entailed by mechanisation, industrialisation, modernisation, urbanisation and consequent wave of hedonism, consumerism and xenophilism in the society.
(*vii*) Effects of castes, creeds and class structures on the social structure and exploitation of masses by the political parties.

(*viii*) Importance of creative activities for enculturation.
(*ix*) Roles schools can play in these situations.

FOLLOWING SHOULD BE INSTRUCTIONAL FIELDS

(*i*) Core subjects like mother-tongue, humanities, social studies, mathematics, physics, chemistry, biology, botany and one or two foreign languages.
(*ii*) Some subsidiary subjects like art, craft and orthography, drawing.
(*iii*) Co-curricular activities and cultural programmes, and extra-curricular activities like sports, yoga, games and social services, which are necessary for health care.

The curriculum should be planned and constructed taking into consideration all these aspects. There should be a committee to review the existing curriculum, which may suggest ways and means for the improvement of the curriculum according to social needs. The committee should coordinate with all concerned agencies.

Every woman has to play many multifaceted roles in her married life. She is born and brought up in one home and due to 'unity in bio-diversity' her rest of the life journey is covered in another home due to patriarchal social structure. Every women has to play various difficult life roles as child bearing, child up-bringing, inculcation of viable life attitudes, household management, sociability, hospitability and religiosity. The present school formal education cannot educate the girls about all these roles. The girls can be made aware about these life roles of women through co-curricular and extra-curricular activities. Therefore, the girls schools should arrange related co-curricular and extra-curricular activities in school instructional programme.

IMPLEMENTATION OF WOMEN EDUCATION CURRICULUM

Implementation of school curriculum, specially for girls education, can be done through proper logical action. Classroom teaching, which should always be student oriented involving the students in knowledge development and by organising the required educational activities like aesthetical activities, that is, art and craft activities, co-curricular activities, extra-curricular activities like social services, health care activities as, daily exercises, yoga, meditation, pranayam, sports and games. Besides these, educational tours, excursions, trips, participation in cultural activities like dance, drama, solo-acting should be arranged during the school session. The school should also organise some religious festivities, like Basant Panchami, Holi, Id-Ul-Fitr, Christmas, Guru Nanak Day, Diwali and community gathering. On these occasions the students should participate house-wise and should do some decorative work like alpana, rangoli, displays, mobile hangings etc. On Guru Nanak Day all girls should be involved in cooking for the *langer*. Also some house-wise competitions as blackboard writing, writing essays and making greeting cards. Also some community gatherings as parents' day can be arranged. Some sort of melas can also be arranged in which different kinds of food items can be prepared by the girl students. The income from such melas can be used for public interest as 'Tsunami relief' flood relief and for helping the poor students.

Since the present system of formal school education for both boys and girls, is extremely examination oriented all schools lay emphasis on the preparation for the examinations. All schools, be it girls schools or boys school want to see their students to perform very well in their examinations, come in flying colours and add always a new feather in school's crown. The schools always devote on classroom teaching, and not generally all on other educational activities like co-curricular activities. As such, this trend is generally encouraged by the authorities, like the Directorate of Education. The schools, both boys and girls, do not arrange such educational programme sincerely. Only some activities are arranged in namesake by few schools. As such, the schools must arrange all such activities very sincerely. Specially the girls schools should never ignore all such educational activities as these activities can only help the girls in their life roles. The school should do for the implementation of school curriculum as under:

TEACHING

The teaching and education are two different concepts. These are supplementary to each other. For educating the students teaching is essential and, and the teaching cannot be done without education. As such, education of the students is done through teaching in all boys and girls schools. The teaching is the development of the word 'teach', which is a derivation of the Greek word 'Taccon' meaning passing on of one's acquired knowledge to a person who is unaware about that knowledge. If this process of passing on acquired knowledge to a person, who is not aware about it, does not innovate and motivate the person, who is being informed, to think, reason, analyse, comprehend and learn such process of teaching can never lead to education. This kind of teaching may be termed as 'teacher oriented teaching'. In such a situation the students accept what is being taught and they remain passive. In such a situation it is necessary to do teaching in such a way which could innovate the students to think, reason, analyse, comprehend and to know through self-learning. As a matter of fact education is a process of taking out individuals' latent or hidden potentialities. And if teaching is done through one way method the education can never be possible. So the teaching should be so designed in which the students can be actively involved. This kind of teaching can be said two way or bi-polar teaching. For this kind of teaching following steps should be taken.

LESSON PLANNING

Under the present formal system of education a teacher has to teach a specific subject content or prescribed subject content in one academic session. The school session starts from April and ends in March every year. The school session is divided into three terms. The first term starts from April and ends on 30th September, which has also two months summer vacation. The second term continues from October to December. And the last term goes on from January to March. The subject content which is to be covered under the planned curriculum in the full school session is further divided term wise. And finally the teacher has to teach the subject content, prescribed for one term. He further divides the subject content to be taught lesson-wise for which the teacher has to prepare lesson plans for every lesson. The main purpose for this kind of day-wise demarcation is that the teacher could cover or teach the whole subject content prescribed in the curriculum in a logical way through which two way teaching could be possible.

FORMAT OF LESSON PLAN

The lesson plan should have the following format:

Lesson Plan

No.................. Date................ Class................ Period................

1. Name of School ....
2. Subject content to be taught (topic) ....
3. Teaching method to be applied ....
4. Teaching aids to be used/Blackboard work ....
5. Process of introduction of the topic to be taught ....
6. Main aim of the teaching of the subject content ....
7. Introduction ....
8. Other aim ....

Process of Teaching to be Applied

Questioning	*Elicitations*	*Presentation*

9. Recapitulation ....
10. Home assignments ....

Approval of the lesson plan with suggestion from the senior teacher or the principal, if necessary, be obtained.

The teacher should prepare the lesson plan for the topic he or she is going to teach in advance. The blackboard work to be done should be recorded on the left side of less on plan book.

LESSON DEVELOPMENT

After the lesson planning, the process of lesson development should start, which should be aimed at the maximum elicitations from the students. It is, therefore, would be better if the students are also informed in advance about the lesson development topic which the teacher is going to teach them. Before, starting lesson development the teacher should write the heading of the topic on the chalkboard (blackboard). This will motivate the students about the topic of the subject content which is being developed during the course of teaching. They will start thinking and will be prepared to contribute in the lesson development. While introducing the topic of the lesson, which is being developed, the teacher should ask some questions one by one, which should be topic related. The teacher should contemplate on these questions before the lesson development or teaching. After asking the questions the teacher should wait for a moment, so as to give time to the students to think and respond. And when the students start replying, the teacher should clinch these responses and should write the responses on the chalkboard. The students who could not respond should be given a chance to write these responses in their notebooks. After this the subject content should be developed through two way presentation—presentation by the teacher and consequent assimilation of elicitations bit by bit. The students should be encouraged to respond as much as possible. As such, two way communication should be applied in the lesson development as much as possible. Related teaching aids as charts, role-up blackboard, models, pictures, maps, posters and samples etc., should be used in lesson development one after another. Showing of teaching aids should be done one after another as required. Showing or displaying all teaching aids at one time always confuses the students. The whole process of lesson development should be based on two way communication. The students should be encouraged to note down the important clinched points emerged during the course of lesson development. The teacher should write all clinched point on the blackboard. After the process of lesson development is complete, the teacher should try to know whether the students have grasped what has been taught to them. This process is called 'recapitulation' of the lesson development. Doing this the teacher should ask questions in the classroom and the students should reply to these questions. The students should also be given some written and practical home assignments. After getting these assignments the teacher should examine these assignments. If the teacher does not follow this and, teach the students without asking questions and securing elicitations, that will be called one way teaching and will be only mere information, that will not lead the students for self-learning and education.

After proper lesson planning and, teaching the students accordingly, using bi-polar communication system, involving them in self-learning and knowledge development, the first face or stage of education covering one part of curriculum can be achieved. But education only is not limited to teaching the academic subjects like language, humanities, mathematics and science and, giving the knowledge of 3 Rs education is much more. It covers all life-building processes of the individual which starts from the early age of the child from his/her family through familial education. And the mother plays a key role in this process of the child development, who is our future guardian. In the present hedonistic age, the joint families have totally broken. Majority of the mothers fail in doing balanced parenting and, by showing too much love to their children, in their nuclear families, they spoil them. In the earlier days even the elders from the extended families and community elders used to contribute in the life-building of the youngers. Now, even the grand parents do not have any say in the life-building process of their grand children. They are not allowed to speak in this regard. Hedonism and consumerism is the only aim of the present nuclear families. No work habits, no axiological norms, no epistemological eagerness, sociability and no desire to respect the elders and love youngers are inculcated in the youngers by the mothers. Only the modern children are prepared to eat fast and junky foods. With the result they do not develop any required sane life habits. They fail to avail the opportunities of higher education. They cannot acquire any skills to earn their livelihood. Such spoiled children only prepare themselves 'to eat drink and be merry'. And when they do not get any chance to earn they become criminals.

It is, therefore, has become very essential to educate the present girls about their future ideal motherly roles. Due to the present formal system of education of the country, which actually is an alien system of education, which only lays stress on teaching subject contents for annual examination, no life-building measures are in the present formal system of school education. In some boys and girls schools such measures are arranged in ostentanious manners in namesake. If this condition is allowed to continue, days are not far off when the whole society will become barbarous, because the life-building processes and enculturation techniques have no place in our present formal system of education. Therefore, it is very necessary that our present girls are suitably made aware about their future life roles. These roles cannot be taught or inculcated through classroom teaching. These can be inculcated through arranging the appropriate co-curricular activities, creative activities and extra-curricular activities in every girls' school. To decide, what kind of such activities should be, when and where these should be arranged, is a tedious job because the present school activities are largely dominated by teaching for preparing the students for their annual examinations. Such school education even does not make the students social and moral. For protecting the health of the society, it is very necessary to make the girls aware about their future life roles. This can only be done by arranging appropriate co-curricular activities regularly. Few of such co-curricular activities as mentioned below are:

CO-CURRICULAR ACTIVITIES

Morning Assembly

Morning assembly in every school be it a boys school or a girls school can be a torchbearer for the life-building process of the students. So, every school, especially girls' school should start school teaching with arranging morning assembly. Every teacher and student should attend the morning assembly compulsorily. The girls can be made aware about the days activity. They can be punctual. Through, morning lectures the girls can also made aware about their life roles. In the beginning the Principal should assign to look after the morning activities to a teacher. She should be assisted by one or two junior teachers. All these teachers should chalk out the morning programme term-wise. Some lady teacher should address the morning assembly. The morning assembly should start with the singing national anthem. The morning assembly committee should encourage the students to address the morning assembly on women education. As such, the morning assembly in the girls school can be useful in educating girls about their future life roles.

Thought for the Day

A thought for the day is very essential for inculcating good life attitudes in the girls. A teacher should look after this activity. A chalkboard or blackboard should be fixed at such a place from where all students enter in the school building. Girls students should be asked to write some thoughts about the life roles of the women. Sayings of some prominent women can also be written on the thought boards. If the school compound is very big two or more thought boards can be installed and same thought or thoughts of the person should be written on these boards. These thought boards should be properly maintained. These should be dusted and painted regularly.

Written Banners

Written banner pertaining to the life roles of the women can be prepared in the school art room and can be displayed on insulation sheet pieces. These banners should be prepared in bold writing and should be hanged at appropriate places.

CULTURAL PROGRAMMES AND ACTIVITIES

Arranging the cultural programmes and related activities are very essential for the implementation of co-curricular activities in all boys and girls schools. Through these activities social sanety, sociability, morality, work culture, cooperation may be established in the society, through the cultural programmes and related activities. The future citizens of the nation can be made aware about the national culture. Through these activities, social conflicts, separation and alienation can be removed. The aspirant behaviour of the students, who are future guardians can be well-established. Through these activities the process of enculturation of the youngers can be put in right gears and the students can be motivated to build and develop the national culture. In comparison to boys schools, arranging the cultural programmes and related activities in girls schools are very very essential, because the girls have limited scope of social exposure.

Culture is a complex pattern of human social activities. It is an embodiment of human behaviour, that is, learned behaviour, shared behaviour. As an explanatory concept by culture we mean those historically created concepts or processes that channelise man's reaction both to external and internal stimulations. Culture contains human behaviour, character, social traits, traditions and art and craft activities. Ralph Linton pointed out that for majority of the people it plays a role of guide. It lays norms of human behaviour and provides the mechanism for survival. Man's or woman's survival is not possible without culture. It promotes human roles in the society. As such, culture is liberator. It frees a person from biological determination. If a person is to be benefited from the society he or she is to abide by the social norms. But the cultural liberates as well as enslaves a person. Culture is the builder of the civilisation. Therefore, a civilisation is a secondary phenomenon. Every culture is a way of life. As such, it is obvious that within this cultural whole, there are elements like prayers, rituals, some social customs, observing of some functions on religious as well as social occasions as marriage of the girls. These elements are called social traits or cultural traits. The combination of these traits is a cultural complex. Ruth Benedict said that embodiment artistic design is very important for a culture.

The human behaviour is moulded by cultural activities. As such, the girls should be involved in cultural and creative activities while they are being educated in school. Cultural activities have a wide spectrum as art activities, craft activities, make up, stage setting, dance, drama, folk arts, debates, seminar, decorations and reception and hospitality. Such co-curricular activities open wide avenues of life building by crating many routes of enculturation. With the help of cultural and creative activities, which can be arranged under co-curricular activities, the teacher can inculcate many life attitudes as, work habits, spirituality, epistemacy, aestheticity, sociability and motherly roles like balanced parenting in the girls who are future managers of their households. The following co-curricular activities can be arranged in girls schools which may entails value cultural activities. A few of such activities are mentioned below:

Singing

Singing is considered a symbol of joy and happiness. When a person is endowed with something new by the nature or Almighty God he/she feels happy and he or she tries to express his/her gratitude to Divine Authority and sings. On special occasions like, on birth of a child, on marriage of a young, on some religious occasion the ladies sings folk songs. As such, singing is considered very auspicious in all religions in all societies. So, singing specially in girls schools should be given a special place while organising co-curricular activities. Also the morning assembly should start with the singing of national anthem in which all girls should participate. As singing always symbolises joy and happiness, the girls in the girls schools should be encouraged to sing. Symbols of Saraswati should be displayed in art rooms and assembly halls of the schools. It is also sure that some teachers might be knowing some folk songs like Haryanvi folk songs, Punjabi folk songs and Rajasthani folk songs. They should demonstrate such songs before the girls students who will learn. Because the voice of the girls is sweet and melodious in comparison to the boys, the girls schools should always encourage the girls to sing. Singing always modify the psyche. With the improved psyche the girls will be able to adjust with their family members in their married lives. In the girls schools, the girls should be encouraged to sing on occasions like Orientation Day, Raksha Bandhan, Bhaiya Duj, Diwali, Basant Panchami, Id-Ul-Fitr, Guru Nanak Day, Parents Day and on Valedictory Day etc. The lady teachers should teach the girls singing.

Dancing

Dancing is another important cultural activity in which the girls can participate. In India, there exists many forms and patterns of dancing. Almost every state has its own specific form of dancing, and folk dances are performed. If we look to the east, every state, like Arunachal, Mizoram, Nagaland, Meghalaya and Manipur, has its own dancing forms and patterns. Specially the tribal states has a rich heritage of dancing. If look to the West—Punjab, Haryana, Jammu & Kashmir, Himachal Pradesh and Uttaranchal have also their own specific dancing patterns and forms. Punjabi Bhangra is famous throughout the world. In south the similar situation exists. In the west in Gujarat and Rajasthan specific pattern of dancing are found. If in schools, specially in girls schools, such dancing patterns are taught to the girls, this will enhance the national unity and integrity and will promote 'unity in bio-diversity'. Foreigners, who come to visit India, generally enjoy the heterogeneity found in Indian dancing. In November, 1962, The Government of India had organised 10th World Educational Conference at the Central Institute of Education (NCERT), 33 Chatra Marg, Delhi University. The delegates from all over the world except China (because of

1962 India-China war) had attended this conference. The students of the Central Institute of Education had presented folk dances of all states in Miranda House Hall (as C.I.E. Hall was small one). The writer under the guidance of late Shri H.A. Gode helped in stage settings for dancers of all states. This programme continued for four or five days and all the delegates had enjoyed it.

Also the dancing is very essential for the health of the girls, as well as, for the health of the nation. The dancing can be solo-dancing and group-dancing. The dancing opens the avenues of enculturation of the students and integration of the nation. As such, the dancing is very essential for the life-building of the girls. The dancing can be done on various occasions, on which singing and dramatisation is also done. Therefore, the girls' school authorities should keep dancing on the agenda of the school co-curricular programmes and should give a chance to the girls on various occasions. An image of Natraj should also be installed in dancing hall.

Dramatisation

Dramatisation is a process of presenting the past and the present social spectrum before the audience. Many auspicious historical happenings like Ram Lila are considered necessary for the life-building of the masses. Also the presentation of recent social happening are considered useful. As the human beings learn quickly more through per se, rather than by telling, many good and bad aspects of human life can be presented before the audience and the students and make them aware about the social, as well as, their life situations. Dramatisation help the students to be epistemic and learn desirable life attitudes. There are many kinds of dramatisation which are done in the society. The religious dramatisation like Ramayana, which is called Rama Lila depicts human nature, and make the human being aware about the nature of human beings. The human being are rational beings in comparison to other living beings, but they are greedy. Greed is a sin and human beings should try to get rid from the greed. The human beings should always think of common good. This is why dramatisation of 'Ramayana' which we call 'Ram Lila', is arranged in the second *paksh* of month *Asoj*. Not only in mother India, Hindu countries like Nepal also celebrates Ram Lila. In Muslim countries like Indonesia, Java and Sumatra and in Buddhist countries like Sri Lanka and Thailand 'Ram Lila' is arranged.

In school co-curricular activities programmes, especially in girls schools, the dramatisation should be given a due weightage. In dramatisation focus should be on life-building process. In girls schools, the girls should be made aware about their future roles as motherly roles, balanced, parenting, balanced handling of the household, cordial relations with their life partners and in-laws, through dramatisations. The girls schools should also organise some programmes through which the girls could learn home science. There should be some functions like Basant Panchami, Guru Nanak Day and Annual School Mela in which the girls should participate in cooking and serving food to all students and staff members. The girls school should also organise some seminars on women life roles. In such seminars some lady experts on gynaecology, women empowerment and role of women in life-building should also be invited to contribute. Another most important factor is creative activities. The girls are more interested in creative activities. The girls are generally very very innovative in picking up new creative activities like knitting, cutting and tailoring and in doing decoration activities. In the field of cooking the girls always do wonders, as such their intelligence should be exploited.

16

Gender Bias and Education

The term 'gender bias' is a combination of two words 'gender' and 'bias'. The word gender is a derivation of French and Latin words—'Generi' and 'Genus', meaning, a kind or sort or a sex, 'a male or female', or a category of differentiation of living beings, or of human beings. Generally all males are 'masculine gender' and all females are faminial gender. Both have retrospective sex organs to enable them to have reciprocal sex to breed. One has to give, another, one has to accept. The unions of both, male and female, is a 'unity in bio-diversity' which is necessary for reproduction. It is reproduction which makes social existence possible. Males and females in human beings, in spite of being bodily topsy-turvy, live together lifelong hand in hand and, contribute the members of the society who leads a social life. In males and females there is a category who are devoid of sexuality and cannot reproduce. Such living beings are infertile and non-breeding and are called 'Hizde' (हिजड़े). Many girls are denied education due to gender bias.

The word bias is also a derivation of French and Latin words 'biais' and 'bifax' meaning 'weight or load tilted to one side', 'prejudice', 'to treat in a startling manner', or 'oligarchy'. Both the males and females are different genders who have different topsy-turvy bodily structures. The nature has made such bodily structures to discharge different life roles. The body of the male is broader at his shoulders as he is supposed to do difficult manual work. The body of the female is broader at her hips as she is supposed to bear a child. The topsy-turvy bodies of males and females are indicative of their different life roles. The union of male and female is must. Without their union life is not possible in the world. As such, males and females should get equal opportunities to grow and to sustain in their lives. But this does not happen. Women being bodily weaker than men are generally not well-treated by men in all societies. In some sections of the societies throughout the world women are beaten and tortured by their life partners. Generally it is seen that there is a gender bias against the women. The women are not well-treated throughout the world. And there are some social reasons for this worldwide spread of gender bias. A few of these are mentioned as below:

PATRIARCHAL SOCIAL STRUCTURE

Generally all social structures in the world are patriarchal. In a patriarchal social structure men play a dominant role. They generally remain dominant in all household affair. The women being bodily weaker than men are generally not well-treated by men, rather they are often tortured by their husbands. Times of India, in Delhi Times edition dated 23.7.2005 reported that a husband started beating his wife on the first day after their union and continued beating his wife till she went back to her parents. This is not the solitary case of torture and harassment of a wife by her husband. Many such cases are seen in the society. In a patriarchal society, the girls are born and brought up by their parents. When they become young they are bounded with the young male members through the institution of marriage, which is an 'unity in bio-diversity'. They after their marriage have to say goodbye to their parental homes and go with their husbands and live in their new houses lifelong. This is why the girls are considered anta-property (पराया-धन). Being anta-property the girls are not equally treated with the boys. The parents always consider the girls as another's property. This is why many girl's parents skip their parental duty of educating their girls equally as the boys are educated. This is why the girls are considered inferior to the boys and are not given full attention and due care. Mostly girls in poor families are devoid of education. It is estimated that ten percent of the girls population in rural areas do not see the gates of the primary schools.

MARRIAGE AND DOWRY SYSTEM

Marriage is a culturally approved relationship of a man and a woman who are biologically topsy-turvy. So marriage is a process of 'unity in bio-diversity' of family. It legalises the sexual intercourse between wife and husband which is requisite requirement for pregnancy for the birth of a child. So marriage is must for social existence. Through marriage a matricentre, which consists a mother woman and children are created. This kind of 'unity in bio-diversity' is a common natural feature, and all living beings—animals, beasts, insects, bees and human beings do this kind of 'unity in bio-diversity'. But only human beings as rational beings, do such unity under some culturally established social norms.

In India, under socially and culturally established rules, the priests prepares rules for the young boy and girl for marriage which occurs according to astrologers advice. The priest asks if anybody has objection to the proposed marriage. Ritual ceremony starts before the sacred fire (हवन). Bride's father washes grooms feet first, while the priest recites holy mantras, comparing the groom to Lord Vishnu. The bride's father presents his daughter in grooms' lap (कन्यादान) and finally give her as a gift to the groom, binding them together. The groom wears three sacred threads symbolic to three pledges—love, protection and permanent union. Bride's *sari* is tied with groom's *patka*. Couple go around the fire (हवन कुंड) seven times. The marriage is solemnised. The priest and the present audience greet them by reciting an arti called 'manglacharan' (मंगलाचरण). Audience pray for their safety and prosperity. They, shower rice and barley over them. Bride goes to the groom's house permanently. Though in the beginning she stays for few days (not more than ten days). Her brothers go to her in-laws house (*Sasural* ससुराल) to fetch her back for few days. Again the astrologer decides for her *gona* (nuptial tie). After this the girl permanently reside with her husband. All this ritualistic procedure confirm that the groom is put on a higher life paddle and the bride is put on a lower level. The groom is considered at the protection foundation or giving end and, the bride is at the receiving end. This shows a clear gender bias against the women.

Dowry system has also added fuel to the gender bias. Dowry system was not prevalent in India only but many other countries also have the custom of dowry. The word dowry has been developed out of the 'Latin' word 'dower' meaning a gift to be given to the girls. In the west, in European countries, there was a social custom to give gifts to the girls at the time of their marriage.

People used to buy Indian artistic handicraft items in European countries. These Indian handicraft traders brought the idea of 'dower' from the western countries and spread it in Arabian countries and in India, which ultimately became a common social feature. And the Indians and Arabians started giving 'dowers' to their daughters on the occasions of their marriages. Now the dowry has became a social permanent menace. And almost all Indians, irrespective of caste and creed, have to give dowry. The system of giving dowry according to the resources of the bride's parents has gone totally topsy-turvy. Now the grooms parents put a dowry demand in advance and the bride's parents will have to give it in any way if they want to marry their daughter. Since the girls being an anta-property (पराया-धन) are to be married and sent to another house being anta-property (पराया-धन), the parents have to manage the dowry at any cost. Even after giving the dowry on the occasion of the marriage of their daughters, many parents face very dangerous situations. The dowry thirst of the in-laws of their daughters is not satisfied and they continue to harass their daughter-in-laws for bringing more dowry further. And due to this many brides are murdered. As such, many parents consider that having a daughter is a great financial liability. Due to such thinking in many cases girl baby foeticides occur. And those who allow the girls to take birth, take the birth of the girls as an unauspicious happening and no joy celebrations are arranged, as are arranged on the occasion of birth of the child boys. It cannot be denied that the girls, that is, women are the genesis of the human society, but they are the victims of this serious gender bias due to dowry system.

INSTITUTION OF MARRIAGE

In Indian human society, the marriages were arranged by the parents of the girls and the boys in a simple manner, the *Gandharva Vivah* (गंधर्व विवाह). This system was generally prevalent in the whole middle classes. The marriage were arranged by the parents of both girls and boy. While deciding the bond the *totams* (गोत्रा) mothers and fathers of both the sides used to be saved. The grooms side did not demand any kind of dowry. After the settlement both sides used to go a nearly Rishi Ashrama for solemnising the marriage rituals. The girls' side used to arrange a very simple vegetarian *bhoj* (lunch) in Rishi Ashrama. After solemnising the marriage ceremony the audience used to bless the newly married couple with a recitation (मंगलाचरण) *manglacharan* and used to give a coin to the girl. After this the audience used to recite a common prayer for the lifelong happy living of the couple, and lead an auspicious married life. And after the marriage ceremony, the grooms side used to treat the bride as their own important member of the family. As such, there was no gender bias.

LIFE ROLES

All living beings, be it animals, beasts, birds, insects, bees or human beings, that is, men and women have to play some specific life roles. They play these roles gender-wise. All fair or familial genders have to play familial roles as bearing of children, bringing them up and, to manage the household affairs. The women and men cooperate in playing these roles. They live together throughout their lives. But, in other living beings this does not happen. Their union is very short, only for reproduction. In human beings the women specifically play familial roles, and majority of them generally remain within the four walls of the house. The men are generally supposed to do muscular roles. They are supposed to earn for sustaining the family. As such, familial roles performed by women are not considered as important as muscular roles performed by men. As such, women are considered weaker than the men. And it can be said that it is a gender bias. Though in the materialistic age the woman are not behind the men in performing life roles and earning.

HUMAN PSYCHE

Human psyche also plays a very positive role in establishing and perpetuating gender bias in human beings species, that is, bias against women by men and against men by women. The Almighty God has made both men and women as rational beings. They can both think, rationalise and act logically. But the Nature or the Almighty God has empowered the human psyche with greed and self-centredness. Generally majority of the human beings, excepting very few, become mad for the self-interests and greed. And very often certain human beings cross the humanistic limits for the attainment of their desires. They can cross any borders for attaining their self-interests. Men can go against women and women can go against their life partners to any extent. Very shameful happenings occur in the society due to greedy psyche of the human beings. As man is physically well-built and is stronger than women, he usually tries to exploit the woman being weaker than him. Many men exhibit and apply a kind of unsocial barbarous behaviour towards their life partners. Not only this many barbarous (*jungli*) men do not hesitate to rape their daughters and nieces. In cities like Delhi, it is very difficult for the women of all ages to go out of their houses in early morning and in the evening for walking. Recently a seventy years old women was raped by a twenty-three years old boy. Rapes and molestations especially of young women have become a common feature in the present hedonistic materialistic society. All this can be termed nothing but 'gender bias' against women by men. In the present society, the girls being anta-property of patriarchal social structure face a gender bias. They are married to male partners and are thrown in their in-laws' houses like biological garbage. After the marriage, the girls are abandoned. Nobody tries to be affectionate or remember the girls after their marriage. *The Times of India* dated 23.7.2005 reported that, a four months girl was abandoned by her mother in Deccan express at Church Gate Railway Station in Mumbai, when the train was being shunted for being placed it in railway yard. After sometime, the girl started weeping. A cooley heard the crying baby girl. He picked up the girl and took her to the station superintendent, who sent the girl to child care department in the Sir J.J. Hospital, Mumbai. Such kind of treatment of the fair sex is a common feature in the society. This can be said 'gender bias' against the fair sex. And the girls are becoming the victims of the gender bias from the very beginning. First they are not well-treated in their parental homes; and later on they face the same problem in their new homes, that is, in their in-laws homes (ससुराल). There is an urgent need to meet this social fallacy. This can be done through proper education of both male and female members of the society.

ROLE OF EDUCATION TO FACE THE GENDER BIAS

Gender bias against women by men is a very serious problem and social evil. It cannot be rooted outer either by enforcement of civil laws or by imposing social decrees. It can be mitigated by changing the mindsets of men and women. They should be fully made aware about this social evil. This can be done by educating them about the present 'gender bias' against the women in the society and about its killing implications on Indian culture and, on total Indian social milieu. This education cannot be done by school teaching alone, which entails only teaching of few subjects and no enculturation. Mere subjects knowledge cannot meet this social challenge. Epistemological knowledge concerning sociological, economical, political, axiological and teleological arenas pertaining to 'gender bias' is required for both men and women. Above all this, women should be trained in self-defending. The girls should be made self-supporting.

Sociological Aspects of Gender Bias

Sociologically both men and women are two parts of a sociological unit which we call family. Their biological union, which is an 'unity in bio-diversity' for happy lifelong living and for reproducing the new human beings as the new future members of the society. Though both of these human beings—men and women, who constitute one human union' are equally important, but the genesis of the existence of human beings lies in the women. The woman is an equal partner of the social unit which is called family, then why should there should be 'gender bias' against women by men? The men should be educated to be very fair towards women. And the women should be educated about their social rights. This should be done at all level right from the familial education up to high education. They should be educated about their life roles.

Economical Aspects of Gender Bias

From the very beginning the man is considered most viable to earn and contribute in household sustenance. As such, he is considered economically viable in the family for the running of the household. And the woman is supposed to manage and run the household. Since the man is supposed to earn, he is considered superior to women. This situation has contributed to the evil of gender bias. But, now in many families, the situation has altogether changed. The women are not behind men in earning. Still their male life partners consider themselves superior to their female partners. They do not contribute in the household work. In spite of earning, the ladies have to do all housework. In such a situation, the gender bias is quite illogical. Both men and women should be educated about this fact at all levels.

Political Aspects of Gender Bias

Due to gender bias the women are generally devoid of their political rights by men. Very few women get chance to become members of political bodies like Gram Panchayats, Municipalities, Municipal Corporations, State Assemblies and Parliament which are temples of our democracy. The women should be given a chance to become members according to demographic picture. For the last so many years there is a hue and cry to reserve 33 percent seats for women in all these civic bodies. But still, it appears a mere show. Also, there is a whispering in the society for women empowerment which also appears a men show. The Indian demographic scope shows that women are equal in numbers to men. Therefore, there should not be any kind of discrimination against women community. The women should also be educated about this also.

Axiological Aspects and Gender Bias

Axiology is the science of ethics which entails, morality, sanety and social homogenity and above all good behaviour, love, affection and sharing and cooperation. For all these there is a need of right life attitudes. Therefore, it is very necessary to inculcate right life attitudes in both boys and girls from the very beginning. First of all, the mothers should inculcate good life attitudes in their children under the familial education. They should innovate and motivate their children to develop in their good work habits, sane social traits and good behaviour. The children should be asked to speak true. They should learn to respect their elders and the ladies. The girls will have to follow all these life attitude in their new homes, that is, *Sasural* (ससुराल). The children should be asked to give due respect to the siblings. Simple living, high thinking should be the base of inculcation of good life attitudes. Equality should also be given due importance.

After this familial education the school should perpetuate all these life attitudes. The school should also tell students to skip from 'Gender Bias'.

Teleological, Knowledge and Gender Bias

Until and unless the youngers know the teleological truth that all living beings and flora fauna are the creation of the Almighty God. The Almighty God, that is, Soul (*Paramatma* परमात्मा) is present in every human being in the form of soul (जीवात्मा). As such, all are equal in this physical world. One who has come will have to go positively. Therefore, one should not dominate or harass or exploit or ignore anybody. Telelogically, the 'Gender Bias' is against the Divine Almighty God. As such, all women should be equally treated. They should not be discriminated at any stage. The youngers should be educated about this teleological truth from the very beginning and later on at school and at college level.

Self-Defending

And finally the women should be educated in self-defending at school and at college level by the physical education teachers.

17

Women Education and Equality

Inequality is a cancerous human disease, which has been going on continuously since the inception of the human society. Inequality is a common feature in all societies. Out of all living beings, the human beings are said to be the rational beings, as they can think, rationalise, comprehend and act accordingly. But it is observed that many human beings are irrational and they behave like animals. They are very greedy and self-centred. For their own benefits, they distort even the social structure also. Knowingly they do not act righteously and sanefully. Many of the human beings due to their greed and self-centredness act so illogically that they create undesirable inequality. And inequality has been a common social feature throughout the world. The stronger has always also been the beacon of inequality. If we peep into the world social history we will find that inequality has ever been there in the every nook and corner of the world.

It is blamed that some self-interested seers had introduced the social stratification based on 'varna' system which was converted into caste system. The *Rishis* and *Munis* appreciated this social stratification as it was analogous to human biological whole. It was supposed to be a logical social stratification. But the upper *varnas* changed it into birth based permanent caste system, which created a permanent syndrome of inequality. This caste based of inequality has its roots too deep, that the degraded castes still could not yet move forward. The upper caste, though illiterate and unable to do any handwork are considered superior. This kind of social stratification has also affected the women badly. On the analogy of upper and lower castes the man was considered women weak and inferior. The women have always been considered a living being which has been sent for the enjoyment of man. So the women are given lover status than the man. Still the women are supposed to bear child, to bring the child and do all household work. Though, the girls are equally intelligent as the boys are. Many of them do well in the field of education. Annual examination results of the Board Examination are the proof of it. They, after marriage they do jobs also, but are considered inferior to man due to gender bias, and are not equally treated as the men are treated. Inequality of women has a wide spectrum in India, which need detailed discussion. But before doing it is necessary to give a sociological view of inequality.

Professor Andre' Beteille in his article 'inequality and social change' (Oxford University Press, Delhi) said that study of inequality occupies a central place in Sociology when we are committed to compete equality for saneful living in society which is most rigidly hierarchical in the world. Professor Andre Beteille says that inequalities are inherent in human nature, also inherent in conditions of existence. As such, human beings are unequally endowed, both physically and mentally. Sociologists, only have interests in individual differences, in life styles of the people which result due to different positions, they occupy in society—as land owners and labours and also like Brahmans and Harijans. Individuals differ in their ritual abilities and aptitudes. Socio-psychological researches show that there is no difference in intelligence between races as, Whites-Negroes, higher castes and lower castes and between males and females.

Inequality is to be studied with some basic structural phenomena—such as class, status and power and gender differences which co-exist in all societies. These may be described as social fact. These are social facts because these exist independently. What individuals think or feel about them cannot be changed to the will of other individuals. Each society has particular type of social stratification based on status, castes, classes, upward and downward mobility. An individual can do or accept anything or hierarchical level in which he lives. Patterns of social stratification vary from society to society. Also the patterns of social stratification change with the passage of time, as changed in many countries like U.S.A., Scandinavian countries, Russia and India. As such, pattern of inequality change in time. Different pattern may co-exist in the same society. Only sociologists consider inequalities of power and status, economy, income social status and occupations. Economic factors cover income and occupation.

Karl Marx lays emphasis on economic aspect of social life. He explicitly rejected the use of income and occupation a defining criteria for defining social class. He emphasised the social position enjoyed by the individual in the organisation of production unit or due to property one has rather than income. Ibu Khaldun, an Arabian historian said that inequality occurs due to distribution of power and authority. Status factor and prestige creates inequality, many believe rather than wealth and power. Ritualistic purity and pollution also add to the inequality as existed in traditional India. In Medieval Europe honour and Chivalry was the cause of inequality. In modern industrial societies gradation of status is the cause of social inequality. Max Weber said class power and status is the cause of inequality. Ossowski describes three dichotomies: (1) rich and power, (2) rulers and ruled and (3) those who work and for those they work. There exist difference of opinion between Marxists (reductionists) and thinkers like Max Weber (pluralists). Marxist do not deny that gradations do not exist, they emphasis on deprivation of facilities. Max Weber says that status and power are closely related and closely interdependent but, distribution of power lead to inequality. As such, it cannot be denied that inequality is an universal common feature. It can also not be denied that the sociologists have not said anything about the gender bias inequality. This need to be discussed to some extent in Indian context.

Inequality is hardly found in animal world. But human beings have been continuously exploiting their fellow beings for their self-interests and, also of and on their life partners, that is, females. As such, the women have been the perennial victims of inequality from the very beginning caused by their life partners. There are reasons for the inequality the women are facing from the very beginning. Some of the reasons are mentioned below:

PATRIARCHAL SOCIAL STRUCTURE

In other living beings, that is, animals, beasts, birds, insects and bees there are no specified social rules to be followed for having relation between opposite sex. In animals a father can have sex with his daughter. And after doing this he disappears. This cannot happen in human beings. The human beings have set social rules for 'unity in bio-diversity'. A female girl is to be married with a boy who is to be from a distant family, though may be of the race, but should have different *totams* (गोत्रा). As such, the bride has to go with the groom's home. And the girls due to this reasons are considered a liability being anta-property. The patriarchal social structure is dominant throughout world and the girls after their marriage have to go to their husband's homes and leave their parental homes. This social custom of marriage spreads a wave of inequality against the girls in the society. There are few tribal tracks like some hilly tracks in District Dehradun, Uttaranchal and some tribal tracks in Kerala in India, where matriarchal social structure exists. Under this structure the groom has to go to bride's house. This system shows inequality against man.

ANTA-PROPERTY

The girls are considered anta-property (पराया-धन) as they have to leave their parental houses after their marriage. The girls parents always consider them as a liability which gives a signal of inequality for the girls. When a woman conceives she tries to know about the gender about the infant, and most of the ladies get foeticide of the girl baby. The girl baby is not allowed to see this world. If a girl is allowed to take birth. Her birth creates an atmosphere of sorrow and grief in the family. Whereas, on the occasion on the birth of a boy child an atmosphere of joy and happiness emerges. Ladies of the family and of the neighbourhood sing songs and enjoy the coming of a child. A *drastouthan* (दृष्टि उत्थान) ceremony is arranged in which the people are invited for a lunch. All this shows that there is an inherent atmosphere of inequality against the girls the society because of their being anta-property (पराया-धन).

GIRLS EDUCATION

Due to a sense of anta-property and a liability against of the girl's education is largely ignored by their parents. The people think that the girls are to be sent to another homes after their marriages and they will be boon to another homes so they will not be benefited if they are highly educated. Some people think that the girls are to give births to the child and do their household work, elsewhere. So there is no need to educate them. As such, largely girls are deprived of education. In rural areas at least 10 percent girls are not allowed to see the gates of the schools and they remain illiterate. Ignorance of girls for elementary as well as higher education is nothing but a sign of social inequality in the society.

MARRIAGE

The marriage of the girls has become a very serious problem. The demographic picture of the shows that the ratio of fair sex is coming down day by day. As such, there should not be any difficulty in arranging the girls marriages. But the situation is quite topsy-turvy. The institution of dowry has made the girls marriage very very difficult. The grooms' parents always keep an eye for high (hi-fi) amount of dowry which the brides, parents find very difficult to give. But without dowry marriage becomes impossible. For arranging dowry the girl's parents starts accumulating the dowry items from the very beginning and also start depositing money for dowry. All thus leaves the girls in a very degraded position which creates an atmosphere of inequality for the girls.

SOCIO-ECONOMIC STATUS OF WOMEN

The socio-economic status of the girls and also of women is not good. The women have hardly any property rights. Even the future generation is named after the name of the father. In many cases, the old aged widows are thrown out of their house for the sake of property by their sons and daughter-in-laws. Recently the *Times of India* reported such a case. An old widow mother was thrown out of her house by her sons and daughter-in-laws in Ashok Vihar, Delhi. The neighbours came to her rescue and reported the matter to the police which helped her.

POLITICAL RIGHTS OF WOMEN

The women's population is nearly half of the population of the country. The genesis of the society lies with the women. Even though they are not given political rights equal to man. Women representation in our temples of democracy like municipalities, town area committees, gram panchayats, state assemblies and in Parliament is very less. The years passed the male members in the

Parliament are singing the songs of thirty-three percent representation in these institutions, but they also create hurdles in women's representation. It is nothing but inequality for the women.

EDUCATION AND INEQUALITY

Keeping in mind the rampant wave of inequality against the women in the society and, also increases in heinous crimes against women like rapes, molestations, beating, side-tracking in property matters against them, it has become very essential to educate both men and women to meet such challenges. In newspapers we read cases of rapes, looting and deceiving women. Times of India reported on 3.8.2005 that two boys of eight years looted Rs. 37,000/- from a lady in Paschim Vihar. Also two domestic servants looted an old lady, ransacked her house in Sainik Farm house. Old ladies are not safe. So our educational programmers should prepare the youngers to meet such barbarous unsocial activities. For meeting the challenge of inequality against fair sex, the girls should be made aware about all such unsocial happenings. They should be prepared to meet the inequality phobia. They should be fully educated to be self-sufficient. Every girl should be educated in self-defending at the school level. The girls should also be educated to be liberal, social, just to all family members and to believe in equality. The boy should be educated to respect and protect the girls. Both the boys and girls should believe in spirituality, axiology and sociability.

18

Relevance of Co-Curricular Activities in Women Education

All teachers in boys and girls schools and in higher institutions of learning, teaching is done according to prescribed curriculum generally designed to teach subjects and prepare the students for annual examinations conducted by recognised authorities as State Education Boards and Universities. A curriculum is a pre-planned, chalked out programme of teaching, whereby the stipulated content of general as well as science subjects are taught by the teacher. If the teaching is done continuously without any break or variance the pupils get bored and also the teacher is tired. Moreover, only teaching the general subjects or science subjects is not education. Education is a wider activity. If the teaching is only done for the preparation for the annual examination and does not inculcate social and moral values and, it does not entail enculturating activities, it cannot socialise and moralise the youngers and cannot be said true education.

Earlier, the family and community used to inculcate desirable social, moral and cultural values through familial education in the children from the very beginning. Now, because of dys-functioning of joint family system and, due to over-engagement of the parents in nuclear family system for earning money, the familial education has become redundant. All schools are supposed to impart all types of education including familial education, that is, inculcation of social, moral and cultural values. And it has become very difficult, rather an arduous job to teach and prepare the students for annual examination and also to enculturate the students in social, moral and cultural values. This is because the teacher has to carry on teaching throughout the day, at least in six periods out of eight periods. Also enculturation of social moral and cultural values is very necessary, because if the school products do not become rational, the school and the teachers of the schools are blamed by the society. This can be done through co-curricular activities. The school co-curricular activities are generally pleasing, joyful and meaningful. These can ease the students from boredom, and from tiresome of continuous classroom teaching. Now-a-days the teacher's job is measured by subject content she/he teaches in the classroom, how glaring examination results are achieved through her/his teaching. In many cases, the school authorities as well as the Directorate of Education and also the parents expects better glaring examination results. This process goes as a die-casting process of annual examination results as of mechanisation in workshops. Both the teacher and the students are victims of this soul killing process. When the students come to school they have to carry unbearable load of books and exercise books to the classroom. When they return to their homes they become extremely tired. In spite of this many parents, especially the mothers, lay stress on them to study and to do assigned homework. As a matter of fact the teachers generally expect that the parents of the students should also help their wards in preparation of annual examinations. As such, the present process of teaching, under formal system of education is very awkward and tiresome for the parents also. Some, so-called programme schools, lay emphasis on progress methods of teaching desiring good examination results. The schools provide excellent teaching aids too. But cumulative efforts of teaching in spite the use of teaching aids, entails boredom and tiresome, as there is no relief from continuous teaching. The teacher and the school principal are not to be blamed for this agony of teaching boredom of which the students and the teacher become victims. It cannot be denied that they are not aware about this fact, but they are forced to do examination oriented teaching and ignore the life-building process of the students. They are aware about the importance of social, moral and cultural values for the society but they generally ignore due to examination results. Parents are also enable to carry on these values in students due to the rat-race of money earning. As a matter of fact inculcation of social, moral and cultural values in girls in the utmost necessity as they are to become mothers and do life-building to their children. The girls, like boys, after passing out the examinations have also to knock the doors of many employers. They also stand in queues of employment exchanges. Due to lack of co-curricular activities neither the students can enjoy some cultural and artistic activities, nor they can learn social, moral and cultural values which are necessary for character building, personality development and for saneful social living. As such, the implementation of co-curricular activities is very necessary especially in girls schools.

Lack of awareness about the co-curricular activities may be due to the nature of teacher's own experience to some extent. Some teachers are not made aware about co-curricular activities during their teacher education training. Some teacher's training institutes do not have provision for co-curricular activities in teacher training programme. Such institutes generally impart theoretical knowledge. As such, many teachers are totally unaware about the relevance of co-curricular activities in school teaching for inculcating social, moral and cultural values in the students. Of course, the teachers might heard and read about the co-curricular activities but many of them do not get opportunities to experience these. Though many of the teachers of the girls and boys schools and principals of the schools realise that the co-curricular activities are very necessary for enculturation and culture building but they do not get green signal from the authorities due to examination phobia. It is also unfortunate that many sub-standard teachers training colleges do not have provision for co-curricular activities in their teacher training programme. Some such colleges were training the teachers through correspondence courses approved by certain universities. Now the National Council for teacher education banned all such colleges.

It is very important that every school, college and teacher training college should make a provision for co-curricular activities. Another most important point is that every teacher should be called upon to join the co-curricular activities and should perform some activity in this direction in the school. There is no reason to believe that a particular teacher or some students should not be involved in co-curricular activities. Every student should be involved in some sort of co-curricular activities. There are great advantages of co-curricular activities. Through these activities exposure to handwork is possible. The students can express their emotions. Co-curricular activities can provide out of the classroom involvement to the students. Regular scheduled programme of these activities can create aesthetic sense in the students, which usually generates a sense of cooperation and sharing in the students which increases a sense of morality and sociability in the students. These increase the desire for togetherness. The use of teaching aids can be a boon for co-curricular activities. The involvement of students in co-curricular activities increases a sense of epistemacy and aestheticity in them. Doing so, the students discover beauty in physical things. Even they try to use ugly things for creativity and they become creative. When they become creative they naturally become inventive. Being inventive the future guardians, that is, the students become national assets. All this can be done by encouraging the students to do creative work. Emotional release is only possible through creative expression, which is very necessary for the development of balanced personality. As for the balanced life development of an individual it is necessary to inculcate some traits of aestheticity, morality, epistemacy and sociability. If a person or a student is highly intelligent, diligent but, he/she is socially withdrawn, egoistic and megalomaniac, he or she cannot be said fully educated. The society can never function with such persons. Such persons can be elites but they can never be sane and humane persons. Generally the girls are very very intelligent in creative activities. They perform very well in dance, drama, folk arts and solo dancer and debates etc. If the girls are involved in co-curricular activities regularly they can easily learn their life roles.

Absence of co-curricular activities from the school programme is a tragic event. These activities are joyful, meaningful and bring happiness and harmony in the society. Their missing is tantamount to soul killing. These activities can fill up the gap which has been created by the dys-functioning of our institution of joint family system. No development of healthy human attitudes, good manners, sane habits and emergence of cultural traits are possible in the present social flux in which only material aspirations are most important. One reason for the non-presence of co-curricular activities in schools these days may be lack of awareness about these. The principals and headmasters of the schools can be blamed for this. They should not remain blind to ultra anti-social flux which is making the man materialistic and hedonistic and, which may be tantamount to the savagery in the society, in future.

Co-curricular activities are not conspicuous at degree colleges and teachers training colleges, and also at schools. It is complete neglect of an important activity. It is found that many technical universities and technical institutions have better co-curricular activities than the other educational institutions of national fame. Some teachers training colleges yet to pick up the chords of co-curricular activities and, about their roles in socialisation, moralisation and enculturation. This can be done only by educating and apprising such institutions about the importance of co-curricular activities and about their roles in socialisation, moralisation and enculturation. This can be done by making the teachers, schools, teachers training institutions and other institutions which are fully aware about co-curricular activities and motivate them about these. Therefore, there should be a comprehensive orientation programme relating to co-curricular activities in teacher training colleges from the beginning of the session, so that, these activities may be carried out throughout the session. These are necessary for character building. The co-curricular activities need to be included as a form of entertainment and to relieve the students and the teachers from the boredom and monotony of the classroom teaching. Pedagogic values need these activities throughout the year. Maintenance of pedagogic values should be the prime concern of school authorities. The students should also opine in selecting these activities. The co-curricular activities should always reflect the taste and interests and also aptitudes of the students. The teachers should implement these activities very sincerely. The teachers and the students should be guided by the school principal or headmaster or by some expert senior teachers. The teacher in-charge of the co-curricular activities should also guide the students for various co-curricular activities so as mono acting, dancing, acting, singing, debating, performing instrumental music and games and sports. On special occasions, if some chief guest is invited will be good. And on some special occasions if some important person is invited will be good. Such occasions may be as orientation day, foundation day, parents-teacher day, alumnus day and valedictory day etc., etc. There should be arrangement for stage setting, for doing make up of the participants. The art teacher should help in these activities. Above all there should be good lightening arrangement. Actual participation in any of these activities should be compulsory for all students. And such activities should be compulsory for all teacher training institutes.

For optimum presentation of co-curricular activities, these activities should be given an appropriate place in school teaching programme during the full session. And the following co-curricular activities should be organised:

- Debates, lectures, symposiums and study circle be organised,
- Mock courts, mock parliaments, mock panchayats and mock gathering can be organised,
- Weekly wall magazines, periodicals, bulletins, news letters and annual magazines may be displayed.
- Dramatics, solo-acting may be done for enculturation,
- Vocal and instrumental music, sports and games be arranged,
- There should be arrangement for guiding and counselling for the students,
- Scouting and guiding camps be arranged,
- Excursions, educational tours and specific visits,
- Annual gathering by arranging melas etc.,
- Celebration of important religious festivals like, Janamastmi, Pongal, Diwali, Milad-ul-Nabi, Id-Ul-Fitr, Guru Nanak Day and Christmas Day,
- Observation of National Days like, Independence Day (15th August), Mahatma Gandhi's Birthday (2nd October) and Republic Day (26th January) every year,
- Parents Day, Alumni Day, Teacher's Day (5th September) and Red Cross Day etc.,
- Birthdays of great leaders like, Tagore Day, Vinobha Bhave Day, Aurobindo Day, Netaji Subhash Chandra Bose Day, Tolstoy Day and Lincoln Day,
- Melas, Fetes and Sports Day,
- Painting Competition Day,
- Orientation programme in the beginning of the session,
- Valedictory Day at the end of year or session,
- Decorated on special occasions as Parents Day with alpana and rangoli,
- Foundation Day of the educational institute or of the school,
- Social services activities like cleanliness, get together and social precautions as self-defence,
- Decoration by alpana, rangoli, mobiles and mosaics before the special occasions like Foundation Day of the Institute or of the School,

- Arranging hobby clubs like art club, sports club, craft club and writing display club and photography club,
- Chalkboard (blackboard) writing competition, and
- Painting competition.

All these activities should be arranged, under a scheduled co-curricular activities programme, house-wise. All student population should be divided in houses like Tagore house, Gandhi house, Maulana Azad house, Vivekananda house, Rajgopal Acharya house, etc., etc. No student and teacher should be allowed to ignore or skip the co-curricular activities. There should be recording of individual participation of the students and teachers in co-curricular activities. Hobbies like photography, painting decoration and gardening should get a prominent place in co-curricular activities. Each house should have one teaching staff supervisor who should guide the students to organise co-curricular activities. Besides this, special committees should be formed for special occasions, functions as Foundation Day, Teachers Day, Parents Day, Independence Day and Republic Day etc.

For the encouragement of co-curricular activities there should be students *versus* teachers competitions like: (1) cricket match, (2) sports, (3) tug of rope, (4) music and poetry etc., etc. In such competition both teaching and non-teaching staff should take part. The whole staff should help in stage setting and make up. At the Central Institute of Education, late Shri Mehar Chand ji, office superintendent, was expert in make up. He used to help the both female and male students in their make up. The teachers and other staff should cooperate and contribute in functions like annual day, sports day, arranging *langars* (feasts) on the occasion of Guru Nanak Day and Basant Panchami.

There are some odd jobs like receiving the guests, doing seating arrangements, serving refreshments and guiding the visitors. On the occasional gatherings arranging of special cultural programmes should be performed by special artists like singers, musicians as musical instrument players and *nautankis*.

There is a need for giving special attention to the co-curricular activities programmes at all levels of teacher training that is, Nursery School Teacher Training, Senior Teachers Training and in all teacher training institutions. This can only be materialised if the teachers of teachers training institutes are fully trained in co-curricular activities and are enculturated to do these activities. Also the co-curricular activities can only be done if the school authorities are interested in these. Then only these activities will be gainful for the pupils, teachers who are going to be appointed as teachers in schools. The schools should give equal weightage to these activities. These activities do not hamper in school studies rather the students are encouraged to be epistemic and aesthetic. Both the school authorities and the parents have a bias against these activities. They believe that these hamper the students studies. On the contrary such activities always give moral strength to the students and generate a creative, innovative and diligent spirit in the students which build a sound personality.

Therefore, the teachers training institutions, colleges of art and all schools should provide adequate co-curricular activities for their students. These should maintain a record of participation of individual students as per proforma given below:

RECORD OF CO-CURRICULAR ACTIVITIES

1. Name of the student .... 2. Class .... 3. Section ....
4. Name of the institute .... Academic year...........................

Activities	*Occasion*	*Date*	*No. of participants*	*House*	*Remarks by the in-charge of co-curricular activities*
A. Music					
B. Dance					
C. Dramatics					
D. Specialities					
(*i*) Debate					
(*ii*) Symposium					
(*iii*) Recitation					
(*iv*) Mono-acting					
(*v*) Solo-dancing					
(*vi*) Literary activities					
(*vii*) Artistic activities					
E. Display					
(*i*) Magazine					
(*ii*) Bulletin Board					
(*iii*) Morning thought for the day					

(*Contd.*)

(*Contd.*)

Activities	*Occasion*	*Date*	*No. of participants*	*House*	*Remarks by the in-charge of co-curricular activities*
(*iv*) Press Club					
(*v*) Alpana					
(*vi*) Rangoli					
(*vii*) Sculptures					
F. Visual Aids					
G. Art and Crafts					
H. Excursion, Picnic, Tour					
I. House-wise Contests as					
(*i*) Blackboard work					
(*ii*) Mobile displays					
(*iii*) Display banners					
J. Physical Education					
(*i*) Attendance					
(*ii*) Participation in Inter-group					
(*iii*) Proficiency in sports					
(*iv*) Participation in self-defence activities					
K. Participation in other school activities					

These activities should be judged by the Co-curricular Management Committee at the end of the session.

19

Educating Women for Sane Behaviour

The way how a person behaves with another person is called behaviour. To behave means to act or to deal with another person or fellow being. If a person deals with his fellow beings nicely and, he or she does not become angry or rough and talks politely, his or her behaviour will be called a sane behaviour. As such, the human behaviour can be said as one of most important cultural ingredients. If a person behaves nicely with her/his fellow beings and life partner, she/he will be called a civilised person. If he or she does not behave well with her/his fellow-beings and life partner she or he will be called uncivilised or barbarous or a *jungli* person. So it is very necessary to educate the youngers to behave well with her/his fellow beings and colleagues from the very beginning. She or he must be educated that it is nice behaviour which can develop a good culture and a sane personality.

Behaviour of a person is the outcome of her/his psyche and social milieu. The psyche and social milieu of a person, female or male differ due to their biological organism, sociological, economical and political situations and consequent life roles. As already explained both females and males have different life roles. So, it is natural that their behaviour patterns are also different. But, because of 'unity in bio-diversity' they have to live together lifelong. There should not be any sort maladjustment in their lives. So it is necessary that both wife and husband should live amicably together. It can only be possible if they both behave well with each other. Because of gender differences the behaviour patterns of males and female may be different, but for lifelong adjustment woman and man both need behavioural adjustment. So their behaviour patterns should be acceptable to each other. It is also seen that due to divergent, adamant and rude behaviour of wife and husband, many wives and husbands usually fail to adjust themselves which always creates disharmony and discord in them. They always fight before their children, which develop a wrong psyche in their children. Such a situation also spoil the future of their children. Their children neither get a balanced personality now develop good work habits which are necessary for living.

FAMILIAL ATTITUDES

As such, for a desirable viable social behaviour, for both female and male it is necessary to inculcate good behaving habits in the children from the very beginning through familial education. The women are the life givers and life moulders of the future guardians. So, it is very necessary that the girls should be educated in their early age in the family. For doing so first it is necessary that the family should be conflict free. All members of the family should behave well with all family members. They should always love the youngers. The wife and husband should never develop a dispute between them. Their family life should be free of conflict. If the mother and father fight each other before their girl or girls, naturally will also develop a sense of fighting with her would be husband. Main reason of this kind of attitude in girls is their being egoistic and megalomaniac. Egoistic and megalomaniac girls shall never desire to adjust neither with their husbands nor with the members of the families of their-in-laws. Such girls always try to combat their husband, even before their children. Their (parents) aggressive behaviour is transmitted to such children who are generally spoiled. Such children neither become epistemic nor hardworking. They will always prove unsuccessful in life. Mrs. Kiran Bedi published an interview with such a girl in *Times of India*, Delhi, Times dated 9.8.2005. The girl renounced her parents and started living with a boy friend. She refused to come back to her parental house. Likewise, many boys and girls are spoiled by the conflict ridden parents. As such, for transmitting good sane social behaviour in the children, the parents should never fight each other. Many mothers prepare their daughters to fight with their mother-in-laws. They are trained in the childhood to live alone. And in many cases, it is noticed that the brides hardly live with their-in-laws for a week. The girls parents provide the necessary household infrastructure. Such brides live alone keeping their life partners as obedient husbands. As such, this kind of attitudes should not be allowed to develop in the girls which becomes a hurdle in the development of good social behaviour in the girls. The girls should be prepared to live amicably in the familistic social whole that is, family. As such, familial attitudes which generally develop in the young girls in childhood play a very prominent role in behaviour development.

UNSOCIABILITY AFFECTED BEHAVIOUR DEVELOPMENT

Unsociability is the main reason of the non-development of good viable sane social behaviour in youngers. Now-a-days people want to have relation only with the people of their status or class. A car owner would only like to talk to a person who owns car. An elite class people would like to talk to an elite, that too, of his/her status. This is the gift of materialistic culture. The materialism has entailed hedonism, consumerism and xenophism. The present generation only believe in 'eat, drink and be merry'. This was the philosophy of 'carvacs' in ancient India. They were atheists. They believed in earning. Their motto of life was 'eat, drink and be merry'. They did not have any concern about their neighbours or of the nation. 'Carvac' is one of the atheistic schools of India.

In Europe, the protestant movement had emerged against the catholic dogmatism. A group of moderate Christians had started this movement first in Germany which later on spread in many other countries. Their philosophy was also based on 'earn, drink, eat and be merry'. The propagator of this life ethics was St. Calvin, who said that the Almighty God has created everything for human use or for the use of mankind. Even the Almighty God had sent Eve to Eden Garden for the use of Adam. As such, St. Calvin had advised his followers to exploit the natural resources to the maximum. The men and women should work throughout the day diligently, earn money and enjoy life in this materialistic world. The men and women should go to the church only on Sunday once a week. This made the Westerners very greedy. They totally became acquisitive and materialistic. They occupied many eastern African countries.

After the occupation of many Eastern and African countries, the Westerners tried to exploit the natural as well as human resources of these countries. For doing so they tried to impose their culture on their subjects. The English rulers, on the advice of Lord Macaulay had imposed their language through their system of formal education on Indians. And they have been so successful in acculturating the Indians, that we Indians have totally, if not completely have totally forgotten our national culture. The western cultural diffusion has totally killed our culture. We are now completely accultured. Acculturation is a virus killer of socio-economic trends. Our all original cultural traits of including human behaviour have been totally vanished. Because we have adopted the Western behaviour traits, under which a man is to be greedy, acquisitive and self-centred and non-sociable. Our cultural patterns have also totally changed. This effect of western culture has been so much, that is affected our women and men that they do not like to establish familial amity. We have stopped talking to our kith and kins and elders and also neighbours. Because of materialistic desires and hedonistic trends we generally remain busy in finding avenues of earning money. We do not have time for talking, mixing and sharing the life problems with our family members and neighbours. Genesis of good behaviour lies in saneful talking, sharing and also cooperating with the near ones. Now no avenues of catharsis remained opened. In the past, the Indian society in spite of rigid caste structure was said to be a homogenous society. The people of different castes used to talk and mix up each other. They used to share their life problems and used to help others. All this used to help the youngers to be social. They used to develop a sane behaviour. Now due to unsociability the youngers—girls and boys both are devoid of sane behaviour development. How can this stigma of unsociability be rooted out from the society and sociability be restored, is a difficult question. Without restoring sane sociability proper behaviour development cannot be possible. It is, therefore, necessary that the parents of the girls' should inculcate a spirit of sociability in their daughters so that they may develop a sane behaviour. The school should perpetuate it through the co-curricular activities.

CHANGE IN LIFE PATTERNS

Due to ugly acculturations we Indians have totally lost our original life patterns. Earlier, 'simple living and high thinking' was the main life pattern of Indians. They had set life rules as: (1) early to bed early to rise makes a man/women healthy, wealthy and wise, (2) to get vegetarian food makes men/women healthy, smart and diligent and (3) sane sociability and morality makes women/men happy beings. Now due to hedonistic attunement the life attitudes of men/women have totally gone topsy-turvy. They sleep late in the night and rise late up to early noon, they like fast and junk foods and due to materialistic hedonism there is no sociability. People have no time to talk. These trends have affected both girls and boys. Due to modernisation the girls have totally forgotten female sanety. They wear modern dress and live in Western style. Therefore, the modern life patterns of the girls have affected their 'behaviour development'. The parents should realise this change. They first should change themselves and restore original life patterns. Then only there can be a good behavioural development of the girls.

FRUSTRATIVE EFFECTS ON GIRLS

As the girls are fully convinced that they have to leave their parental homes one day for 'unity in bio-diversity' through the institution of marriage. And they have to live with their husbands permanently. Also due to this there exists a gender bias against them in the society. Due to which the girls do not get their due treatment neither from the parents nor from the society. Such girls get frustrated. Though this does not happen in all cases. This mental emotional frustration set in deep layers of their minds. Such mental frustration develops a specific psyche in them. They prepare a mind-set to achieve in their married life what they could not achieve in their parental homes. Often such girls becomes greedy too. After becoming brides their life aim becomes to live alone with their husbands in nuclear families. They develop a kind solitary behaviour. From the very beginning of their marriage they start behaving with their mother-in-laws, anti-in-laws (चचिया सास), sister-in-laws in such a way which could help them in achieving their dream of separate living. Such girls break the joint family system. Such behaviour is not good for sane social living. As such, their girls should be educated to avoid such unsocial an inhumanistic behaviour. For the development of a sane behaviour first of all the society would eradicate the gender bias against the girls from the society. The girls should be given fair treatment as is given to the boys. This is very necessary for bringing the sanety in the society.

EFFECTS OF FAMILIAL RELIGIOSITY ON BEHAVIOUR

Man for conducting his life has evolved certain mechanisms. He developed economic organism. He developed, for developing economic organism some sort of technologies for harnessing the natural resources to meet his biological needs. He developed language for communication. He also developed education, social organisation and political organisation. Being a rational being he also developed religion as he apprehended the super power who has created the living beings and all natural flora and fauna. The man ultimately come to the conclusion that there is a Divine Authority who creates all living beings and flora and fauna. That Divine Authority is Almighty God.

The word religion is derived from the Latin word 'religio' which itself is derived from the root 'leg' which means 'get', or 'together' or 'count' or 'observe' or 'from the root of a big' which means to bind together. In former sense the implication is 'belief' and observance of or signs of Divine Communication which later on blinds all together. In other words, religion means a feeling of reverence to a Supreme Being or a recognition to God. In other words, religion means a recognition of a Divine authority which is an object of worship, love, obedience and of faith and worship. On such faith, there are religions like Hinduism, Greek religion, Jews, Mohammedans or Islam and Christianity. And religiosity is tendency of mind towards the observance of religion. There are many religion related concepts as: (1) *Theism*: acknowledgement or belief in God, (2) *Atheism*: disbelief in God, (3) *Monotheism*: belief in one God, (4) *Henotheism*: belief in many gods and goddess and (5) *Polytheism*: belief in many religions. The man always desires to acquire many things as offsprings and material things. So he/she starts worshipping many gods and goddess. All religions consists of mental attitudes towards the supernatural power. These attitudes manifest in the shape of belief rituals. Sometimes the belief is called myth. All religions, primitive and modern, have the base of ritual and beliefs:

Rituals: Rituals are done for the observance of religion according to prescribed manner or traits as Hindus do morning and evening prayers called 'Sandhya' (संध्या) and do certain religions rites as yajna for establishing a liaison between the individual or individuals and the super-natural power—the Almighty God. The Muslim offer *Namaj* five times in a day to Almighty God. Christians do pray in Churches.

Beliefs: Beliefs are charter of rituals and also rationalisation of the same. The beliefs ensure that the rituals are observed regularly.

Difference between religion and higher religion depends upon variety of philosophical speculations. The beliefs have this. The primitive man has not philosophical speculations regarding religion. But the presence of religion of one kind or another is there. Various thinkers put forward their opinions about the concept of religion.

1. According to Durkheim, "a religion is an integrated system of beliefs and practices relating to sacred things, that is, superb and taboos which unite human beings in one moral community. Sacred things are symbolised with Divinity not necessarily to know ends and relationship cow is symbolised with distinct reality. Jung said that religion is essential feature of human life without which attainment of full integration of human personality is not possible. Tylor said origin of the religion seems to have originated with belief in the soul (*anima*), hence the concept 'animism' for this theory emerged." Tylors' arguments about religion as follows:

> Primitive man experienced in sleep or dream about other beings, while awake he heard his voice, saw his reflection in water. He thought there must be some unseen thing in him which must have escaped 'unseen' making him dead. Such thing is called soul. The primitive man must have thought of two souls—one 'permanent' one 'perishable'. The idea of *Paramatma* (परमात्मा), permanent soul and *Atma* (जीवात्मा) or personal soul is the outcome of such thinking. There are many religions theories which cannot be written here.

In olden times, mostly the Indian people were theistic. They used to believe in monotheism, that is, one God. The main aim of religiosity was to prepare the human being humanistic, axiologist, social by developing a sane ideal behaviour in them. Since all families were religious and they believed religiosity, they used to involve their youngers in religious rituals and used to enculcate in them some religious traits which used to develop a sane ideal behaviour in them. They used to inculcate in them some good habits like, early to bed early to rise, simple living and high thinking, sociability, work habits and sense of cooperation with the fellow beings. The girls were not behind the boys in gaining all these, rather they were ahead.

Hereclitus, the Greek philosopher said that everything is in flux. All living beings, flora and fauna, social structures and sense of religiosity change with the passage of time. In the past we Indians were religious. We used to pray by doing 'sandhya' (संध्या) in the morning and evening. Due to acculturation a sense of deep greed has gripped us. Now, mostly all of us are in the rat-race of money earning. "Earn more, eat, drink be merry" has become the life motto of all people. The people earn in the day and count the money in the night, go to bed late in the night and rise very late in the morning. As such, there is no time to pray the Almighty God. Also mostly all have adopted the Calvinistic ethics "earn throughout the week and pray once on Sunday", we Indians have crossed this limit also. We try to earn throughout the year and at the end we arrange a 'kirtan', or 'jagrata' and give *prasada* to the people who attend the *kirtan*. Someone also tries to arrange a common *langar* (lunch). As such, there remains no place of true religiosity. People have renounced monotheism and have adopted henotheism or polytheism. There remains no place to give religious education at home. In schools, one cannot talk of religiosity due to policy of secularism. Religiosity is very necessary for the development of sane behaviour in the youngers. But it cannot be done in the present changed accultured situation. It is also not desirable that the important aspect of life-building, that is, behaviour development be ignored. Something should be done in this regard. It should be done by the whole society just and later on by the schools. The society should know-how sane behaviour can be developed and some necessary collective steps be taken by the whole society. The elders of the society should take some steps to revive the joint family system and should advise the housewives to develop good behaviour in their children.

ROLE OF SCHOOLS IN BEHAVIOUR DEVELOPMENT

Now in the present social dys-functional situation when the joint family has been totally crumbled down and nuclear families have emerged, and this has happened due to bad familial attitudes, unsociability due to hedonistic temper, acculturation, change in life patterns, frustative effects on housewives due to anta-property social status of women and lack of religiosity in family life. Craze of money earning has totally side-tracked the behaviour development of the youngers. But how long it can be ignored? It cannot be ignored permanently. In the present situation the onus of the behaviour development lies on the girls and boys schools. The schools cannot teach behaviour development as school subject. The schools can inculcate some life attitudes, for building the behaviour, through co-curricular activities. As such, the girls schools, as well as the boys schools should give proper place to behaviour development through co-curricular activities. These activities may be wide and varied. These co-curricular activities should reflect the character of national personalities like father of the nation, M.K. Gandhi, Aurobindo, Vivekananda, Swami Dayananda Saraswati, Acharya Vinobha Bhave, Netaji Subhash etc., etc., the co-curricular activities should also lay stress on enculturation reflecting our national culture, and some cultural activities on this aspect be organised. Cultural activities which are to be arranged should generate sociability, axiology cooperation and sharing. All these activities should give a chance to the students to mix up with all students and talk each other. Activities like games and sports can provide such opportunities. For girls such activities are important because through these activities they can mix up with their peer group and can get a chance of behaviour development.

20

Some Priorities of Women Education

The woman and man are two equal life partners of human social life. Neither woman or man can survive alone nor any of them can ignore each other. They are a combination and a whole of 'unity in bio-diversity' which is done through the institution of marriage for the human social existence. This is happening since the inception of the human society. The woman conceives, gives birth to the child, brings up the child, mould the life of the child, so the onus of the genesis of the human society lies in the woman. All women have to perform difficult life roles, so there are some priorities for their lives development. These priorities should be look into deeply and should be attended by the educational administrators and by the school teachers and school principals. As the girls have to play very specific roles in their future lives, the lady teachers should educate the girls very carefully and sincerely. The main priority of the girls education should be to educate the girls about their prominent future life roles as given below. These priorities are in addition to main school education priorities as teaching, reading, writing, remembering and comprehending through thinking, reasoning and analysing, in others words self-learning.

1. One of the most important aim of girls education should be to make the girls aware about their matrimonial aspects. They should be made aware about 'Sharda Act' under which early child marriage of girls and boys of age below 18 years age girls and 21 years age boys cannot marry. If this happens this is very dangerous for the health of the girls. The girls should be advised not to accept early marriage.

2. It is also certain that the girls to be married in outside vicinity. They have to go to different homes, from their parental homes. As such, the girls should be fully made aware about their future life roles as: (1) household management, (2) bearing and bringing up the children, their life moulding through inculcation of good life attitudes, (3) good sociability and homogeneity for the familial integration, (4) respect to elderly ladies and male members and equal love to all children of the family.
3. To maintain homogeneity between wife and husband. The husband and wife should not develop any kind of discord between them.
4. To behave well before their children. Sometimes many ladies who consider themselves megalomaniac start arguing with their husbands. This affect the future life of their children.
5. To prepare the girls for happy, sweety saneful living. It is necessary to inculcate in them good life attitudes as sharing, cooperation and tolerance. For all these, to inculcate sane sociability is necessary. These can inculcate a desire for singing, extra version, that is, talking with the peer group and habit of laughing, are necessary.
6. To prepare the girls to enjoy natural beauty. For this arrangement of educational tours, excursions and picnics are necessary.
7. To generate a desire in the girls to be epistemic about their natural surroundings. For this the girls should be innovated and motivated by the teachers to know about the natural phenomena.
8. To be epistemic can only be possible, if necessary work habits are developed in the girls by the teachers, to know about physical things.
9. The girls should be encouraged to speak true fearlessly.
10. The girls should be prepared to face all life situations bravely.
11. Efforts should be made, at the school, through co-curricular activities, to develop healthy mind of the girls for human bonding based on love and affection for the family members and the neighbours.

12. To educate the girls to face the causal health problems through health care practices as yoga or daily health care practices. The school should organise health care classes in the schools as extra-curricular activities. Such health habits will keep the girls healthy throughout their lives.
13. The teachers should also advise the girls to be satisfied with their life situation.
14. The teachers should encourage the girls to believe in sound works habits.
15. The teachers should generate a spirit of hospitability in the girls students.
16. The girls should be educated to face any kind of awkward life situations bravely.
17. Of course, the French Philosopher Rene Desecrates said that "the doubt is the foundation of epistemacy", but it should not become a psychological problem for the girl students, as well as for boy students forever. The students should be told that doubting should not be a permanent lifelong feature. Only one should doubt when one is trying to know something new. Doubt should not be entailed beyond the knowledge acquiring process.
18. The girls generally are afraid of tackling difficult problems. The teachers should advise the girls not to be weak minded. They should be advised to tackle all life problems with brave heart.
19. The teachers should educate the girls not to be acquisitive and greedy. Acquisitiveness and greediness are against to our culture of 'simple living and high thinking'. As such, the girls should limit their desires.
20. The main priority of girls education should be to make the girls happy in their coming life situations. For this the girls should be educated to be cooperative, accommodative, sociable and extrovert.
21. To generate humanity and homogeneity in the girls, the lady teachers at the girls school should also apprise the girls about the teleological reality about the living beings. One who has come in the world will have to go positively from this world, that is, all are mortal. Then why should be greed, acquisitiveness in the human beings. All should lead a same homogeneous life.

22. Generally, it is seen that the females are not fairly treated in human society. The girls should be educated to be prepared to face any kind of gender bias against them.
23. In the present industrial society generally the fair sex becomes the victims of crimes like molestation, rapes and looting. A number of men have become barbarous and commit such crimes. The morality does not touch them. In cities like Delhi the girls cannot come out of their houses neither in the morning nor in the evening. They become victims of such crimes because they are considered physically weak. As such, the girls should be trained in self-defending at school level as well as community level. They should be trained in 'karate' and 'jogging' etc, etc.
24. At school level the girls should be educated not to be mentally sick (चिन्तामई).
25. The girls should be educated, innovated and motivated to judge what is good or bad, not only for them but for all.
26. The present psyche of illiterate women is that 'there are only those who were born out their womb'. This limited thinking make them self-centred and greedy. Such ladies play the role of dys-functioning of joint family system. The teachers should try to eradicate this mentality of self-centredness of the girls. This can be done by arranging related co-curricular activities.
27. The girls should be educated to discharge all of their familial roles very sincerely.
28. Finally, the girls should be educated and prepared to respect all elders and to love all children.

Now-a-days, in the industrial age and consequent hedonistic temper of human beings, there is a crucial dichotomy in all educational fields, that is, education of girls and boys. The education is considered limited up to teaching some subjects for passing out examination and consequent certification. This trend leads to cut-throat competition in the job market in the society. This kind of education is imparted through formal system of education which has no place for inculcation of necessary life attitudes in the pupils and for enculturation. The true education is that which is done for life-building. The education is a process of taking out students' hidden potentialities and motivating them for self-learning and life-building by acquiring some relevant life attitudes, manners, good behaviours, good character and spirit of taking logical actions. Therefore, it is necessary that the elders should be aware about all these necessary educational priorities of the girls, and first of all they should carry on the life-building priorities of the girls. Since the women are life givers, life-builders and life protectors, there should not be any kind of carelessness in girls' education. The girls are future women and mothers. They will have to play very distinct life roles, which are no less than the roles played by the women's counterparts. Therefore, every care should be taken to educate the girls keeping all women education priorities in mind.

The girls are to be educated by the lady teachers. The lady teachers are considered ideal teachers. But due to their familial problems, the lady teachers have some problems. First, they do their household duties as making refreshment and preparing lunch packets for their husbands and children. Thereafter, they come to the school partially tried. Their husbands do not cooperate at all. After the school teaching when they go to their homes back they go tired. Again they have to do all household work, such as cooking, washing of clothes and purchasing necessary things for the kitchen. As such, the lady teachers hardly get any time to study and proficiate. They hardly play their teaching roles as per teaching professional ethics. Such problem can only be tackled if theirs husbands come forward to cooperate with their housewives in all of their household work. Then only the lady teachers can look to the priorities of girls' education at all levels. The educational administrators, principals and husbands of the lady teachers should look to this serious problem in the educational field.

21

Women's Behaviour Development

The term behaviour is the development of the word 'behave', which means to conduct or to apply one's self in dealing with others. Different ways and modes of human behaviour such as talking, laughing, anguishing and meeting are used while dealing with others in the human society. Behavioural norms are also noticed in other living beings, such as animals, birds, beasts, insects and bees. Since human beings have developed language and speak with his/her fellow being, the human behaviour has reached to new heights. Behaviour of a person is the dictums of one's personality. It is the indicator of one's inner emotions, morality, sociability and the mode of character. If a person behaves well with his/her fellow beings, she/he will be considered a nice sane gentleman or gentlewoman. If a person dose not behave with his/her fellow beings, he/she will be considered a rude uncivilised person. Also the ways of behaving of men and women may be different. The reason of such behaving may be their different psyche, personalities, ways of sociability, greed, physical appearances, self-centredness, sanity and humbleness. But it is an accepted fact that one who behaves well with his/her fellow beings is always considered a gentle person. Behaviour of such person is always appreciated in the society.

The roots of such nice sane behaviour or rude behaviour of persons of any country are found in the religiosity of the people and social and economic structure of the country. Indian culture is one of the oldest cultures of the world. The Indians were and still are, theistic. As such, they believe in religiosity. They believe in the duality of the soul (जीवात्मा) and believe that all living beings are part of the 'Bigger Soul'. That is, 'Paramatma' which is immortal. So this teleological belief motivates the Indians to religiosity. They believe that all individuals are part of the Almighty

God, so they deserve equal treatment in all respects. So the human behaviour should be sane homogeneous and kind. This is why the Indian people still used to behave with all nicely. In the past Indian people used to be very hospitable with their fellow beings. In the olden days the hospitability was considered tantamount to divinity in India. Honouring a guest was considered a 'Guest Religion' (अतिथि धर्म). The guest was to be honourably welcomed. He was given food and shelter. And the guest was well-behaved and trusted. Still when a person goes to another's house, the owner of the house receives him/her honourably and extend to him/her due hospitability. First of all the guest is offered a seat, either on cot or on the chair. Thereafter a glass of water is offered. After this tea is offered. The guest is well-behaved. In the past, the guest offered milk in the winter, and 'sharbat of sugar' (sugar water) in the hot days. Such a behaviour was considered necessary according to Indian culture. And the Indian women used to play prominent role in such a behaviour of hospitability. This is why the sane temper of human behaviour entailed hospitability seriously in India. And the Indian women were the source of such hospitable behaviour. Many foreigners praised the Indian hospitable behaviour. Few years back, the American first lady Mrs. Hillary Clinton, the wife of the former President of U.S.A. Mr. Bill Clinton was so much impressed by the Indian hospitable behaviour that she advised the Americans to adopt the joint family system and hospitable human behaviour. She was very much impressed by the Indian culture also. In 1954, Mr. Albert Coommer, a disciple of late Professor (Dr.) S. Radhakrishnan, the former President of India, was very much impressed of the sane hospitable behaviour of his teacher (*guru*). He decided to visit the country of his *guru* and met him at Delhi. His teacher late Dr. S. Radhakrishnan was then the Vice-President of India. He had also decided to visit behavioural institutions in India Gurukula Narsen, Muzzafarnagar, Gurukul Kangri Haridawar, Shanti Kunj and Swargashram Rishikesh, and such other places as in Prayag, Varanasi, Mathura, Madurai and Rameshwaram in Tamil Nadu. During the month of July 1954, he started his journey from London on foot. After crossing the British Channel he came to India covering many European, Arabian and Asian countries. He was looted at eight times upto Khyber Pass on the western border of Pakistan. After entering Pakistan he was given due warm hospitability during the course of his journey to

India. After crossing the Wagha border, he came to Amritsar. He stayed for few days at Golden Temple, Amritsar, where he was impressed by the Indian hospitable behaviour. Likewise, he was nicely treated and was given hospitable treatment by the Indians. Finally, he reached New Delhi and met late Dr. S. Radhakrishnan, the then Vice-President of India and former Professor in Philosophy at Cambridge University, London. After staying with him about a fortnight he decided to resume his journey to northern part of India to see Gurukula Narsen, Gurukula Kangri Haridawar, Shanti Kunj and Swargashram Rishikesh. Dr. S. Radhakrishnan had offered him vehicle to go to Rishikesh, but he declined. He argued that he wanted to see the landscape and socioscape of the area. He started his journey from New Delhi to Rishikesh on foot. On the first day he stayed in Duhai village in the night. He was very eager to meet the Indian people. Next day he came to Govindpuri (Modinagar). He entered the Government Training-Cum-Production Centre, Govindpuri, where the writer was working as a Carpentry Instructor. He saw radio, electrical and sheet metal classes first, and after this he enter the carpentry class. The writer asked him (Albert Coommer) whether he would like to eat something, while offering him water. He replied, "anything you can offer". Thereafter the writer asked his attendant Kothari to take Mr. Albert Coommer to his residence, give him a cot to take rest and cook rice and *dal* and offer him. Mr. Kothari made the *dal spicy* and Mr. Albert Coommer could not eat rice with the *dal*. In the afternoon when the writer and his companion Mr. Lohani went to their residence, they both asked Mr. Albert Coommer whether he had taken something. He replied 'no', he could not take because the food was too spicy. In the evening he was offered non-spicy food. Mr. Albert Coommer stayed with Mr. Lohani and with the writer for three days and he was given due hospitability. On the third day, he asked to bring *jaggery* for him which was not known neither to the writer nor to Mr. Lohani. Ultimately they both took Mr. Albert Coommer to the market where he pointed out *jaggery*, that is, *Gud* (गुड). Next morning he again resumed his journey for Rishikesh. He was offered to travel in Bus upto Rishikesh but he refused bus journey. In his valedictory talks he said that India is one of the most hospitable country in the world and Indians behave so nicely that their behaviour is a hospitable behaviour.

This is an accepted reality that for sane homogeneous social living good, nice, sane and hospitable behaviour is a social dire necessity. Without a sane good behaviour people cannot live together amicably. But nowadays due to acute acculturation we Indians have forgotten our original culture and have become desirous for material things for leading a hedonistic life. This social change has also badly affected the women also. Today's modern hectic life is full of stress, and women are not free of it. The effect of acculturation of western culture is not less over the women. They also dream for a hedonistic life and want to be rich. This is why women are found in job market extensively to meet the needs of present hedonistic life. The Almighty God has endowed the human beings with some bodily faculties. Human beings are rewarded with bigger brain to think, rationalise, comprehend and act accordingly. The human being have erect posture and moving hands for acting. But the Almighty God has made the human beings very greedy. Men and women both are prey of it. As such, the human beings have forgotten all traits of morality, sociability, brotherhood, good behaviour and sane character. The women which were once sane behaviourists have also now become totally self-centred. They consider their own children as their own. Due to their greedy nature they are now the dys-functioners of joint family system. The idea of common good has now changed into own good. The women now are fully determined to live alone in nuclear families. So, the notion of ideal fair sex has totally gone. When the women do not like to talk to their original family members, how can they behave well with others. There is no sense of cooperation, sharing and renouncement in the present women. As such, concept of ideal hospitable women is no more. This is not the case of illiterate women, the so-called educated women are also sailing in the boat of self-interest and unsound behaviour.

It is, therefore, very essential to take some steps towards women behaviour development. The school education cannot do when the parents of the girls have become totally self-centred, and do not want to establish sociability with the neighbours. For the sane female behaviour development it is utmost necessary to educate the parents of the girls first. It seems quite impossible because the institution of joint family, which can do this job, is no more and totally crumbled. The people do not have time to attend the religious discourse because of their busy life. Religiosity is no more perfectly in the houses. The people are not ready to listen to the elders of the community. So in absence of familial education on the women behaviour development appears to be very difficult.

In this regard something can be done through enculturation. The nuclear families due to their involvement in money-earning cannot do it. Now only this difficult job falls on the soldiers of girls school's lady teachers. Of course, they are also very busy in teaching schools, but where there is a will there is a way, they can do this job by establishing good rapport with the girls and thereby apprising them about the tenets good women behaviour.

22

Ideal Roles of Women Education Teachers

Every girl is to be a woman and mother. A mother is always an embodiment of love and affection, sacrifice, dedication, diligency and aestheticity. The genesis of human existence and human society lies in the mothers. They give birth to the future guardians of the society. They bring them up and mould their lives. The women inculcate all life values, such as, work habits, morality, sociability, epistemacy, aestheticity, diligency, sincerity and spirituality. So a mother is an ideal social being. So the girls, the future women, need appropriate ideal education. For an ideal education an ideal teacher is needed. The girls, the would be mothers, have to play many multifaceted life role in their married life. They are to be life givers, life builders, life moulders enculturators of the youngers. So the life roles of the girls are much more difficult and auspicious than the male members of the society. Their educational needs are different than the boys. So the girls need to be educated very cautiously about their future life roles as housewives and mothers. In their lives they have to deal with a genetic whole of being women, housewives and mothers. They need to be educated, to be kind, humanistic, considerate, cooperative, epistemic, aesthetic, sociable, and spiritualistic so that they may able to strengthen the social whole, that is, society and its unit, the family, and keep these intact. In the present materialistic and hedonistic age, under the present formal system of education, the emphasis is laid on teaching specific subjects like science, mathematics, humanities and languages etc. The life-building processes are not given due importance in formal education.

Swami Vivekananda said that the main aim of education is the "wholesome development of the individual". Father of the nation,

Shri M.K. Gandhi said that "education is drawing out the best from the individual". Prof. E.A. Pires said that "education should inculcate the ideas in the individual for making him self-conscious human being. The individual should be kindly to his fellow being. His/her soul should discern common spiritual good. Without good ideas an individual can never be a good person. The essence of good education should be self-discovery, self-direction and out one's own limitations. The good education should be wholesome and integrative development of individuals' personality and self-built character, ideal development of one's personality". Since the teacher is the beacon light and torch bearer of the pupils, some ideals are very necessary in the life of the teacher. So the teacher should always cherish for all sane, and unique important ideas.

It is necessary to give etymological explanation of the term "ideal" first of all. The world ideal is an adverb of the word 'idea'. The word 'idea' is a derivation from the Greek word 'Idus' meaning 'a mental form' or 'appearance of a thought of a person', 'a thing', 'a kind of species', 'a root', 'a model of thinking in mind' that which is comprehended by individual faculties in philosophical terms. An idea is generally aimed at to designate objective notions with or without subjective validity. An idea is a thought acceptable, appreciable belief by the majority of the people. There are schools of philosophy like idealism, realism, dogmatism, naturalism, empiricism, communism, pragmatism, terrorism, socialism and capitalism etc., etc., based on specific ideas. Idealism is one such philosophical school which is based on common good. Acting according to ones' inner consciousness, believing in spirituality for common interest and good without any personal gain or inclination is a form of action which may be called 'idealism'. As such, the term 'ideal' is that which is noble, good for all and is always non-inclinature. Many governments adopt an idealistic constitution. Ideal thinking always entails a belief which is circumscribed around the wish of common good and not doing anything which may harm or hurt others in the society. An ideal person is one who has always has good ideas and works for the common good. Such person is always considered an ideal man in the society. He is liked and loved by the majority of the people. An ideal man/woman is the embodiment of goodness. An ideal man should have a well developed personality. He/she should possess the following qualities:

1. A perfect admirable sane character.,
2. An integrated personality which should always entail:
   (*a*) a balanced behaviour,
   (*b*) non-inclinativeness,
   (*c*) deep desire for common good,
   (*d*) respect to the fair sex, and elders,
   (*e*) an intense deep desire to help the weak, poor, ill, elders and fair sex,
   (*f*) should love every child as his/her own child, and
   (*g*) believing in simple living and high thinking and life.

An ideal personality should be of worth respecting by all in the society. Sane sociability, morality and living for the common cause and good should be the life motto of an ideal person. A fully developed human being is only possible if a person develops socially, morally having the sensitivity for the truth, beauty, justice, love, affection, cooperation, tolerance, non-violence, thinking, reasoning, comprehending and a sense of kinship affection for students teaching. The teaching should be based on the principle of sharing. All these qualities are essential for an ideal woman teacher. In the modern time of industrialisation which entailed modernisation. Due to modernisation the simple living and high thinking has been renounced by the people. It made the people too much greedy, self-centred, utilitarian, hedonistic, xenophilic and megalomaniac. Due to this social idealism has been renounced by most of the people. Instead of being idealistic, the modern man and woman have become pragmatics for material gains. The old religious beliefs based on spirituality and monotheism have been replaced by hedonism, polytheism, xenotheism which are practiced for personal gains. Daily prayers are generally being discarded due to busy materialistic life of man. These have been replaced by weekly *satsangs* on the pattern of western Calvinistic philosophy of exploitation of natural gains for material gains and, for praying in Church once a week on Sunday. For material gains the modern man/woman does not spare time even for their own kith and kins. It is seen that the wife does not hesitate in killing her legal husband for personal gains. Son dos not hesitate in killing his own father for gaining property. Neighbourly relations have almost been vanished. Now old caste structure is being replaced by class structure. The old norms of social living are vanishing day-by-day. An elite person does not want to maintain relationship with his neighbourly elites because of megalomanism. An owner of a car always liked to talk to a person who has a car. A person having bicycle, though he may be intelligent, diligent, honest and an ideal person now is considered fool by the well-settled, and economically well-settled persons, with the result there is a rat-race for maternal mobility. This trend has, more or less, eliminated sociability, morality, ethnicity from the society. The present man/woman has become totally self-centred, egoistic, greedy, acquisitive and meglomaniastic. This is because of present system of formal education, which was imposed on Indian by the British government. This system has no ideas to generate sanety in the students. Our women teachers while teaching in girls' schools should be made aware about all these socio-economic and cultural aspects. This should be done by the teacher training colleges while imparting teacher education.

Our present system of education only breeds love for maternal gains which entails cut-throat competition. It lacks socialisation, axiology and moralisation which is the soul of integrated sane social life. The corruption is so rampant in the society that, there is hardly any field which can be said corruption free. Incidents of loot, dacoities, burglaries, chain snatching, pick pocketing and molesting have become a common social feature these days. Acculturation has engrilled the whole society very badly. Sixty-years back one used to afraid of wolves and beasts in the country side. Now in country side human beasts have taken place of jungle beasts, nobody can dare to go out after sun set. Loot, kidnappings, snatching have become a common feature in country side. Kidnapping for ransom has become a rewarding business. This happens in rural and urban areas equally. In cities, like Delhi, the girls and even old ladies are not safe. They are being raped by so-called emerging backward classes. A week ago seventy-three year old women was raped by twenty-three years old boy. And such criminals are not punished and roam scot-free. The women teachers should make the girls aware about such awkward social situation.

In such a pathetic social situation there is an urgent need of idealistic behaviour in our lives. Since the women are the real teachers of the youngers, the women, teachers should teach the girls to give an idealistic mould in the behaviour of their future offsprings. But it is very difficult. At present, there is no congenial atmosphere for building idealistic behaviour in our younger generation. It is, because of ostentatious and xenophilic life styles. The joint family system has more or less crumbled down. In place of joint families nuclear families have emerged. Both the parents are in the rat-race of money-earning. They want to earn more and more. They generally ignore their younger ones. The socialisation and moralisation which used to start at home and, the family members used to do it, is now missing. Where are the younger ones are going is neither the concern of the parents nor of the community and society? The rulers always look to the consolidation of their governance. Parents, community and the government generally expect school to do everything for the younger generation as, education, socialisation, moralisation and enculturation. Also the schools should prepare the students to face the competition. As such, the teacher has to devote most of her/his time to prepare the students for annual examinations so as to enable them to face the job competitions. The teacher does not have time to devote to life-building activities like socialisation, moralisation and enculturation. If a younger becomes criminal, generally the school in which he/she is studying or studied is blamed, but the parents are not blamed. It is observed that the mother plays a vital role in making a younger a criminal. If she offered him fast and junky foods and does not develop sociability, work habits and diligency the younger shall not be able to earn in his life and to meet his requirements of hedonistic life, he or she will become a criminal. But it is observed that if a younger becomes criminal, his teachers and school are blamed. When the consumeristic habits are developed in home by the parents, the student will generally sleep and will not study at all. Such hedonistic habits spoil, mostly, all of the intelligent students. The school women teachers can play motherly roles. They should be very cautious about these while teaching the girls. Of course, due to hedonistic climate of the homes, proper inculcation of desirable life attitudes and habits are not done in homes. The women teachers should not ignore this aspect at all. They should make the girl students fully aware about all these aspects. Making the students aware about sane life attitudes is the prime need of the day. The schools should organise parents-teacher days at least once in a term and make the mothers aware about their ideal motherly roles. Only inculcation of ideas, attitudes and work habits in the youngers can save them from dirty aspects of hedonism and consequent consumerism. The dirty virus of materialism which brings acculturation in the society, can be rooted out. There is no way out of sane ideas and inculcation of good life attitudes. Only enculturation and inculcation of good life attitudes can save our youngers from materialism. The materialistic trends are robbing our society of our national culture. Habit of simple living can help in this regard. The woman teachers should advise the girl students to develop a habit of simple living and high thinking. In fact, the school teachers be it male teachers or female teachers are occupied in preparing the students for annual examination. In the past there was no examination system in Indian in old education system. But due to the climate of epistemacy, India could produce more brilliant educated men. The present examination system is the gift of foreigners. Our educationists should look to this aspect seriously and should devise a method which may reduce the burden of examination. By doing so, the teachers will get time for inculcation of good life attitudes and for enculturation.

The teacher is a nation builder, a trend setter and character builder of the youngers. And women teachers have a special place in this aspect as they teach the future mothers. It is the mothers who either can do proper life-building of the youngers or can spoil their lives. If not all but many mothers due to their hedonistic and consumeristic life attitudes either spoil their children or make them lazy. They shower too much of love over their children which is always poisonous. Many of such children become redundant future citizens. They do not like to do any work themselves. Their only desires remain to eat fast and junky foods. They are not taught by their mothers to respect elders. This is a very serious social situation which is seen in the Indian society. Many educated women create such an awful situation in the country. Such women are generally megalomaniac. They do not listen to the advice of their in-laws. Such women are those who are generally born and brought in poor families, but after marriage they find a place in well to do families, and because of availability of everything they forget everything. Some educated women exhibit such behaviour. The women teachers should apprise the girls about such undesirable life situations.

If we peep into the past history of our Brahmanic education system, we find that old *Gurus* (teachers) were the idealistic personalities. They were epistemic, well-read, spiritualistic, monotheistic, *yogis* and were dedicated to teaching profession. The old teachers were sincere, didactic, elicitators, non-inclinative, sacrificers, helpers and guides to their disciples. They used to act as spiritual and social *gurus*. They never thought of any social, gains and enjoyments. They did not have any degree after passing examinations. They always encouraged debates and discussions (वाद-विवाद). They always respected fair sex and allowed outside women to participate in debates and discussions which used to take place in Gurukulas. Main objective of *shikshan* (teaching) was socialisation, moralisation, economic upliftment of the people in the olden days. In other words, it can be said it was purely a life-building process which used to help people in their socio-economic upliftment which was/is necessary for social mobility.

The old teachers used to follow the teaching professions' ethical code. Now the situation has totally changed. It is quite topsy-turvy. Now the teacher, be it a female teacher or male teacher is a public servant. Whereas in the past the *guru* (teacher) was a true professionist, an idealist and a spiritualist. He was a widely respected. The present teacher be a lady teacher or male teacher because of her/his minimum economic gains is not respected by the economically affluent members of the society. In spite of all this the teacher, male or female, should not forget the roles performed by the old teachers, the *Gurus*.

It is the teacher, especially the lady teacher, who can raise the people from social degradation, as they teach the girls who are going to be future mothers. The teacher should cherish and aspire a well-balanced personality. If a teacher has a well-balanced personality, then only she/he can mould the personalities of the pupils by presenting herself/himself as an ideal model before them. The teacher, be a lady teacher or male teacher should constantly build herself/himself for being a constant helper of the children and pupils. This can be possible if she/he has a sympathetic ear towards the pupils. The teacher should listen and understand the problems of the pupils and, then respond to their problems sympathetically. The teacher should see that the pupil is mentally undisturbed and is spiritually bold. Therefore, the teacher should try to take steps to prepare the young pupils as fully developed human beings. The full development of the pupils is only possible, if they are developed socially, economically and morally. For this end the teacher should have a sensitivity about truth, beauty, justice, goodness and a sense of kinship for the pupils. With these qualities an individual can be a true sane citizen who will aspire for the common good and will dedicate to the national development.

No teacher can be said to have a real role of teaching profession, if she/he is not inspired by the ideal real roles of teaching profession. The teacher must be aware about the credentials of the teaching professions which are as under:

1. A profession is a relationship between an expert and an ignorant client. Of course, the teacher is supposed to be an expert in the subject she/he is teaching. But her/his client, the student is not an ignorant client like that of medical man, or a lawyer and a priest. So the teacher has to be more expert and proficient in the subject, she/he is going to teach, for this she/he has to continue her/his studies for becoming proficient in subject she or he is teaching.
2. Therefore, the teacher should continue her/his studies, so that she/he may be proficient in the subject she or he is teaching.
3. The teacher should be very sincere to her/his clients that is, students, she/he is going to teach. If the teacher is not inspired by the ideals of teaching profession and, not dedicated to the pupils and the society, the teacher cannot mould the future guardians. This can be done when a teacher posses:

    (*i*) a sense of good character,
    (*ii*) a sense of sympathy and kindness towards the pupils,
    (*iii*) a sense of self-introspection and restraint,
    (*iv*) a sense of epistemacy and desire for gaining more and more knowledge and practical experience in aesthetic and creative field, and
    (*v*) a teacher should be sympathetically appreciative of multi-patterned life situations. She/he should face the life situations very courageously.

4. A teacher should be non-inclinative. She/he should not aspire to do tuitions.

In addition to this the teacher should be sympathetic to animal life also. She or he should always keep in mind that as a builder of the nation and the future guardians her/his sources are essential for the society. These should be discharged with dedication. The teacher should always keep in mind that her/his duties are not only limited within the four walls of the classroom in the school alone. These go beyond the school. The teacher is the builder and enlighter of the whole nation. Therefore, the teacher has to be most sincere, active, intelligent, diligent and a social minded citizen. The teacher should be broad minded, kind hearted and socially active person.

A teacher must strictly follow the code teaching ethics, which requires proficiency, sincerity to the students and to the society as a whole; and above all she/he should be non-inclinative. But in the present materialistic age generally the male teachers do tuitions to meet their hedonistic needs and the lady teachers as they have to look after their households. They do not get cooperation in their household work, they usually remain semi-active and not fully active in their teaching and other school duties like co-curricular activities. As a matter of fact, the co-curricular activities pertaining to women's life roles are very very essential. These should be arranged with sincerity in girls' schools. Many lady teachers also tries to commercialise education. They open preparatory schools in their homes. Instead, the lady teachers should innovate and motivate the girls to know about their future life roles and should encourage them for self-upbringing. A lady teacher should always cooperate with her colleagues. She should never be megalomaniac, that is, believing that she knows every thing. If a better teacher advises her, she should not ignore the advise, rather she should be thankful to her colleague. A teacher who is megalomaniac can never be a good teacher because she/he will not try to know and add to her/his knowledge. This dictum does not only apply to the teaching profession. It also applies to all other professions and vocations. For example, if a carpenter or a cabinet maker or fabricator or a mason thinks that he is the master of her/his area of action, her/his megalomony will kill his/her thinking, reasoning, analysing and acting. This will ultimately put a halt on her/his actions and creating. So a teacher should always avoid megalomony in her/his area of action should be open for thinking, reasoning, analysing and criticism. A teacher should not be afraid of criticism by his disciples and colleagues. Rather a teacher should welcome and appreciate the open criticisms and suggestions. This will unveil the doors her/his brain for self-introspection and consequent thinking. The teacher should apply such methods of teaching as, heuristic method, project methods, discussion method etc., etc., which could motivate and stimulate the students' mode of thinking, reasoning, comprehending, analysing and responding. These can help the students in learning. For this process the use of teaching aids is necessary. The teaching aids can initiate the teacher-taught interactions which will lead to elicitations. The teacher should be liberal. She/he should allow the students to discuss the other matters as social, political, moral and integration. The teacher should innovate the students for social integration, economic development and enculturation. The teacher should spend her/his leisure time for the development of creativity.

Culture of any country is its soul. If the culture of any country disappears, the nation also dies like a human body dies when its soul (जीवात्मा) leaves it. Therefore, it is very necessary for the teacher to know about the national culture, having wide variety of national interest. The teacher should be made aware about all cultural activities during teacher education at a teachers' training institute. Then only the teacher can enculturate the students. The woman teacher can play a vital role in enculturation and cultural development.

The democracy is the slogan of the day. A democratic of government is a 'government by the people, for the people'. Because of human animal nature many political leaders to want to make the democracy as their property. And for keeping their hold intact for remaining in power, they do not hesitate to criminalise the political institutions. The teacher has a great responsibility in this regard. She/he should inculcate democratic norms in the students by developing belief in democratic institutions. The school authorities should initiate this process by establishing students democratic institutions as students panchayats. The teacher has a great responsibility in this regard. She/he should help in making the school democratic institutions like student panchayat functioning. She/he should inculcate democratic norms and habits in the students by developing belief in democratic institutions. The teacher should prepare the future citizens for ideal democratic living, making them aware about the criminals, economic criminals, unsocial elements and political criminal dens and to fight with such bad elements. The women teachers should prepare the girls to fight the unsocial criminals such as rapists. All girls schools, school should introduce self-defence classes for the girls through co-curricular activities, group discussion, seminars, workshops and symposiums. The women teachers should make the girls aware about the versatility of sociability, truthfulness, punctuality, regularity in life such as 'early to bed early to rise makes a man/women steady, wealthy and healthy and wise. The women teachers should also motivate the girl pupils to be regular and punctual and inculcate in them some habits of good living. All these can be inculcated through co-curricular activities in the school.

Teaching is a creative process like that of creative arts and fine arts. The teacher should always apply creative process in educating the students. Generally the girls are creative, so the women teacher always should inculcate creative spirit in them. Then few of them will become creative thinkers, artists and other professionalists. The women teachers should always keep in mind the great teachers, the *gurus* of olden times, while teaching. Also the teacher should also make a reference of the great person. This will help in the character building of the pupil. The teacher should always keep good rapport with the students and their parents. She should apprise the students about the evil effects of modernisation and consequent acculturation which occurred due to cultural diffusion with the western culture.

Finally, it would not be wrong to assume that roles of an ideal teacher should be honesty, sincerity, simplicity, proficiency in the subject, sociability, morality and truthfulness and also dedication to the teaching profession.

23

The Role of Lady Teacher in Socialisation, Enculturation and Moralisation of Girl Students

Teaching of school subjects can never be said complete education. The complete education of youngers is much more. Besides subject knowledge education is a life-building process. And the school education should have a complete provision of life-building process in school curriculum for the students. This should be done according to the future life roles of the students, both boys and girls. Since the times immemorial the men and women both have ever been doing the life-building of their offsprings by socialising, moralising, inculcating good life attitudes and life attitudes in their children. They have been socialising their offsprings by enculturating them for culturally prescribed patterns, language, skills, social norms, moral values, customs, traditions for generating in them a capacity to perform many social roles, social relationships and creating an atmosphere for strengthening the collectivity of individuals, that is, society. This is all done through socialisation of the individuals, by generating in them social norms, values, sociability, cooperation, and especially the morality and diligence. This process had deep antiquity and, is used for regulating the human behaviour. If we peep into the history and trace the educational ideas, we will find that our old seers, thinkers and philosophers have always been constantly trying to profitiate new ideas for regulating the human life. This is because the man by nature has ever been egoistic, greedy, self-centred, hedonistic, acquisitive, consumeristic and a xenophilic being. The strong man has ever been exploiting the weak man resulting in social discontents, social conflicts and disharmony in the society. To overcome such awkward social situations, the wisemen have always been devising steps and ways and means. They have always prescribing certain social norms for social homogeneity. They have always been profitiating and prescribing certain social sane norms of good social behaviour. They have always been devising ways and means for developing an acceptable social behaviour in human society. Such patterns of human behaviour and character are generally called morals. And moral building is done through enculturation of the culture of a particular society. Prominent moralist like Immanuel Kant, H.E. Moor, Shopenhauer, Hegel and at home and all of our Gurus and Acharyas can be said as moralists. Our present teachers both, male and female teachers, have also to play a prominent role in infusing morality in our youngers.

The culture and civilisation are often mised together, though these have sharp distinctions. Even though these two are taken in wide ethnographic sense as similar. But it is culture which contributes to the development of civilisation. The culture is that complex whole which includes knowledge, beliefs, art and crafts, morals, laws, customs, traditions, social traits behaviour and many other capabilities and habits acquired by men and women as members of the society. Clyde Klukohan and W.H. Kelly say that it only confines to a single cluster of people or a group. A culture is a historically developed system of common ways of living which tend to be shared by the members of a groups says Ralph Linton. It encompasses the groups' languages, traditions, customs, manners and institutions including the institutions motivating ideas, beliefs, values and their embodiments and also art and artefacts.

The word civilisation was used in 19th century in its familiar sense referring to the aggregates of characteristics displayed by the members of the society in their lives, advanced ways of life of the people of a historic periods, for instance Greek civilisation at the time of Pericles, Hebrew civilisation, Mohen-jo-daro and Harappa civilisation of India and, Chinese civilisation. The term civilisation as it was used, E.B. Tylor refers to it is to show the total achievements of the most advanced people, to date it, as if the civilisations were uni-liner development of the past with later people at different stages of development. To me "the culture building is an inherent process of enculturating which always done through non-inclinativeness like a creation, a piece of work of art". When this process goes in the material welfare of the society it becomes civilisation. This would be wrong to compare a piece of craft with a piece of art, as a piece of craft is always done with inclinativeness and greed and, as a piece of art is always done with non-inclinativeness. As such, a material urge or desire or aspiration always convert a culture into civilisation. This is done for the welfare of the people. This it is because, as we notice, that all civilisations existed for the material welfare of the people in the past.

Due to this fact, in view of human animal nature, we have to consider socialisation for moral civilisation and have to look to the needs of morality for a civilisation, because a civilisation has always material overtones. Man being a member of a society builds a civilisation, but always has selfish ends in view. He will always look to his selfish ends. He will always keep his interests first then the good for others. In such a situation there should be some moral bindings on the deviating members of the society. Therefore, for a prosperous civilisation a sound culture is very necessary which could also enculturate people. It is the function of the culture to generate ethics and morality in the members of the society through the sound process of socialisation. And the schools, especially the girls schools and, the school teachers can play a prominent role in enculturating the students along with the other agencies of the society.

If we look to the history of ideas, the thinkers have always been contemplating on the tendencies, and suggesting some ways and means which may stop creating disharmony and disintegration in the society and, continuously devising some ideas of conduct for their members of the society. They have been continuously suggesting certain social traits, traditions, social sanity and some ideal manners for good behaviour entailing ethical norms which creates morality and moral laws.

Herodotus, a Greek thinker and philosopher was the first person to suggest ethical values in the society, for the solidarity of the society. Thereafter, many thinkers like Socrates and his disciples—Plato Isocrates, Crito, Permendes and many others discussed and showed the need of ethical laws in the society for the solidarity of the society. Their ideas are reflected in dialogues—like Phaedo, Symposium, Justice, Meno, Law, Beauty and Republic etc., etc. Debates in these dialogues are intimately connected with the views about the nature of the society, state and the ends for which the citizens should strive to attain. The educational theory was discussed in dialogues. Phaedo, Meno and Republic is based on these ideas so as to bring cohesion and cooperation in the society. Plato's views about the division of citizens of the state into classes is designated to emphasise that there are different kinds of services which the citizens perform should be well-organised as: (1) to develop reasoning capacity in the individuals through sound education, so as to make the individual aware about good or lead, (2) to know about the justice and injustice and (3) and to know about truth and beauty. This was to subside the self-interest tendencies in the society and to encourage brotherhood, cooperation and good neighbourhood. This kind of thinking had emerged in Greece due to counter terrorist troubles by Spartans. The lashing of terrorist problem by Spartans in Greece entailed a war between Greeks and Spartans which continued for thirty years about 500 B.C. At present India is also facing the similar problem of terrorism, which can be said a proxy war from a neighbour.

Axiological thinking also proceeded in India simultaneously as proceeded in Greece, as India was also not free from personal greeds, social feuds and conflicts. Our classical epics like Ramayana and Mahabharata and Hindu kingdoms show how kings fought each other ignoring common interests of the people. On the other hand, Rishis, Munis and *Gurus* (teachers) showed the way for common good enunciating good social traits, customs, good sane life norms, laws and ethical codes. In Indian society many ceremonies like *Darasthouthan* (दृष्टो-उत्थान), *Yyagavpavitram* (यज्ञोपवित्रम), *Guru Diksha* (गुरू दिक्षा) and *Grah Pravesh* (गृह-प्रवेश) are performed. These ceremonies are the source of developing moral civilisation. In Indian society very few cases of divorce and suicides are still seen. If such rare cases occur, these occur due to materialistic influence and consequent acculturation. Moreover, in spite of rigid caste structure, the Indian social structure is homogenous as it is based on rural agro-economy, which is based on cooperation, sharing, self-sufficiency, non-competitiveness and respect for the neighbours. Still it is considered best in the world. Karl Marx had praised the Indian social structure saying it as communistic.

In the west many thinkers contributed for the sane social order in the society. Thomas Hobbs (17th century) described the primitive man as solitary poor, nasty and short of ideas—no art, no culture, no letters and no society. Everything has resulted from human perfectability which entailed certain norms and values. According to John Gottfried Von Herder (German Theologist) man is a divine creation. He must have a purpose on earth namely his own perfection in tune with humanity. Voltier (French philosopher) assumed that enlightenment in mankind for upward progress is necessary. Turgot says that the manners are the result of human good behaviour. These bring the nation together, nearer and closer through creating good conditions. He described three stages of human development, savagery, barbarous and civilisation.

There have been movements for the equality in human society. French revolution was one of these. Prostant reformation movement was another in Europe. Here at home in India, many reformers tried to improve the conditions of the repressed. Guru Nanak, Chaitenaya Mahaprabhu, Swami Vivekananda, Swami Dayananda Saraswati, Acharya Vinobha Bhave were among those who tried to socialise people for morality. In 18th and 19th centuries some people tried to generate axiological perspectives in the society. It was an important happening in the human history. Man is the product of nature, and according to Jean Jacques Rousseau (French philosopher and giver of Naturalistic Philosophy), the man is born free, healthy, sane and incorrupt but he is enslaved and made corrupt by human institutions like family, community and society. He said that the "child (future man) is born free but finds himself in chains". His saying is an indication of mans' greed and selfishness and, it needs a change from material trends to axiological trends.

Auguste Comte (1798-1857 A.D., French) who gave the social science called 'Sociology'. The name of sociology and its basic principles strongly influenced the conception of human progress, which are the basic principles and tenets of human social development. The French Revolution had repudiated the monarchy and Christianity, and had installed worship of reason'. According to it, man's historical development has three stages: (1) theological, (2) metaphysical and (3) scientific and with the source of positivism ultimate achievement is secured:

1. *Theological Stage*: All cosmic phenomena are brought to be governed by Divine Will—such as like man, first of all things axiomatic (Fetish) living, and intelligence, secondly the invisible things govern (polytheistic view) and only the Almighty God govern (monotheistic view).
2. *Metaphysical stage*: All events are no longer governed by super natural forces by fundamental abstract idea, essences and energies.
3. *Positivist Stage*: Finally in positivist stage phenomena are exclaimed by cause and effect which are diversified by observation, per-se (perception), hypothesis, experimentation and synthesis.

Out of these three stages of development, man is in the third stage. He should apply his reason and, should act for social harmony. The ethical values are necessary in human life. E.B. Tylor (1832-1937—England) and Lavis H. Morgan (1818-1881) were the exponents of cultural stages, found in the evolution of human kind. Their main concern was cultural development in general and individual culture in particular. Man could survive out of the savagery and barbarism because he could do and adopt some of the same social customs, traditions, good manners and morals.

Charles Darwin invented the term 'survival of the fittest', which was followed by Herbert Spencer (1820-1930—English thinker). He told that an "unknown and unknowable absolute force is continuously operating in the material world producing variety of coherence, integration, secularism and individualism."

Karl Marx (1818-1883 AD, German) saw that the principles of economic organisation represented by a social class which builds idealism leads to slavery. This is done by a partisan class of landlords, nobility believing in capitalism raised by the entrepreneurs and by masters who were exploiters and tortures of their slaves. This leads to class war. The two classes are formed 'bourgeois' and 'proliterates'. This situation can be overcome when there is a consideration about exploitation of proliterates by the bourgeois.

Lester F. Ward (1841-1913, U.S.A.) and Albert W. Small (1854-1926, U.S.A.) considered man as an animal. They opined that, there is a need to change such man as a rational, social man through tele method of social planning. For such a social change sociology has to play a dominant role.

Max Weber (1864-1920, German) saw rationalisation as a tool for the change of man to be amoral man. He asserted that (1) it can be done through charismatic method, (2) leadership be developed by traditional way and (3) legalisation.

Emile Durkheim (1858-1917, French) saw the division of labour as the main cause of disharmony in the society. He advocates for mental dependence puts forward the theories of collective consciousness for social organic solidarity. This can be done when man becomes objectively aware of social values—such as sharing, adherence to ethical values and believing in collectivity. Then only conflicts can be resolved. Mechanical solidarity is followed by organic solidarity. The interests are followed by restraints in the form of laws imposed by the Government. Therefore, collective consciousness is necessary.

Also many other thinkers contributed to moral education. Important of them are Immanuel Kant (France) G.E. Moor (England), Fred Clock (England), Swami Vivekananda, Swami Dayananda Saraswati, Swami Agnivesh, M.K. Gandhi, Aurobindo and Swami J. Krishnamurthy, Guru Nanak, many saints and sufis contributed to moral education. All of them contributed towards socialisation for moralisation for making the society a sane society.

Today, amongst all other things, there is a need for a fresh outlook at the condition of moral values in the society in order to carry on harmonious economic and social development in Indian society. The Indian society has a pluralistic corporate composite culture shared by various linguistic, religious and ethical groups. After 58 years of independence we are still following an alien educational structure which was imposed by foreign British Government for their own ends. Their rigorously applied neutrality was devoid of any suitable educational programme for cultivating spiritual, moral and vocational values through their imposed formal education, which was and still is a state imposed system of education. After independence we followed the policy of neutrality and adopted secularism, but there should have been a long and deep researching for moral values and socialisation along with it. These are very necessary for our system of education. Old Vedic and Brahmanical system of education had this. The various committees and commissions have strongly recommended the inculcation of moral values in the youngers through education. But the examination system always became a stumbling block in achieving this end. Our teachers, both male teachers and female teachers do not find time for inculcating moral values in the youngers and enculturating them, due to preparation of the students for examinations.

As early as in 1815 AD, Lord Moria had observed this social situation and suggested ethical maxims in education. Education Commission 1948-49 headed by late Dr. Radhakrishnan reviewed the situation of religion, education in historical perspective viz., as existed during ancient, medieval, and modern periods of Indian history and considered the constitutional positions and, practices prevailing in other secular countries as America (USA) and Australia. The Commission also considered the thinking of the father of the nation late Shri M.K. Gandhi on this aspect. The Commission observed "what makes a man truly virtuous is the purpose for which he lives and his general outlook on life. If we look to our historical development and, even after this exclusion of spiritual training in our educational institutions, it appears such exclusion would be untrue and illegal in view of our whole history of educational development. Indians believed and to some extent, and still believe if one has done his duties faithfully as a householder (*grahasthi* गृहस्थी) and has been a good citizen, a good father or mother, a good provider for the family and how hospitable he or she will be good citizen. The beauty and mystery of life in the universe lies in knowing the meaning of life and death, the aspirations of the human soul and the feelings, wishful thinking and sound mindedness that are beyond the ordinary knowledge. Only positive knowledge can provide an insight, that is, self-introspection, that there is realm unseen forces which we feel but can never know completely.

If the education of the individual is diversed for the material perfection and not for moral, social and axiological values, it is defective and, is rather harmful for social harmony. How can it be improved? What we actually need is not mere imparting of instructions or teaching? We need transmitting of vitality in humanity. We must civilise the human hearts for harmonious living in the society, which can only be accomplished by socialising man morally and apprising him of unnecessary greed. The lady teacher or male teacher while working in a school, which is an instrument of state for achieving the desired ends through formal education can accomplish it, provided he/she is given opportunity to do this. She or he can do it to be a saver of society from the social evils. Education Commission (1948-49) recommended as stated below in this regard.

SILENT MEDITATION IN MORNING ASSEMBLY AND YOGA CLASSES

A silent worship or meditation can lead to morality. Every morning, in school a short period of silent worship or meditation can be fixed every day in morning assembly or in daily yoga classes. A morning assembly should be a permanent feature in every school and college time table. For a few minutes we may distract the mind from daily life and, attend to the forces which determine the meaning and value of life. The morning assembly should be conducted regularly before the teaching starts. It should be managed by a teacher or a team or teachers who should work under the guidance and supervision of the principal of the school. Students should also be encouraged to deliver short lectures or talks on morality and sociability. This will give them training in self-expression. Like-wise, in *yoga* classes, after the *asana*, there should be a *dhyana* practices, which should include meditation. After this there should be *Hasya Yoga* (laughing practice). In the school or college there should not be any religious practice nor any kind of religious criticism. All religions should be respected and then annual religious functions like Janmastmi, Guru Nanak Day, Diwali, Holi, Basant Panchami, Id-Ul-Fitr and Christmas should be celebrated. All should take part in these functions irrespective of their religious faiths.

STUDY OF GREAT BOOKS

A reverent study of some essentials religious books would be uniquely rewarding as a step towards social harmony and tolerance in different religious sects, long divided due to dogmatic limited views. This is in consonance with the spirit of 'unity in bio-diversity' in the country. I. Tsuang tells that the University of Nalanda was the meeting ground of different sects and creeds with different possible and impossible religious doctrines. University of Taxila had the similar character where many foreign scholars from West, North and East used to come to study. A Greek thinker, most probably Permendes had come to Taxila to escape conscription during the thirty years war between Greeks and Spartans during the rule of Pericles. The Spartan had spread terrorism in Greece which was the cause of war. It is believed that this Greek thinker had stayed at Taxila for eight years. During his stay he had studied all theistic schools—Sankhya Yoga, Naya-Visheska and Vedant and Advit Vedand and all atheistic schools Buddhism, Jainism and Carvac. He had also read all Indian scriptures like—Puranas, Shruties, Upanishads, Brahmans and Epics, Ramayana, Mahabharata and finally he studied Shrimad Bhagwat Gita and had come to know about the immortality of human soul (जीवात्मा). He had gone back to his country with the idea of immortality of soul. He had offered to go to the war front to fight the Spartans. He had also conveyed to Socrates that the human soul is immortal. And Socrates in the due course of time this discussed with his disciples which could produce the dialogue 'Phaedo' in which the proofs have been advanced about the immortality of soul, out of which in one proof 'law of reminiscence' the genesis of education has also emerged. As such, the study of different books are always useful in enriching the epistemacy of human beings. Generally the study of all religious books makes man more tolerant and kind. It is the self-centred religious dogmatic readers who make the society intolerant. Thoughts of the great men and women should be made known to the students in schools. Some common religious tenets should also be known to the students, specially the girls need to be taught not to be greedy and self-centred. They should be reminded of motherly roles. The teachers, especially the lady teachers, should be broad minded regarding social dealings.

The Secondary Education Commission (1952-53) headed by Dr. A. Lakshmana Swami Mudaliar considered that the healthy trends in regard to religion and moral behaviour spring from three sources:

1. The influence of home which is the dominant factor in life-building.
2. The influence of the school, through the conduct and behaviour of the teachers there, and life at the school community as a whole.
3. The influence exercised by the public of the locality and to which the public opinion prevails in all matters pertaining to religious and moral codes of conduct.

The Committee on "Religion and moral instructions" headed by Shri Prakash, set up by the Ministry of Education, Government of India examined: (1) the desirability and flexibility of making provisions for teaching, moral and spiritual values in educational institutions, (2) if it is found desirable and flexible to make such provisions then the educational institutions should:

1. Define broadly the content of instructions in morals at various stage of education.
2. Give a place to moral education in school education programmes.

The Committee revived the whole situation and suggested that religious and moral activities should be left to home, since the parents very often observe and celebrate various religious functions and rituals at home. The Committee felt that moral and spiritual values are essential in life. These should be inculcated in the individuals right from very early age. The family members have to influence the child first. Good manners are very important for moral education. It is not unusual tnat often when people become free after attaining freedom after long years of bondage, suddenly they become self-willed, arrogant, intolerant and inconsiderate and usually inclined to become materialistic and hedonistic. To meet this situation good manners and ethical values are necessary. Graciousness, charm of social behaviour and good social relationship have largely disappeared from the western countries due to materialistic and consequent hedonistic and xenophilic craze of which we Indians are now also prey at large extent. The Committee recommended that:

1. The teaching of moral and spiritual values in educational institutions is desirable, but with certain limitations.
2. Creative and sympathetic study of lives and teachings of great religious teachers should be arranged in schools and in other educational institutions through functions and seminars. For good manners social services and patriotism should be inculcated through talks, displays, radio, T.V., cinema by voluntary organisations.

   In writer's village the trio freedom fighters late Shri Maharshi Harishchandraji, late Pt. Shri Babu Ram Sharma (Munda) and late Shri Thakur Malkhan Singhji used to arrange such talks for the removal of untouchability and gender bias from Village and P.O. Bhalswa Gaj, Distt. Haridwar, Uttaranchal.

There should be a compulsory Rashtragan in the morning assembly in schools. There should be two minutes silence after singing the national anthem (*Rashtragan*). The students should be asked to meditate during the silence (मौन) time. The school principal and the teacher in-charge of the morning assembly should deliver a talk on axiology, may it be brief talks.

3. Suitable books on spirituality and aesthetics should made available in school and college libraries, so that the students may be encouraged to read about morality, sociability and aestheticity. The class teacher should encourage the students to read by giving some related assignments which may entail related book reading.
4. For inter-religious understanding, religious functions selected from all religions should be arranged and celebrated annually in schools and educational institutions. This would create a spirit of understanding of other religions and of tolerance.
5. Some form of physical training should be compulsory for all students in schools and other educational institutions at every stage, so as to bring cohesive bonds among students and physical fitness. Now-a-days physical education is more or less ignored in school and in other educational institutions including teachers training institutions. This is why we fail to do any viable performance in games at the international level. Parents, too, do not permit their wards to play due to examination studies at home.
6. There should be some clubs like sports club, arts and crafts club, social services club and folk arts club for promoting activities which may bring unity, cohesion amongst the students and their enculturation may be done.

Many ills now-a-days are seen due to which the world, systems of education and also the whole national system of education are suffering these days because of lack of social and moral values in the society. These result in wide spread corruption, non-sociability, cheating, frauds, disregard of religion and spirituality, disappearance of the institution of joint family and non-rapportistic attitude towards own family members and neighbours. All these making the society dys-functional. Now-a-days the men are not united and social bonds are disappearing day-by-day. All these social lacking is a matter of great concern. God knows what will happen of our nation in future.

The Emotional Integration Committee headed by Dr. Sampurnanand, appointed by Government of India in 1961, looked education as an agency of strengthening and promoting national integration. It recommended that education should foster mutual appreciation of various religions in the society. Every student who has taken up science for study should have background humanities compulsorily. Adult education should be organised nationwide. Religious education cannot be part of formal education, but without this the education shall remain incomplete.

The Education Commission 1964-66 headed by Prof. D.S. Kothari also looked into this matter. It recommended for inclusion of social, moral and religious values in the educational system as under:

> The weaking of social and moral values in the younger generation is tantamount to creating many social problems. It can create social, ethnical, and economical conflicts as happening in some western countries. The Commission felt that ethical and moral values are necessary for social harmony. The Commission also felt that modernisation does not mean renouncing of social and moral values. These should be promoted for self-discipline and social harmony.

SECULARISM AND RELIGION

In a multi-religious society, like Indian society, it is necessary to define the attitudes of the state towards religious and religious bodies. The adoption of secularist policy, that is, in political, economic and social matters, all citizens irrespective of their religious faiths will enjoy equality of rights that, no religious community will be favoured. Secularism implies that there should not be any kind of religious education in school. But it does not mean that there should not be any place or provision for spiritual moral and social values in the life of a person. The State should make a distinction between religious education and moral education. The former is concerned about the religious traits and the later is concerned about religious values which are essential for good life. They should encourage tolerant attitudes towards the study of all religion. Ignorance and misunderstanding about it should be removed and clearly statement about own religion should be given.

SOCIAL, MORAL AND SPIRITUAL VALUES IN SCHOOL CURRICULUM

A serious defect in school curriculum is absence of provision for social, moral and spiritual values in education. In the life of majority of Indians, religion is a great motivating force and ultimately is bound up with the character formulation which can be done by enculturation and inculcation of ethical values. A national system of education that is, related to life needs to look to the aspiration of the people. It cannot afford to ignore this purposeful objective. The Commission therefore recommended:

1. Moral education should be imparted through methods such as suggestions, discussions as well as teaching orally.
2. Congenial school atmosphere, that is, behaviour and personality of the teachers and the administrators.
3. Every teacher, whatever his/her teaching subjects are, all should be kept in mind, the integrity points, be considered.
4. Sense of social purpose should always be reflected in school programme as well as in curriculum activities.
5. Honesty, integrity and cohesion should be the motto of every teacher.
6. At least one or two periods should be set aside for telling stories.
7. There should be story telling contest in curriculum activities programmes in the schools. A teacher should look after this.
8. And in addition, the Principal of the school should find time to attend the morning assembly.

Committee of Members of Parliament on National Policy on Education constituted in 1967 suggested ways and means for inculcating moral, social and spiritual values in children for inculcating good attitudes for character formation. Some steps should be taken to give due emphasis in school education process. Proper studies of humanities and social sciences including great universal religions, participation in games, sports and hobbies can contribute to the development of right attitudes, development of religious tolerance, cooperation and spirit of sharing in students. Also these contribute to the right values and attitudes towards fellow-beings including sane sociability, sharing and cooperation. The curriculum development, by the National Council of Educational Research and Training, New Delhi, in 1975 and recently in 2004-2005 for school education programme was a good exercise in this regard.

THE WARDHA EDUCATION CONFERENCE ON BASIC EDUCATION, 1937

Following resolution was adopted for Basic Education:

1. Free and compulsory education for all for seven years,
2. Medium of instruction should be mother-tongue,
3. Education should centre around manual work and production work, most probably should be related to control or promote localised handicrafts.
4. The conference felt that the production would meet the salary of the teacher or teachers.
5. The school teaching will not contain teaching of religion. Gandhiji believed and affirmed that all religions are same. The teacher must have faith and respect for all religions. The teacher must have an ideal character to influence the taughts.

In the last it would not be wrong to stress that home is the first place where the first lesson in social, moral and ethical values pertaining to one's life starts and where it attains maturity. The parents should do an ideal presentations to their children, to other children in social, economical and moral values. If the parents are religious, they should inculcate religious values and traits in their children. They should also inculcate a spirit of forbearance, tolerance, sharing, cooperation and kindness in their children. If the parents are addicted to bad habits as drinking and smoking, fast food junk, eating and engaged in some unlawful unsocial activities like corruption, adulteration, they should renounce such bad habits bit by bit and should not expose such nefarious activities before their children. It is also essential that mother and father of the children should not fight or argue before their children.

The idea of Basic Education advanced by the father of Nation late Shri M.K. Gandhi was unique. It was in line of our national culture based on sane axiology, work culture and, was a suitable tool for rooting out alien system of formal education. It was aimed at to develop a skilled workforce in the country and inculcate sanety, morality and moral values in the youngers. But the then rulers were so much influenced by the Western culture that they preferred the alien system of formal education and cremated the Basic Education along with the dead body of the nation Mahatma Gandhi. The Basic Education was quite different from the pragmatist education advanced by John Dewey, just after the World War First. The pragmatist education was just introduced for material gains and not for axiological gains. Though, we Indians renounced the Basic Education, and we have been totally accultured by the foreign formal education, but the African country Kenya and in an east Asian country's province Bali in Indonesia are still following the pattern of Basic Education which aimed at axiology based economy. In Indonesia, in Bali, it was introduced by a retired Police Officer and, in Kenya, by a Negro who was influenced by Mahatma Gandhi's movement in South Africa.

On the whole it is true and logical that socialisation for sane sociability, morality, cooperation sharing and enculturation should be the prime of education and the teacher, especially the lady teachers should educate the girls about these.

24

Role of Administrators in Women Education

The present school education of both girls and boys, under the present system of formal system of education, which is an alien system of education, has rooted out our national culture. The Indian culture which was once considered the topmost cultures of the world, as it was famous for hospitality, sociability respect and regard for the elders and fair sex, economic self-independence through non-formal education and for promoting religiosity and simple living has now been crumbled due to greed and self-interests. We Indians have totally adopted the western culture, and have been completely accultured. We Indians are now totally grabbed by greed and self-interests. The youngers even do not respect their parents. They have become chronically ill of fast and junky foods. On many occasions it becomes difficult to recognise who is a boy and who is a girl? Of course, according to a Greek philosopher it is true that everything is in flux at every movement. But there should be a limit for a social change, it should not be at the cost of the national culture.

The women who are life givers, rationalisers and life builders are now becoming the social dys-functioners. Instead of enculturators, familial educators of the youngers, now they are involved in western life styles builders, believing in western fashion, self-interests. With the result the dys-functioning of joint family system is occurring in the society daily. And our present system of school education is helpless to do anything to protect our culture. Therefore, it is necessary to examine our present system of education which can only be done by the educational administrators.

The educational administrators have great responsibility to meet this social challenge. They, in addition to educational administration, also plan the educational infrastructure. They should work as pioneers in educating the girls who are going to be would be women and mothers. They should play a parental role in this regard. They can contribute in the field of women education, a lot. Rather it would not be wrong to assume that proper women education cannot be possible without monitoring the girls education by educational administrators. They should not act as bureaucrats act in offices and in industrial and economic organisations. They should work as guides and pioneers. Now-a-days all educational administrators lay emphasis only on good examination results. In their view each and every school should try for good examination results. The good examination results phobia has made the educational administrators quite unaware about true concept of education. It is they who pressurise the school principals and teachers to devote wholeheartedly for good shinning annual examination results. For this end the teachers are required to teach the students very sincerely. They lay emphasis on teaching some important topics likely to appear in examination papers. Due to this the teachers generally ignore all other prime educational aspects as inculcating good life attitudes, good work habits, development of good behaviour character and, enculturation. Also for achieving the good examination results of their pupils, the teachers leaving aside their teaching professional ethics keep themselves actually engaged in teaching examination school subjects. They always whole heartedly desire that their students should achieve a remarkable success in their annual examination and should add glaring wings to the crown of the school. As such, the teachers always pray that their students should come in flying colours in their examination. This trend has also made the parents quite ignorant about the familial education. They always have a craze for the good examination results of their wards in their annual examination. Some mothers become mad for the glaring examination results of their children. Such mothers do not inculcate necessary work habits in their children. This kind of education practice aimed at good examination results, under the present system of formal education has badly affected the total Indian socioscape. This has completely rooted out desirable work culture from the Indian society, as the youngers do not get any motivation for doing any hand work due to examination phobia.

This is happening because the social milieu has been totally accultured to western culture. The people have totally forgotten the cultural traits of national culture. And generally the educational administrators add fuel to this non-stoppable fire of acculturation, because they generally pat and praise the schools whose students perform well in their annual examination. The examination system has become a kind of social concern. It has brought the 'Laisseze Faire' thinking in the Indian society, which has engrilled the Indian society in cut-throat competition. In the olden days, there was no examination system at all in India under the old Gurukula system of education. Also, there was no need of examination under the non-formal system of education through which the artisans used to train their youngers. And the students in olden days used to prove their epistemacy and proficiency in their future life. Old Indian seers—Rishi and Munis who had contributed in the field of epistemacy and religiosity were never examined. Neither the artists and artisans who had contributed in the field of art and culture were examined. They were trained in non-formal way. But due to training of artisans in industrial institutes in formal way, the non-formal system of education used in training the wards of artisans has been totally gone. And examination system has totally vanished it. Because of this, skills acquired through non-formal way in family occupations have totally gone. In other words, the present system of formal education based on examination has totally rooted out the main life-building concepts of education. In other words, the examination system is not at all suited to the Indian social structure which is based on caste system.

The school administrators should look into all these pros and cons of Indian educational system and should try to reform it accordingly. The educational administrators should be eager to do this soon. They should look into the real life-building educational aspects. For this end they should give due importance to the life-building processes. Such life-building process are more important for the girls. These life-building processes can be done through co-curricular and extra-curricular activities in school teaching programme. The educational administrators should give equal importance to curricular and to co-curricular and extra-curricular activities in girls as well as in boys schools, through which the right life attitudes could be inculcated in the students. The administrators should advise the school curriculum planners to give a due place to the co-curricular and extra-curricular activities in school educational programme. The principal, vice-principal, all teachers and non-teaching staff who are interested in co-curricular activities should be involved in these activities. The academic activities and co-curricular activities should be equally treated and should be given equal weightage while assessing the students. The administrator should also find time, if not in all programmes, at least in some co-curricular activities in some schools to attend such activities.

The school administrators should also see that the school teachers are sincerely following the teaching professional ethics. Whether they are sincere in enculturating the students. Whether they are inculcating good life attitudes and developing appropriate work habits. The educational administrators should also try to find out whether the educating of the students is done to achieve the desired educational aims. As such, the educational programme should be planned and worked out accordingly. For girls education special steps need to be taken to prepare the girls for their future life roles. And for this purpose there should be a special provision for women teacher education in teacher training institutes. The school curriculum should have a place for life-building activities.

25

Art, Craft and Cultural Activities

ETYMOLOGY OF ART

The word 'art' is a derivation from the Latin words 'ars' and 'artis'. The word art has also roots in Greek word 'ars'. All these words mean 'to join', 'to compose', 'to fit', 'to create', 'to fabricate' or 'the employment of different things to answer or to meet some special purpose, or 'the employment of some means to accomplish some end'. Art is a system for an arrangement to facilitate a fabrication for aesthetic performance and developing things of beauty for use. All arts, that is, building, architecture, engineering, structuring or fabricating, dance, drama, folk arts, fashion designing and cooking etc., entail creativity. And beautiful usable things done in aesthetic tone are called fine arts.

GENESIS OF ART

The genesis of art is, wide, Artistic beauty is found in all divine creators and in all activities of living beings, that is, animals, birds, beasts, insects, bees and human beings therefore, it is necessary to look into the following views for analysing the genesis of art.

Historical View

Artistic activities are as old as human society, as these go hand in glove with human life. It is very difficult to trace the detailed history of artistic activities, especially the human artistic activities in the universe. These might have emerged with the emergence of human society. Necessity is the mother of invention. When the Almighty God created the universe, he adorned it with multiple beautiful natural phenomenon like high attitude mountains, hilly tracks, snow clad, glaciers, rivers, forests having different types of trees, beautiful landscapes, charming seascapes, flora and fauna and agricultural lands. He also created all living beings, such as, birds, animals, beast, insects bees and human beings, that is, men and women with a bio-diversity, unity of which enables them to produce their future guardians. Human beings, being rational beings could acquire and might have acquired many more things than other living beings, as food and shelter for their existence. As such, the man from the beginning started doing many things, which might have entailed doing some artistic activities from the very beginning. And, as day-by-day the necessities of human beings might have increased, this process which might have entailed a chain of creative activities, which was nothing but art. This kind of trend can be termed as genesis of art in human society, which also brought change in the society and social, economic and cultural development could be possible.

With the passage of time due to special change some sort of social stability took place in the society. The dominant powerful persons became the rules. The rules promoted art and crafts. They got built forts, palaces (*mahals*), temples, mosques, churches, gurudwaras and ashramas etc. For their, as well as, national security, they also required some armaments vehicles, as 'rathas' (रथ) which they got made. Man being a rational being, has ever been regularly visualising natural flora and fauna from the very beginning. He has been thinking abut it regularly and rationalising it for his personal use and has been acting accordingly. In the beginning the man was living in bushes in forests like animals and beasts. After nationalisation, he moved under the shadow of trees. Bit by bit, he visualized the natural things. He thought and analysed his personal problems and also tried to solve his problems. He first of all made hut out of forest grass for his shelter. He further collected some material and improved his shelter huts. And finally he made 'kachcha' house for his living. Likewise, he collected some seeds of cereals. He developed agriculture and made agricultural implements. As such, the man has been thinking and creating new things from the beginning for the use of human beings. And after continued creative struggle the man emerged out of Palaeolithic age to the modern age. In the beginning the man depended on trees and plants for his subsistence and survival.

Slowly-slowly he moved upward. He progressed in every field. He produced a large quantity of cereals for meeting food requirements of the human beings. In the beginning he depended on tree barks and grass for protecting his body from heat and cold. In due course of time he discovered cotton seeds and produced cotton also. He developed the cloth making and developed related infrastructure also. What was all this? This was 'art' based on human activities. From the very beginning the man was very conscious of comfort and for that he always thought, rationalised about the possibility of use of various natural materials. So he always tried to create new things for his comfort, for that purpose he developed multiple arts. His life partner, the woman was not behind him and she continuously did artistic activities and developed arts.

Human Biological View

Out of all living beings, the human beings, that is, men and women are considered rational beings. It is because the nature has endowed them with special biological facilities. It has gifted human beings with bigger brains, with extraordinary capacity to visualise, think, reason, rationalise, comprehend and act accordingly. The nature has given moving hands to human beings to work with, erect posture and steady legs to walk and run. So the men and women have always been thinking, reasoning and acting in innovative creative way. This promoted creative activities which are called art. In spite of human rationality, the nature has made the man very greedy, self-centred, acquisitive and very conscious of self-comfort. And due to all this, it would not be wrong to assume that sometimes, the men and women becomes worse than animals. They become mad for their personal interests. They do not hesitate even harming their sibling and kith and kins. This is due to material hunger in them. They satisfy this hunger by creating new things, and doing art activities. This promotes creativity in the society which promotes new arts. Also the bio-diversical human unity, that is, unity of man and woman through the institution of marriage enables the man and woman to produce their offsprings. All this natural endowment to mankind creates an atmosphere for creating new things for use. This process helps in thc genesis of arts.

Sociological View

A society is a heterogenic whole of individuals having personal individual differences, though being of one race and caste, following one or varied religions, they lack intense unity. Due to this, generally a social structure faces certain challenges like fractured ethnical unity and national unity, because the individuals always try to follow their own paths in their lives. The social whole is composed of different individuals. It is not like a biological whole which is controlled by human soul. All parts in a human body function in harmony with all body parts. The social functions should go in harmony with all body parts. The social situations are quite different to biological whole which is very individualistic dangerous and challenging. It may lead to social dys-functioning or breaking. Many societies are divided due to this reason. Division of India at the time of independence is one such example. As such, to keep a society united is a challenging job. Of course, the human beings are generally self-centred, but few of them are also very rational too. They always think of common good. They take the interest of all human beings into consideration. As such, sane and rational people always try to devise appropriate rules for social living. They develop certain social institutions like community houses, Panchayats, Ashrama, Gurukulas, religious Akharas and institutions for the common good. They also develop educational institutions and social institutions like marriage etc., etc. They formulate rules and regulations for such institutions and chalkout certain cultural programmes. They also develop some social traits, customs, traditions and religious functions which always entails sane artistic creative activities, like music, decoration—like alpana, rangoli and creative activities which finally enculturate people and develop national culture. Artistic creativity activities give life to social composition. These help in their sane personality development. The artistic activities help people in discarding greed selfishness and self-centredness. These help in the development of sanety in people. The artistic activities help people in binding the society together. The artistic activities help the society in keeping the social traits, customs, traditions, educational institutions and culture in tact, which keep the society ever alive.

Economical Aspects

Economical aspects are as old human society, because without sound economy human beings cannot survive. So, from the very beginning the man has been very innovative towards his earnings, and has been developing continuously new techniques and methods to make his economy sound. As such, economic aspects in every field, be it home economy or industrial economy a national economy, also generate conditions for the development of art. Economic means matters related to economy, be it related to home economy or industrial economy or national economy. The economy is a derivation from Latin word 'Economia', and Greek word 'Oikonomia', meaning management regulation and, arrangement which expands economy through judicious application of time, skills, labour, instruments and disposition of works in aesthetical manner through application of good forms and colours. This condition is always applicable to home activities and to industrial infrastructure and also where human beings reside. They always want to keep their residence good looking, that is, beautiful. Likewise, they always want to keep themselves looking good. As such, the parents always inculcate an aesthetic sense in their children which always motivate them to do creative and artistic activities. In industries creative firmament is necessary. If things produced are not beautiful these cannot be sold. So in industry aesthetic temper is essential, if this is applied the goods produced are not sold and money is not earned. So the economic aspects, be it in home or in industry always promote art and becomes the genesis of art.

Cultural Aspects

Culture is a multiple whole—a configuration of many artistic activities and human behaviour, traditions, customs, traits and social life. The term 'culture' is a derivation from the Latin word 'cultura' which was developed out of Latin word 'calo' meaning a 'column' or a constructed stand or pillar to bear the weight in straight or in tilled form as we see in modern constructed buildings. Culture also means a tillage or cultivation, a training including a discipline by which man's moral or intellectual nature is elevated or moulded. The result of such training is enlightenment which may build a rich civilisation.

The civilisation is an act of civilising the citizens from the rude behaviour and sewage life to an ideal life. In the whole world the man is considered a rational being. Even though the man has an acquisitive nature and, he needs to be civilised. A civilised person is one who cares for his/her fellow beings also. In order to civilise a person, it is necessary to inculcate a civic sense in him or her. It can be done by improvement in human activities, traditions, social traits, customs, education, art activities, such as visual arts, dance, folk arts, music, drama and social activities. Therefore, it is necessary to have a systematic programme of enculturation in the society for making the nation strong and united. A nation which looses its culture looses everything and even independence. In the past the colonisers always tried to keep their subjects under their control forever. For this end, they always try to acculturate the people over whom they established their control. In India, Lord Macaulay keeping this fact in view that had imposed the western type of formal education in 1833 A.D. on Indian people.

Culture cannot be taught as a school subject, as other subjects are taught. It can be developed by continuous art activities. This can be done by the whole society and artists can play a positive role in culture building. Also, the artisans class can play a very positive role in culture building. Priestly class adhere religion. Some folk artists, singers, dancers depend on their art activities and earn their livelihood. Some sections of the society can only upgrade their activities with the help of aesthetic temper and artistic activities. As almost all societies depict heterogeneity in their demographic scape even though they exhibit equimanity in art activities.

World's old civilisation like Indian Mohen-jo-daro and Harappa civilisation, Chinese, Greek, Mesopotamian, Egyptian, Roman and Hebrew Civilisations were outcomes of cultures respective countries. And artistic activities generally contributed in the development of cultures of these countries. Culture is a complex whole which includes knowledge, beliefs, art and crafts, moral laws, customs, traditions, social traits, habits, behaviour patterns and other capabilities acquired by the members of the society. Clyde K. Cohan and W.H. Kelly say that culture does not remain limited to a single group. Ralph Lynton (Linton) said that culture is a historically derived system of art and designs for living which is trended to be shared by all members of the society. It encourages groups' common language, artistic activities, traditions, customs, social traits, ideas, beliefs, values and their embodiments as art artefacts. As such, culture of any society is the genesis of art, artifacts and crafts of the society.

Psychological Aspects

Human beings, sometimes, due to undesirable social conditions, behaviours, such as, tortures, frauds and usurping by the near ones, face undesirable psychological phobias. Such conditions disturb human emotions, which generally remain suppressed. As the affected persons do not get opportunity for the catharsis of repressed emotions. The repressed emotions, because lack of catharsis, go so deep that in due course of time such repressed emotions become dangerous for the health of the affected person. Sigmund Freud a noted physician and psychologist said that if these emotions are not taken out early, the affected person will fall seriously ill. He suggested that the best way for the catharsis of such repressed emotions is that the affected person be involved in creative artistic activities. The artistic activities not only take out the repressed emotions, but these can make such person a happy same person. As such, human emotions play a vital role in the development of art and crafts. If a person is involved in artistic activities from the very beginning, he will never be disturbed by repressed emotions. His emotions will never be repressed. He will always remain happy and healthy throughout her/his life. Keeping in view this psycho-medical aspect of mind Sigmund Freud had suggested inclusion of Art in school curriculum from the very beginning. Art education should not be given a step-motherly treatment, he argued. But now in our educational programme, due to industrialisation it has not got its due place. During contemporary materialistic competitive age in all countries stress is laid on teaching science subjects like physics, chemistry, mathematics and biology and, in humanities subjects like English, Hindi, Political Science, Economics and Commerce are taught. Due to the importance of these subjects, art and art related activities like decoration—alpana, rangoli and cultural programmes hardly get any place in school curriculum. Whereas these are very necessary for the girls education for inculcating in them their future life roles. There are very few schools which offer subjects like sociology, philosophy, axiology and folk arts. Teaching of art in both girls, as well as, in boys schools is more or less ignored in almost all schools. The writer once approached a Principal of a Central School and requested him to provide the art syllabus for teaching art in his school. He replied that neither art is a teaching subject nor it is an extra-curricular subject in his school. This revelation was really a shocking one.

Folk Art Aspects

Folk arts are such arts which are performed by common people. Such arts are performed on special occasions such as, marriages, festivals, religious festivities, on the occasion like birth of a child etc., etc. Many of these folk arts are very attractive and inspiring which generally promote aestheticity in the minds of the people and generate a desire or inspire them to learn art. For example, on the occasion of Durga Puja, the Bengali artisans prepare very beautiful images of Ma Durga. These images are prepared with great enthusiasm throughout the country. Likewise, big images of Ravana and his brothers are prepared on the occasion of Dushera for burning throughout the country. People from all walks of life come to see these burning and, are inspired to do art. Huge Rathas are also made for the journey of Bhagwan Jagannath, his brother and sister in Orissa in Puri and in other parts of the country. These are made by the Vishwakarma artisan of India. These artistic creations inspire people to learn art. Similarly dances are performed by folk artists on special occasions such as marriages, birth of the child, entry into newly built house. Mostly in all religions folk arts are performed which are generally enjoyed by all. Such arts generate a good spirit of creativity in the people and becomes a genesis of arts.

Art Heritage View

Art heritage is a staged acquisition of knowledge, art and skills from the ancestors. Therefore, art heritage is a process of getting and learning doing art products and artistic things from the elders. We in India have an immense treasure of art of which we are proud. Therefore, Art Heritage is the genesis of learning and pursuing art.

The word 'heritage' is derivation of Latin word 'Hereditas' meaning which is 'inheridated". Actually Indian social stratification is entirely based on inheritage covering under the caste system. All castes pursue different activities which the youngsters inherit and learn from their elders. These are called hereditary occupations. Under this system every caste member get a heritage which they follow throughout their lives following their family occupations. The system of inheriting artistic and other skills, such as technical trades from elders was unique in the world. The youngers used to learn their family occupations and related skills by continuously associating with their elders. They used to observe a vast spectrum of raw-materials, tools and demonstration and finally attain proficiency in their family trade and occupation. This was the most liked system of non-formal learning. In India it was considered unique when Lord Macaulay imposed the formal system of Western type of bookish teaching, the then British Governor of Punjab (now in Pakistan) had opposed the imposition of formal education on Indians. He had argued that India was world's only country where heritage system of education for learning arts and crafts was followed on non-formal way with good results. In India all types of occupations from artistic, technical and to service occupations are followed on caste basis. Under this system, the youngers used to learn the artistic skills, technical skills and service skills from their elders hereditically and used to attain proficiency. As such, art heritage has been the genesis of art from the very beginning.

In olden days, all kinds of arts like sculpture, wood carving, stone carving, architecture, murals, images, making of temples, construction of forts and dharamshalas, house buildings, all kind of vehicles like Rathas were done by hereditary artisans and professionals. Still we see many artisans doing such artistic jobs. Stone workers from Rajasthan, temple builders from Gujarat, who are called 'Sompuras', musical makers from Madhya Pradesh who are called 'Suttars' and *Dhiman* (धीमान) and *Jangeds* (जांगेड) from Northern India who are *Rathkar* (रथकार). They all follow artistic activities and are the descendents of Lord Vishwakarma. The Vishwakarma artisan community is an unique artisan community of India. Our vast monuments like important temples like Lord Jagannath temple, Puri (Orissa), Sun temple, Konark, Orissa, four dham temples in Uttaranchal, Madurai temple and Rameshwaram temple in Tamil Nadu, temples in Haridwar, Prayag, Varanasi, Mathura, Swarna temple in Amritsar, Somnath temple and Akshardham temples in Gujarat, Delhi and temples of Rajasthan are unique. These temples inspire people to be theistic and creative. Also there are many monuments which reveal social feelings of the people. These are like Khajuraho, Fatehpuri Sikri Fort, Agra Fort, Red Fort, Delhi, Old Fort, Delhi, Qutab Minar, Delhi. As such, art heritage lead to learning of art. People see the monuments of act heritage and get inspired to do some creative work. The art heritage also reveal the history of the country which becomes the genesis of Art.

THEORIES OF ART

Philosophical View and Materialistic Views

Art is an activity which is based on creativity, which has been done or created for the first time. It is way of emotional release through creation of new verbal images, new things or new exposures of rhythm and new expression in new forms. This is done by engaging one's self-mentally, physically, emotionally and wholly done without any inclination with endless creativeness. It is an ideal programme of action which appeals to the senses and imagination. Art generates joy, initiates a good taste and aesthetic sense, and finally results in thrill or an unique feeling of good achievement. Art moulds ones personality. It enriches social and physical environment. It helps in building culture and development of civilisation. Seeing the natural phenomenon sharpens one's sensibility comprehension of natural things and promotes aestheticity out of these. All these lead to imaginative skills and finally lead to the release of human stored emotions. The earliest creative experiences of man in art are very old. Traces of art are found around in human dwellings and natural environment and its flora and fauna. The essential features of human culture and civilisation were visible earlier than speech basic ways of expression which entailed recent ideas feelings of joy, sorrow, living and social traits. Man did art in the past and still do so in crude form in paintings, in dance, in drawing, in sculpture, in music and other daily routine activities like cooking, oral singing. As such, instincts of art have been in human beings as heritage from the beginning. And women are not behind in doing art activities. Art helped in creation of culture, invention, civilisation. Humans progress and development of societies are tied with the development of art. And all old civilisation, Greek, Hebrew, Roman, Indian, Chinese, Egyptian and Mesopotamian flourished due to art. Also all technological development witnessed the contribution of art. But in the present modern hedonistic age art has no place in the present system of education. Also art is extensively used in economic sector but it does not get its due recognition. K.G. Sayaidin Committee on 'Art Education' reported that "Art is so vast that it covers every aspect of life. And due to this vastness many believe that art cannot be defined. Even though many have tried to define art on the premises of emotions. Man is a rational being. He has capacity to visualise the empirical world. He can think, reason, introspect and contemplate and also conceptualise for the younger generation. As such, man tried to analyse various art forms and put forward definitions of art also. All over the world the men created many wonderful things which are accessible to human beings. And others who enjoyed and appreciated these creations of art have tried to define art in different ways. One thing which appears to have been agreed upon is that art is expression of emotions.

Origin of emotions starts with human life circle. Emotions are built up with life events. When man gets touchy with some good or bad happenings or occasion or events either he/she feels delighted or anguished to the concerned agency or person. If the happenings come as a reward to him/her the result would be happiness. If the happening is torturing or harming the individual would be annoyed. He or she will feel discomfortable. Suppose if a person is rewarded by his boss, the person will be grateful and touchy to the boss. His or her relations will also be happy and delightful. Such person will try to do good for others. On the contrary, if the boss's action comes in the form of punishment, the affected person will get the retributory emotions. And in such a situation disastrous actions will follow. The reward and punishment are common features in man's life at the hands of society members as well as by the nature, and these entail respective emotions. The process of emotion building continues throughout one's life. These emotions generate respective psyche in the individuals. The touchiness hatred, social ignorance, family ignorance, kithnic hatred, self-centredness, greed and likewise, love benevolence, gratefulness, kindness, respect from the youngers so on and so forth bring respective emotions. These deep emotions may come out in the form of any kind of expression. These expressions generally happen or occur through sensual perception of natural phenomena and consequently its presentation in the form of creative form, that is, art. This creative work may be in the form of painting, liner drawing, sculpture, dance, music, dramatics, polemics, cooking, writing, poetry, laughing or any other creative work such as novel writing. This becomes the source of emotional release of the person doing the creative work, be it a painting or a sculpture or any other novel work which is being done by the emotive person. When a person is rewarded by the Almighty God, suppose if one gets a child and, that too a male child he or she will be pleased and the person will be grateful to Almighty God. On the other hand, if a person is repressed or cheated or exploited, agony, hatred and dissatisfaction will be the content of his creations. Distortion and disharmony will be the content of his/her creation. Distortion and disharmony will be reflected in his/her work of art—may it be a literary work or art work. As such, all symbolic representation in the form of sublimity, aestheticity as found in good landscapes, seascapes, in good sculptures depicting a sense of divinity and social harmony is the result of good emotions caused due to divine grace and kindness. On the contrary, crude, cut and distorted human forms as we found in the paintings of some western artists like Picasso's torso in sculptures show disharmony in the social set up in a particular society. Likewise, *Bhayanak* (भयानक) or dreadful *Rasa* (रसा) forms in *Nataka* (drama) reflect emotions caused by repressive feelings due to stress and strain caused due to undesirable social interactions. As such, the art expressions always reflect social functions. Art is always is the mirror of the society. On the one hand, it helps in building the composite national culture of any society on the other side. Human habits like sharing, cooperation, adjustment, character building and finally the personality development is the contribution of art. It also alarms the society about repressive elements through tortured or distorted form of art. Art practices help, finally, in developing self-confidence. So the art plays a very important role in the balanced development of an individual personality and consequently in the development of sane society.

Many thinkers have strongly stressed on the importance of art. They said that art is the distinct human activity. Though, many birds, insects and bees display artistic temper in their activities. Some birds build beautiful nests. Bees build very beautiful honey bed. Also some insects build their resting wholes beautifully. Langer said that art is an unconsciously adopted creation. According to her art is an expression and communication of human emotional feelings. R.L. Read's observation is the same about three dimensional art. He said that art is an embodiment created for sense perception based on entire imagination. According to him, art is like an organic whole and is the result of emotional feelings R.L. Read's observation is about three dimensional creations as sculptures and images which are generally made by joining physical material together. For many thinkers art is a distinct activity which is different from a practical activity such as craft, science and technical trades which are done for earning-money. Art is also different from philosophy which very often advances transcendental ideas. An object of art is a significant collectivity not only a sensuous phenomenon but aesthetics also. Every work of art has significant, as Picasso's 'Gurnica' and 'Semoisis' symbols. Greek thinkers codified art as a body of knowledge and skills. They described medicine as an art and, prescribed a professional ethics which entailed 'Hippocratic' oath. In many other skills done observing professional ethics. These can be said or considered as art. Denis said poetry is an art as it is aimed at to achieve certain aims confirming to set rules. Straminsky said that art is the true way of fashioning things according to certain rules acquired by inventiveness and perpetuated by apprenticeship. The art cannot be possible without sincere practice.

Thinkers also have different opinions about the nature of art. Some say that art has its interval arrangements which are based on human emotions. While some say art is an embodiment. Herbert and Mrs. S.K. Langer say that art is an expression of human emotional feelings. Artists' Craftsman's feelings and skills issue a kind of natural beauty appears on the convess. These cultivate harmony, a kind of natural beauty on the convess. These cultivate harmony and grace which entail happiness, joy and sometimes sorrow also. Herbert Read says that (1) first the man respond to shapes, get ideas and then, (2) he creates deliberate arrangements of surfaces, sounds and mass and then he creates strangeness which is, called art, (3) this deliberate arrangement corresponds to his/her previously existing emotions. All this happiness due to his/her perception, imagination and ideas. Also Mrs. Langer agreed to this theory, only she emphasised that it is expression. R.L. Read protested and disagreed with these views of Herbert Read and Mrs. Langer Read said that art is only embodiment. This may be because of his emphasis may be on sculpture which always done in three dimensional form, whereas other surface arts are done in two dimensional forms. Some philosophers like Aristotle, Mathew, Arnold took art as an constructive device. But Mrs. S.K. Langer disagreed with this view. She criticised and said that a constructive device can never be an art. Every constructive device always entails a specific advance planning, whereas an art activity does not require specific advance planning, as a building construction requires. An art activity is a spontaneous emergence of emotional feelings which always inspire to carry out an art activity and gives it a form which is also not already set. In art activity entire imagination is involved. Art is both intellectual and emotional activity, and also an imaginative ordering to do some creative work on sense perception.

Ultimately it can be said that a principle of construction can never be defined as an 'art'. Of course, art always entails craftsmanship but with a specific end. Art is a process of creating new expressive forms, which are created for visibility, audibility and aestheticity, which are imaginatively perceivable and have set forth the nature of human emotional feelings for human perception. Werner Heinsberg said that art is always an idealisation of visual elements. As such, art and craft are two different processes of doing creative activities. Art is that activity: (1) which has been done for the first time, (2) which is new and creative and (3) which is an artistic activity which has not been done for material ends, that is, without inclination. For example, if a person, man or woman creates a new design of sweater for the first time for his/her personal satisfaction, that will be called an art piece.

Craft

A craft is a heterogenic artists activity based on another's creation. "A craft is methodologically consciously chosen means adopted for a fixed pre-conceived end". It requires: (*a*) tools, (*b*) raw materials, (*c*) end for usefulness, (*d*) it may require pre-planning, (*e*) execution and (*f*) pre-conceived form. A craft knowledge need not to be learned formally. A craft can be learned hereditically on non-formal basis, as artisans learn their family occupation (trade) hereditically from their elders. But, still craft is a creative device as Aristotle asserts in 'Poetics'. He says that Greek drama requires action, diction and place. Craft is always done after an artistic creativity, when one thing created is used for productivity for material ends. So craft cannot be categorised as art, as it always involve principles of construction which cannot be considered art. Art is more than craft, even it is more than drawing and painting. It always entails arrangement, selection, design all prevailing truth, and appreciation of truth and beauty.

As such, art is much more than craft. As education is elicitation of knowledge through experience, art is recognition of aesthetic sense, design, decoration, decorative forms, not for inclinativeness and for material gains. Art is always for self-realisation. As such, thinkers have tried to define art in different ways. Important of these definitions are given as below:

Ontological Theory of Art

Indians, from the very beginning, have been theistic believing in Almighty God and in some gods and goddesses. As such, many of them, even being monotheistic, still believe in many gods and goddesses and worship them. They used to get the idols of these gods and goddesses made by the Vishwakarma artisans and used to install these idols in temples and even in their homes and worship them. They believe in invisible deities for gaining some benefits on ontological grounds. They believe that there is a super power who has created the universe, all living being and all flora and fauna. They have been grateful to this super-power and used to dedicate all arts to them. As such, theory of art which was advanced by late Shri Guru Rabindranath Tagore can be said ontological theory of art. All Indians (Hindus) believe in *Paramatma* (परमात्मा) and *Jivatma* (जीवात्मा). And on this principle late Guru Rabindranath Tagore advanced 'ontological theory of Indian Art'. He explained the Indian art as under:

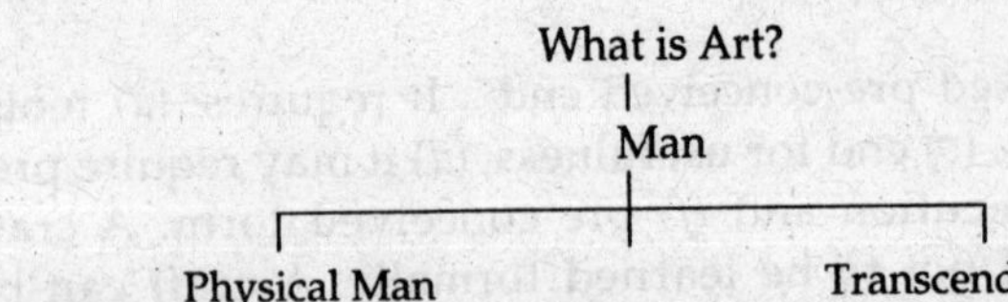

Physical Man	Transcendental Man
• Lives in this word. He is unreal.	• Non-essential, omnipresent real.
• Instinctive, Inclinative. Hedonistic Perceptive, keen in wordly affairs, such as family, reproduction, food acquisitive, hedonistic, xenophilic, perceptive of pleasure and pain, consumeristic, meglomaniace, greedy, self-centred, animal nature. In spite of being rational greedy self-centred, encroacher in others interests, damager of other's interests constant generator of conflicts and materialistic.	• Non-instinctive Non-hedonistic • Non-xenophilic • Non-consumeristic • Gatherer of good emotions • Non-pleasure • Non-materialistic • Ontological and present in all beings and things.

Late Guru Shri Rabindranath Tagore believed that man in spite of being rational always try to look his/her own interests and hurt the interests and, thereby the emotions of his fellow beings. These hurted emotions are always accumulated and repressed in human body and ultimately these emotions are changed into gestrojuices. If these repressed emotions are not out of the body of the individual either by catharsis or through some creative activities, these may become dangerous for the health of the affected person. This idea, it seems, Guru Shri R.N. Tagore has picked up from Sigmund Freud theory of 'repressed emotion'. He further said that when a person is gratified with actions and consequent reward, love, affection mercy his emotions are loaded with gratification. For an example, if a couple is rewarded, by Almighty God, by a male child, they are very gratified and thankful to gods and goddesses. And ultimately such emotions turn into the exposition of greatness of the Almighty God or gods and goddesses. And the man/woman expresses his/her emotion in making or getting made sculptures, images, idols and temples as a reverence to Almighty God. Such art is called 'ontological art'. Late Guru Rabindranath Tagore believed that since the Indian society is homogeneous because of the duality of soul, peoples emotions are less hurted by their fellow beings. If some emotions are affected he/she prays Almighty God, gods and goddesses for redressal of the affected emotions. After getting relief he or she is thankful to Almighty God and this reverence, sometimes, is given through art activities. All Indian temples, sculptures, images and murals installed in temples are proof of the ontological art of India. Besides this on the outside walls of their temples, relief sculptures, sculptures and some other images depict some social scenes of the society, as departure of the bride for *Sasural* (ससुराल) after her marriage show a gratitude to the Almighty God. Also the Indian Art shows the manifestations of gods and goddesses, the attainment of truth, the unity of finite with the infinite harmony with the nature, harmony of Indian society. Indian art delights in eating, living, meditation, cordial family life, easing tension and building good passions. It also shows the greatness of the nature. Indian art also depicts unity in diversity and tolerance. Therefore, it is reflected Indian idols in temples and sculptures reflecting Indian social scenes of Indian life. Indian art has been basically done in stone sculptures, stone relief images and wood carvings. All this was done by the Vishwakarma Artisans of India.

When India came into contact with Muslims and English people the basic main character of Indian art changed. During this period Indian art came into the source of persons. Earlier, it was done for the service of Almighty God. When the art was done for the service of kings and queens their whims intervened in the development of art. Many schools of art came into being such as Pahari, Kangra, Rajput, Bhojpuri and Moghul art school etc., etc., each art school or pattern of art adopted its own style and some foreign motifs as Persian motifs and western styles intermingled in Indian art styles. During the British rule the Indian art was used to the service of the industry. Art schools at Calcutta, Madras, Bombay, Lahore (now in Pakistan) were opened for this purpose and, the Indians were trained as draftsman, orthographic drawing makers, artisans and as creative inventors. Xenophobia in art styles and technique swept in which was largely adopted and is still prevalent. Late guru Shri R.N. Tagore had rightly visualised the place of art in life is not for commercialisation but for the ontological life realities.

Psychological Theory of Art

The psychological theory of art has its inception with Sigmund Freud, who was a medical men. After completing his M.D. (doctor of Medicine) from Vienna University he started working with a Doctor, as an associate doctor. The doctor was handling the cases of hysteria at that time. As the young men and women were suffering from hysteria in large numbers. The main reason of hysteria was sex problems. The doctor with whom Sigmund Freud was working used to rely on medicines. Sigmund Freud thought to go into depth. He suggested this to his senior doctor who disagreed. Thereafter, Sigmund Freud disassociated with him and opened his own clinic for hysteric patients. He started questioning and counselling the patients in camera. Sometimes a patient was to be interrogated for hours. This interrogation used to be done secretly. And finally Sigmund Freud succeeded in finding the reason or hysteria. He wrote two books on such interrogations: (1) Dora and (2) Wolf (fake names). During the interrogation he found that there occurred such happenings in the lives of young boys and girls when their sex desires are not fulfilled and they become emotionally disturbed. The emotional disturbance is the main cause of hysteria.

Sigmund Freud developed 'Psychoanalytic' theory of personality. He observed that there are three stages of consciousness: (*a*) conscious level, (*b*) semi-conscious level and (*c*) sub-conscious level. Conscious level is like an iceberg in a water pot. Semi-conscious level an sub-conscious levels always remained drowned in water at low level. These three stages of consciousness occur due to human depressed emotions. Young man and woman who get attached to each other, but due to some reasons remain separated are consciously affected badly. But due to some social reasons they cannot tell it to anybody and catharsis becomes impossible. In such a situation their emotions get repressed. And day-by-day these repressed emotions submerge in their bodies and they loose consciousness. As such, repressed emotions at sub-conscious level need let out. This led out an be done either in constructive forms or in destructive forms. The western society is anamic. It is feudalistic society. There is a great disparity amongst people in the western society. Some are very rich, some are very poor. This is another reason of hysteric cases in Europe among ladies and gents. Sigmund Freud studied all such cases and recommended art activity as a compulsory activity in schools, because it is art, which can let out repressed emotions in the form of beauty and can avoid destructive happenings. As a matter of fact the psychological theory of art is emotional theory of art. When human emotions are repressed their let out through creative artistic activities becomes necessary for the health of the affected person. Repression of emotions is psychologically dangerous for the human life. And let out of repressed emotion can only be possible through art activities, therefore this is called psychological theory of art.

The Expository Theory of Art

The expository theory of art is based on indirect exposition of social heterogeneity through art forms. When a society is gripped in social stigmas of inequality, the artist wants to say something about social stigmas, he tries to express his emotions in twisted art forms indirectly. It is because, it becomes difficult for him to express his vies about heterogeneous social structure in which he is living. This happens so due to fear of reciprocal actions from these whose who are in power. In such a situation the artist expresses his views through unique distorted new art forms which may catch the attention of general public. This is the current view about the western modern art. This may be called expressive view of art also. In comparison to Indian homogenic society, in spite of Indian caste system, the Western society is considered heterogeneous society where feudalistic system is dominant. The feudals are so powerful they have everything in their command. They are called Barons. They have sufficient landed property, industrial infrastructure and good share in governance in their countries. They made their countries their colonies. And in their occupied colonies they establish hetarchy or document government. The western activists like Picasso etc., expressed their view in twisted art forms which they called, modern art. Under this new unique art theory the western artists exhort that:

1. Art is an unique activity which has been done for the first time.
2. Art is always a creativity and not an imitation.
3. An artistic activity is always done on the principles of art is always for the art's sake.

4. An artistic activity should always be done for personal satisfaction.
5. An artistic activity should never be done for personal inclinative purpose or ends.
6. If any artistic activity is done on already created or existed art forms it would not be art but would be craft.
7. Any art be it painting, sculpture, poetry drama should not be done for any secret purpose.
8. Everybody has got artistic ability and capacity to create and express his/her emotions. Emotions are always imbibed in creativity.
9. Expository theory of art is based cathartic spirit or desire which is based on let out of repressed emotions. These repressed emotions are the result of inequality, disparity, exploitation and alienation due to heterogenic structure of the society.
10. Due to this theory of 'art for the sake of art' many art forms and styles such as romanticism, realism, cubism, collage, modern art, and abstract art have emerged.

Some of the thinkers have opined about art as mental below:

1. *Plato*: According to Plato, "art is an activity or a careful creation which requires a careful theory and practice while doing it (Ref. 10th Book of Republic). According to Plato art can only be possible through practice which requires imitation".
2. *Aristotle*: According to Aristotle art is one of the science as are physics and philosophy; art provides beautiful things for aesthetic use.
3. *Aquinas*: According to Aquinas for creating of right things art is a way of thinking and doing.
4. *Lessing*: According to Lessing every work of art has principles.
5. *Hegel*: Hegel described different aspects of art. These are 'symbolic', 'classical', and 'romantic'. According to him art is an absolute shining.
6. *Schopenhauer*: According to Schopenhauer music is the biggest art.

7. *Nietzsche*: According to Nietzsche art is the manifestation of spiritual soul.
8. *John Dewey*: According to John Dewey art is an experience like any other experiences. With the knowledge of art creation of beautiful abstracts things like architecture can be possible. And an aesthetic sense can only be possible with the knowledge of art. The word 'aesthetics' is a derivation from the Greek word 'aesthesis' meaning a sense of beauty. As such, aesthetics is a sensible experience about the beautiful things. Because, aesthetic things are always beautiful, they always inculcate an aesthetic sense in man.

   The concept of aesthetics was given by Baumgarten Herbert Read also used the term aesthetics. Many thinkers and philosophers have put forward their views in definite ways:
9. *Platinius*: Art is associated with beauty and creates splendour.
10. *Thomas Aquinas*: Beautiful art objects are completely integrated and have perfection.
11. *Shaftebury & Huthson*: Art is the result of inner sense and sensitivity to harmony.
12. *Jacunus Meriten*: Beauty as transcendental is a concrete embodiment and is pleasing to the intellect. It is a sign of something more.
13. *Immanuel Kant*: Art is a sense of harmony in whatever is produced.
14. *Borsangot*: Borsangot was follower of Hegel. He described art as a concrete universal phenomenon.
15. *Croce*: Art in which we find beauty is a specific act of imagination. It is a complete intuition.
16. *Tolstoy*: Art is an impression of emotions.
17. *Santayana*: Art is an objectified pleasure.
18. *Friedrich Schiller*: Basic category of life following morality and feeling are to be existent in art.
19. *Collingswood*: Art is concerned to reality of things and their historicity.
20. *Edward Bullough*: Art represents psychological distances.
21. *Theodor Lipps*: Art is a feeling visualised with self and experience.

22. *H.S. Langfield*: Art is a tentative activity within self and experience.
23. *Sigmund Freud*: Art is an inner drama of human soul. Human repressed emotions force man to create.
24. *Clive*: Art is a significant form of human actions.
25. *Roger Fry*: Aesthetic emotions leads to artistic activity.
26. *Susan and Mrs. S.K. Langer*: Art is a presentation of unconscious symbols.
27. *Ortega Y. Gasset*: Dehumanisation due to modernisation forces man to create and construct new understandings.
28. *Herbert Read*: Amongst all of the thinkers who put forward their views on art, Herbert Read tried to define art. He said that art is a metaphysical concept—an organic and measurable phenomenon. Art is deeply involved in action, perception, thought and bodily action. Art is the main source to provide governing principles of life as it is the builder of culture and civilisation which balance the human life.

Art as a discipline has a very wide spectrum and it is very difficult to bring forward all aspects of art. Art entails multiple activities which are wide spread like our mother earth (soil). Soil is every where around us. We rarely step up to counter art. Art is not something we see not only in the museums and in art galleries or in old cities like Puri, Konark, Madurai, Rameshwaram, Khajuraho in hilly tracks like four dhams in Uttaranchal etc., etc. Art is present everywhere around us to please us and meet desires. There is a hierarchy in art. Many qualities in art had emerged in the past and many new qualities now emerging in the field of art which add new wings in the area of art. The work of art which does not appeal to human senses or physical sensory organ of perception cannot be termed as art. The quality of art is that which appeals to our senses. An aesthetic element is already in perception itself.

The essences of art are so universal so open to all kinds of impressions and are so interwoven with one another and so widespread that is, difficult to assume that art is not found in any nook and corner. It is so interwoven with one another that it is very difficult to say that art is not everywhere. It is because that human mind is like an automatic exchange sending and receiving messages at every moment. In all living beings, the females are mostly involved in artistic activities. This trend is not only limited to women in the human society. The female of other living beings generally do artistic activities. The birds construct the beautiful nests for their offsprings. The insects make deep wholes in the earth for their shelter and safety of their offsprings. Like that all living beings are creative and inventive. They make shelter for them and for their offsprings. In human society generally the women are more creative than men. In other words, the women are the epicentre of creativity and aestheticity. They, from the very beginning following the artistic norms and ethics of art while doing house management and bringing up their children. They always try to reate new things in the field of house management, house decoration, cooking dress making etc., etc. All this they do without any inclination for the sustenance of human society. But due to materialism and hedonism prevalent in the present society the human psyche has totally changed. They have also now become totally self-centred. Love, affection sociability, morality which was earlier engrained in their views have totally changed. Their personality is now topsy-turvy to earlier women's personality. Art can make a person humane, as such, it is necessary to educate deeply all girls about art and art activities, first at family level and later at the school level. As such, all girls schools also should have adequate art teaching as well as doing of art activities arrangements. These should be boosted by the school principals.

ART TECHNIQUES, STYLES, MATERIALS AND ASSESSMENT

For teaching art, it is necessary that the art teacher should have complete knowledge of nature of art, art techniques to be applied in art creative activities, art styles, difference between art and craft, methods of art assessment and also innovative methods to be applied for involving the students in art activities. Then only the art teacher can make the students aware about all these. All these have vide spectrum and, explanation of all these is a difficult job. A few important aspects are given below:

Art Form

Form is a simple and short word. It is a derivation from the Greek word 'Forma' meaning a shape. If somebody plays well, runs well we can say that he or she is in good form. The concept of 'form' is used for all artistic creative activities—like singing, playing, painting, dancing and acting etc., etc. Also all living beings and natural flora and fauna have forms. Therefore, form as a shape should be beautiful or aesthetic. So, a form is the essence of piece of work of art of any sort. A form takes place due to deliberate creative action. And art is the result of such deliberate action. A form is that which pleases the human senses. And good works of art are those which have good forms.

Composition

Getting inspired by the idea of Herbert Read that the nature is main source of artistic activities. I feel that the elements of composition, which are essential elements or characteristics of any work of art are also derived from nature. Nature has opposite elements which co-exist and make the life possible. For example, male and female are two opposites, who are topsy-turvy biologically. But when they are united, it makes their living beautiful and, social existence becomes possible. Because social existence is only possible when they live together and reproduce. Because human existence is only possible when man and woman live together lifelong. There are many things which are found in abundance in natural flora and fauna. Like this the artists use many things for making art works. As a human organic whole contains parts like bones, flesh, muscles and nerves and an art work also is made by joining many elements like lines, colours, plaster of Paris for making sculpture, perspective, balance, rhythm, texture and hues etc., etc. By joining all these an virtual element is created in the work of art which makes the composed art work attractive and beautiful. A form is created through the various elements and this process is called composition.

Proportion

Nature is the main source of manifestation for the artist. But a deliberate imitation of natural form for making things like vessels require use of proportion. But these can only look beautiful if some artistic element is added in newly created things. An imitation is never worth of appreciation in the field of art. Natural things develop spontaneity and force. The artist too, applies the basic laws of mathematics and physics which entail proportion. Take for example a person shaped a figure—a form derived from a fruit (a bear) which has all the features which make a jug beautiful and utilitarian. Like that all organism in nature confers to proportion, which has curious mathematical properties. Ideal situation for the artist is that he/she should learn the principles of proportion and division from natural things for applying in artistic activities.

Types of Artistic Activities and their Application

1. *Sketching*: Sketching is an initial artistic activity. The teacher should tell the students to do sketching first while doing so they should be told about the principles of perspective.
2. Second step should be to do still life drawings.
3. Third step for teaching art should be to teach the students to do landscape or hillscape or seascape drawings. These are necessary for learning artistic activities.
4. Painting (Oil and Water Colour) for painting murals, stained glass, making coloured portraits and doing rural folk arts, painting is done.
5. *Collage painting*: College paintings are done by using cut pieces, composing them together and supplementing with paint.
6. *Designing*: Making creative designs of greeting cards, etc.
7. *Graphic arts*: Print making and applied arts.
8. *Applied or commercial art*: Textile design, furniture design, making publicity matter as poster, hoardings, costume design, stage setting for dramatics and making illustrations for books.
9. *Decoration*: Making designs for doing alpana, rangoli and movable and banners.
10. *Lighting*: Shadow play, various kinds of lighting efforts such as storm, rain and storm etc.
11. *Photography*: To do photography, film making and slide making.
12. *Display*: Arranging exhibitions on special occasions such as foundation day, orientation day, alumni day, parents day, arranging exhibition of work of art and valedictory day.

13. *Restoration and preservation*: Collection of art objects and keeping these in permanent exhibition room.
14. House and classroom decoration through alpana, paper outs, rangoli and through decorative chalkboards.
15. *Education through art*: Helping the teacher in the preparation of teaching aids.
16. Art activities for special occasions such as annual melas, get together social feasts as on Guru Nanak day and Saraswati day on Basant Panchami and also on teachers' day on 5th September, every year.

Art Styles

In the field of art there are many art styles as—realism, cubism, romanticism, modernism, imitation and experimentism, etc. etc.

Art Techniques

1. *Linear drawing and art*: Doing art with lines is the primary source of art. Following types of lines are based in art work.
   (*a*) Straight lines ——— shows stability.
   (*b*) Vertical lines | shows strength and power.
   (*c*) Curved lines/shows action and motion.
   (*d*) Chained lines – – – – – shows continuity.
2. *Painting*: Paintings are—water colour painting, postal colour painting and coloured painting, portrait painting etc.

Art Material

There are various kinds of art material

1. *Pencils*: There are various kinds of pencils as

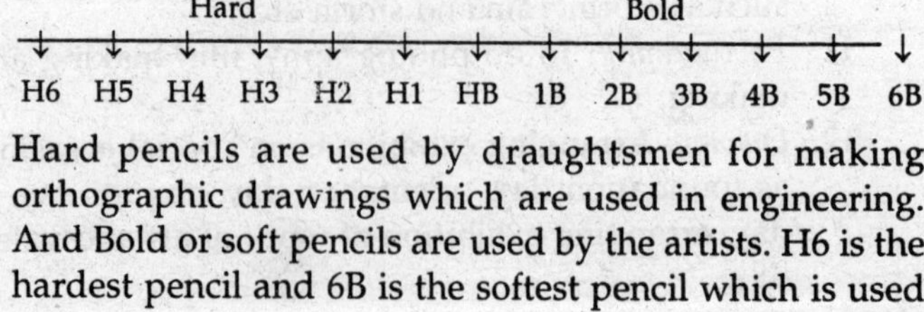

Hard pencils are used by draughtsmen for making orthographic drawings which are used in engineering. And Bold or soft pencils are used by the artists. H6 is the hardest pencil and 6B is the softest pencil which is used for making sketches. HB is the middle way pencil which can be used by all for all purposes.

2. *Paper*: Generally cartridge paper of size 28″ × 22″ of 72 lb weight is used for artistic purposes.
3. *Brushes*: Different kinds of brushes as flat brushes for oil painting and round pointed brushes are used for portal colour painting.
4. *Convess:* Oil painting is done on special convess which has special background. These are framed on special frames.
5. For making sculptures, clay, cow dung, wood, stone and plaster of Paris are used.

As such, art teaching and consequent art activities are the soul of any logical educational programme. The general teaching generally should always be designed for sound education which should be aimed for educational recovery of hidden potentials. For this recovery the artistic activities always prove to be instrumental. These remove students boredom, release emotions and build sound personality. But it is observed that artistic activities in schools, as well as, in teachers training colleges are generally ignored. As far as, girls education, the artistic activities are very necessary as the girls are generally very creative. And their life roles are also creation related. The artistic activities can only boost co-curricular activities in the girls schools which are necessary for enculturation and for inculcating the life roles in the girls who are future women.

The teacher, whether male or female, is the builder of the nation, because he or she moulds the future of guardians of the nation. Therefore, it is very necessary that they be trained in artistic activities during the course of teacher training. The authorities should look to this essentiality of education. The school administration should try to carry forward the artistic activities in the school very earnestly. The art activities will carry forward co-curricular activities. The lady teacher of the girls' schools have a special responsibility in this regard. They should encourage the art teacher and the students.

The artistic activities can prepare the students to be creative, cooperative and sociable. As such, the artistic activities are the boon for the teachers and the students.

26

Teaching Aids in Women Education

Women education, the teaching aids and the teacher all are correlated. Though having different meanings they are also supplementary to each other. The concept of teaching has emerged out of the Greek word "Taccon", which means to 'instruct', 'to impart', 'to tell', 'to apprise', and 'to pass on what one knows'. The word 'education is a derivation from the Latin word 'Educare', meaning to 'bring up', 'to grow', 'to take out', 'to prepare', 'to mould', and 'to dig out'. Teaching is usually done for bring out the hidden potentials of a person by a knowledgeable person. He or she possesses his/her acquired knowledge to a person who does not know, but has some related hidden knowledge in her/his mind. So, education actually is a process of taking out of inner potentialities of a person. As such, teaching is usually done to make a person aware what the person does not know and, to innovate and motivate the person to bring out his/her inner hidden knowledge through thinking, reasoning and comprehending. Education and teaching have different epistemic aspects so these are two different concepts, though supplementary but are contrary to each other. In teaching, the teacher who knows the subject-matter passes his/her knowledge to the students through verbal communication. But if the verbal communication is not supplemented by some innovative techniques, which can be done by teaching aids, the teaching will remain one way communication. In such a situation the students shall remain passive listeners, that is, receivers. One way communication does not ignite, thinking reasoning and comprehending in the students. In such a situation the students remain passive listeners and, they cannot contribute to the knowledge development. But education is a process through which one tries to learn himself or herself. If the school teaching does not innovate, motivate and ignite for self-learning it can never be said education. It will be mere passing out of one way information which will make the students passive. The students do not become active because, thinking, reasoning, rationalising and comprehending do not take place. In the modern sense, functionally the word education has many meanings. It is a way of upbringing of the youngers. It is an instrument of epistemacy. It is a way of upward social mobility, modernity and way of social, economic and political development. Karl Marx said that education is used by the strong for exploitation of the weak. Education is used by the theocrats for promoting their religion. Prof. M.N. Srinivas said that education is a process of transformation of occupational knowledge. Many sociologists assert that education is the vehicle of enculturation, socialisation and economic transformation. As such, education is a process of all-round development of human potentialities and capacities what are already within the biological whole of a person. All this cannot be done only through verbal communication.

There are many mythological interpretations, which may be correct or wrong about the concept of education, as already explained under the topic education. Also some philosophical aspects given in Naya-Visheska have also been explained. The law of reminiscence given in dialogue. Phaedo and the role of soul in remembering as given in Hindu theistic school of philosophy Naya and Visheska that the education is a process of taking out what is already in the human body and mind. In other words, education is a process of taking and what the human soul has acquired through human senses and accumulated within the body. And this process of taking out of accumulated knowledge is nothing but education. For taking out such accumulated knowledge some process, methods and tools are required. Suppose a person has to dig out some hidden wealth from the earth, he or she will require a spade for digging the earth. As such, for the recovery of human hidden potentialities or capacities which are already there in the human body or soul, some innovative methods of teaching and some teachings aids are to be applied.

Teaching and education are complimentary and supplementary to each other. Therefore, education is not possible without teaching and, teaching is useless if it is not applied or done for educating the pupils. As such, educational process involves a sound process of transmission of information which is done through various communication methods as given below:

(*i*) Gestures, symbols;
(*ii*) Through spoken and written words;
(*iii*) By showing concrete things;
(*iv*) By showing pictures, illustrations, photographs, posters and charts;
(*v*) By showing models, republicas of concrete things and dioramas;
(*vi*) By making projects;
(*vii*) Projections and displays, exhibitions and, so on so forth. Teaching is basically done through two kinds of symbols:
   (*a*) Non-discursive symbols (words-spoken or written);
   (*b*) Discursive symbols or non-verbal media-like concrete things or actual things or through contrived experiences of the concrete things. This contrived experience can be given through pictures, photographs, illustrations, posters, maps, charts and flash cards etc., etc., and also through models and dioramas.

In teaching, both kinds of communication, that is, verbal and non-verbal are used. If this is done, then only teaching can be educating. In olden times, conservative methods of teaching were used. But in Gurukulas the teaching always entailed group discussions (वाद विवाद). The teaching was aimed at to pass on cultural heritage, religious norms for inculcating moral values and for sane socialisation. The teacher used to be proficient and an authority on these areas and, used to pass on information about these to his disciples, which was surely to be entailed with debates and discussions. On the whole the teaching was more teacher oriented. Also the students were also not supposed to accept what was being taught by the Guru (teacher). But it cannot be denied that the teaching in olden times was more teacher oriented and less student oriented. Also the students had not to accept what the teacher used to tell because of follow up debates and discussions which used to be lengthy ones. In China also the process of debates and discussions used to follow. But in other countries the situation was different.

In China, teaching was based on showing of actual things. There is a Chinese adage, "What we hear we forget and, what we see we remember". In other countries teaching was basically done through verbal communication. But teaching through verbal communication does not lead to education. It remains merely information. The same thing is happening now in our Indian girls and boys schools due to formal system of education which is merely examination oriented. The teacher is basically over-occupied in passing on more and more information about subject related contents. He or she want to cover the subject content before the stipulated time, assigned as per curriculum content to be covered, so as he/she could do revision. This is done for better examination results of the students.

From the olden days, thinkers have been supporting the showing of connected concrete things in teaching. They believed that per-se. (perception) is the prime source of teaching. Socrates said that "perception is the better source of learning and knowledge". Plato said, "Knowledge is only possible through perception, comprehension and understanding". Aristotle said, "Knowledge is only possible through study of matter". Rene' Descartes said that every person has some innate ideas, these ideas should be tapped through thinking, reasoning and comprehending. Thinking can only be possible either by showing things or their images. John Locke rejected the assumption of Rene' Descartes of innate ideas. He put forward an empiricist theory of perception. He said that a child is a biological whole at the time his/her birth. The child does not have any innate ideas at the time of his/her birth. As the child grows biologically his/her sense organs also grow. Initially the mind of the child is empty and is like a Tabula-Rasa (a blank slate). John Locke said that as the child grows, his/her sensory organs grow and the child perceives the physical things, he/she acquires experience and writes on his/her empty Tabula-Rasa or slate. John Locke advocated that the sensory experiences provide knowledge. Therefore, gaining of sensory experiences should be compulsory for the youngers while they are being taught. If a child is to be made aware about snow falling he/she should be forced to go out of his/her house and should experience snow falling while it is falling. Likewise, the child should be given compulsory experiences in all fields at every stage of life. A.J. Ayer said that true is that which can be verified. David

Hume said that dogmatism should not have any place in education. True education is that which is acquired through sensory experiences. J.J. Rousseau, who was the founder of Naturalism said that "when the child is born is free, but he/she finds himself/herself in chains. The society imposes many restrictions in terms of social traits and social traditions which are to be obeyed by the child". Comenius was the first educationist who first of all thought of the use of pictures in teaching. He also suggested that the text-books should be illustrated. He had introduced the 'deductive method' in teaching out of which heuristic method of teaching emerged. He also had written books on teaching 'Orbis pictus', 'teaching through pictures', and 'Didectus', teaching for self-learning. Froebel said that, 'Child's curiosity for knowing should be exploited by showing him/her concrete things and pictures of the related things. Pestalozzi laid emphasis on child's emotions. He also like J.J. Rousseau said that child should be educated in natural atmosphere and, learning should be based on touch and sensation. M.K. Gandhi said that "all the best should be taken out from child through hard work and correlating this with related issues. John Dewey laid stress on practical approach (pragmatic) in education. He advocated pragmatism in education. But he did suggest application of axiology in education as suggested in Basic Education by M.K. Gandhi. Robin Cook was the first person who utilised his artistic knowledge in teaching. While he was serving in British army in Australia, he had made beautiful landscapes and seascapes. After serving in Australia, he was transferred to Africa where he made pictures of African animals. Later on, Mr. Robin Cook used all these artistic drawing while he was teaching geography in a grammar school in England. Guru R.N. Tagore laid stress on nature and freedom in educating the youngs. With this idea he established Vishwa Bharati University at Bolpur in West Bengal where the students are still taught in natural atmosphere. Feeding with the bookish and informative teaching based on alien system of formal education, which generates acculturations innovated J. Krishnamurti. He established few Rishi schools in *jungles* on the river banks, on the pattern of old Gurukulas, in Andhra Pradesh and Rajghat schools in the *jungles* on the Ganga river banks in Varanasi, U.P. Shri J. Krishnamurti had established these school to counter of formal education. Also by establishing the Rishi schools Shri J. Krishnamurti aimed at using the natural experience in Education. These schools are still functioning on Gurukula pattern. In Delhi Ganga International School located at Hiren Kudna More on Rohtak Road has been established on the pattern of Rishi Schools. As such, many thinkers laid stress on the use of Audio-Visual Aids in teaching.

The process of education is a deductive process which entails self-learning. If teaching does not involve self-learning, it will make the learner a dummy passive receiver who will never think, reason, analyse and comprehend. Such person can never be a creative thinker and a contributor. So, both the girls schools and boys schools should always use of teaching aids or audio-visual aids, during the course of teaching. The use of the teaching aids is necessary to innovate and motivate the students to think, reason, analyse, comprehend and understand for self-learning, which is true education.

All great men were prone to self-learning through the deductive approach. A deductive method is that method of teaching in which there is maximum interaction between the teacher and the students. This can only be possible when the teacher applies progressive heuristic method of teaching. Heuristic method of teaching always aims at to make the students interactive. The students can be interactive if they are given chance of thinking, reasoning, analysing, comprehending and responding to the queries made by the teacher and students in the classroom. This can be done by involving all sense organs of the students as hearing, touching, seeing, smelling and testing. For this, the teacher should use verbal as well as non-verbal ways of communication. The verbal communication should always be used for giving introductory narration of the topic which is being taught. It should be followed by showing related pictures, photographs, posters, charts, flashcards models and dioramas. This would motivate the students to think, reason and contribute in the development of the topic, being taught under a particular lesson which being taught in the class. All great men like Goethe, Homer, Shakespeare, Schopenhauer, Immanuel Kant, Karl Marx, Rene' Descartes, Nietzsche in the West and Kalidas, Tulsidas, Kabir, Gurunanak, Tagore, Ramanujam, Swami Dayananda Saraswati, G.V. Raman and J. Krishnamurti could educate themselves through the deductive approach. Likewise, in the field of science they applied deductive approach in educating themselves in their respective disciplines.

As such, teacher's approach while teaching in classroom should be creative for establishing a congenial atmosphere in the classroom while teaching. The teacher should use deductive method for teaching for clinching the hidden knowledge of the students. He or she should establish a good rapport with the students. It can only be possible by applying progressive methods of teaching, such as deductive and heuristic methods which provide sensory experiences to the students. And for this, the use of audio-visual aids in teaching is must. This can make the students self-learning. For this the teacher must be aware about pedagogic understandings. Peda (a Greek word) means a child and, gogic means an understanding. For pedagogic concept three elements should be studied:

(*i*) Pedagogic epistemological standpoints,
(*ii*) Pedagogic psychological standpoints, and
(*iii*) Pedagogic personalistic standpoints.

Pedagogic epistemological standpoints refer to conditions which promote knowledge. For this, the pupils should be motivated to know. And the teacher must be aware about the appropriate teaching methods to be applied for particular topics. She or he must also be aware what teaching aids can be used for a particular topic which could create epistemic motivation. The teacher must be aware about the epistemic conditions for teaching. The teacher should also try to know about the psychological conditions of his/her clients, that is, the students. The teacher should try to examine the personality of the students. This can be done by having a sympathetic ear and by establishing congenial rapport with the students. To make a pupil psychologically sound, the pupil must be understood as an individual. He or she should be loved and respected. There should not be any place for the use of rode. The pupil should be loved, innovated, motivated, stimulated and encouraged to learn. The pupil should be encouraged for self-learning. The pedagogic principle, implies and aims at knowing the unknown.

Audio-visual aids provide sensory experiences. And sensory experiences from the bases of self-learning and knowledge acquisition. There are five senses—visual (eyes), Aural (ears), Olfactory (nose), Gustatory (tongue) and Tactile (skin) and, these are called gates of knowledge. To begin with, thinking is restricted to concrete experiences, which form the base of abstract learning. Sensory experiences are concrete experiences. Learning experiences appealing to the senses are more effective in abstract learning. Thus, there is strong case for using teaching aids in teaching by the teacher.

Though, all the five senses are important, but in many special cases a particular sense is applicable for knowing, but stress is laid on aural and visual senses, because without these two way teaching and learning is not possible. If a teacher does not use verbal media, that is, verbal communication, the students get it difficul. ιo understand. On the other hand, if the teacher use only verbal communication, the students always remain of the receiving end and become passive listeners. If verbal and non-verbal communication are used simultaneously then only learning can take place. Verbal communication is always non-discursive and does not evoke thinking process which is necessary for the acquisition of knowledge. Whereas, non-verbal communication, that occurs with the use of teaching aids, is always discursive. It forces the pupils to think, reason, and comprehend which is necessary for learning and knowledge development. Comenius was the first educationist who used pictures in teaching the first Pestalozzi used objects and their models in teaching. Captain Cook used landscapes in teaching geography, Madam Montessori laid stress on intensive sense experiences in a play way. In the last two world wars the army generals used visual aids for educating illiterate army soldiers. Before sixty or sixty-five years ago, the teaching in schools was basically done through verbal communication. Now the entire field of teaching in schools is dominated by audio-visual aids. Due to the advancement of science and technology, the progressive methods of teaching have become mandatory for the teachers in both girls and boys schools. It is, therefore, very necessary, rather essential, that all teachers should be made fully aware about the use of audio-visual aids in teaching. The use of audio-visual aids make the teaching easy effective and educative. These accelerate the rate of learning, quick barring and provide longer retention, is the slogan of audio-visual educationists and technologists.

Audio-visual aids are not only beneficial for teaching in schools. These can be very beneficial in socialisation, moralisation and rationalisation and, also in life-building process of those who are still illiterates, irrational and unsane in the present modern society. Most such persons are quite unaware about the desired life roles. Mostly the women outnumber such persons. The illiterate women, generally in villages, become the beacon light of dys-functioning of Indian renowned social institution of the joint family system. Such women can be educated through audio-visual aids. This can be done by social organisations like Gram Panchayats and some religious organisations by apprising such illiterate ladies that the joint family is the backbone of Indian culture. For this audio-visual aids should be used. Such action will be beneficial for the integration of the society.

Considering the sensory experience beneficial for the knowledge acquisition, Edger Dale, an American educationist, suggested a cone of experience which help the teacher in classroom teaching-learning situations through audio-visual aids.

EDGER DALE'S CONE OF EXPERIENCE

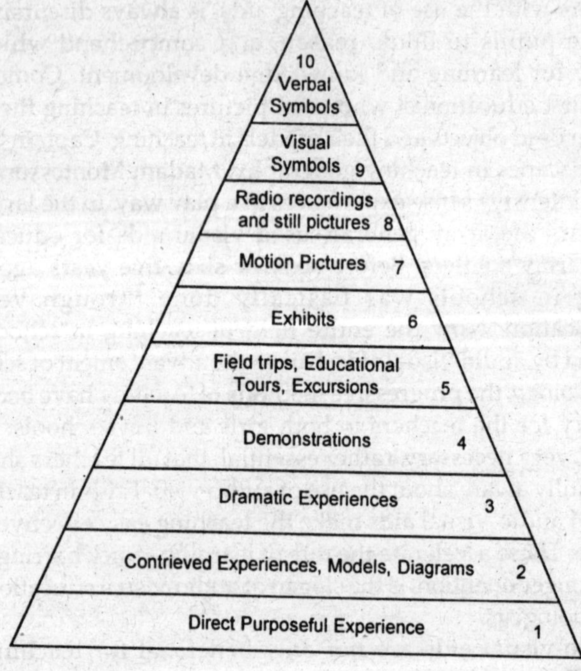

Though all the five senses are important for learning, stress is laid on the aural and visual senses as these are widely used in classroom teaching. Every physical object cannot be shown in the classroom, while teaching. In absence of actual things their pictures, republicas, models or dioramas are shown in the classroom by the teacher while teaching. Teaching aids or audio-visual aids sometimes give dual perspectives and create confusion. A three dimensional model of a thing is also a source of perception (per-se) like that of a picture. It can also be touched and seen. Broadly speaking the audio-visual aids can be touched and seen. These are categorised as: (1) projected teaching aids, and (2) non-projected teaching aids. In projected aids images of things are projected on a screen with the help of projectors like films, film strips, slides and some transparencies come under this category. Non-projected aids form the bulk of audio-visual aids. The projected and non-projected aids classified under types of Audio-visual aids.

In projected aids, the images of things are projected on a screen with the help of projectors. Films, film strips, slides and transparencies come under this category. Non-projected aids from the bulk of teaching aids. Also chalkboards (called blackboards) dioramas, globes, human skeleton, models, specimen of things, charts maps, flashcards, display material come under this category of contrived experience of teaching aids.

UTILISATION OF AUDIO-VISUAL AIDS

Even, the most effective teaching aids become ineffective in the hands of an unexperienced non-serious teacher. The right use of proper audio-visual aids, made of right material at the right time and at the right place contribute four Rs. that is, reading, writing, remembering and recording. A teacher while using the audio-visual aids must keep in her/his mind: (1) educational outcomes of expected, elicitations from the students, (2) nature and complexity of the content to be taught or developed, (3) methodology of teaching to be applied and related experience to be given to the students, (4) the choice of teaching aids should be decided or determined according to the objectives of teaching. How can the teaching aids be related to teaching? There are different scopes of the use of teaching aids according to their

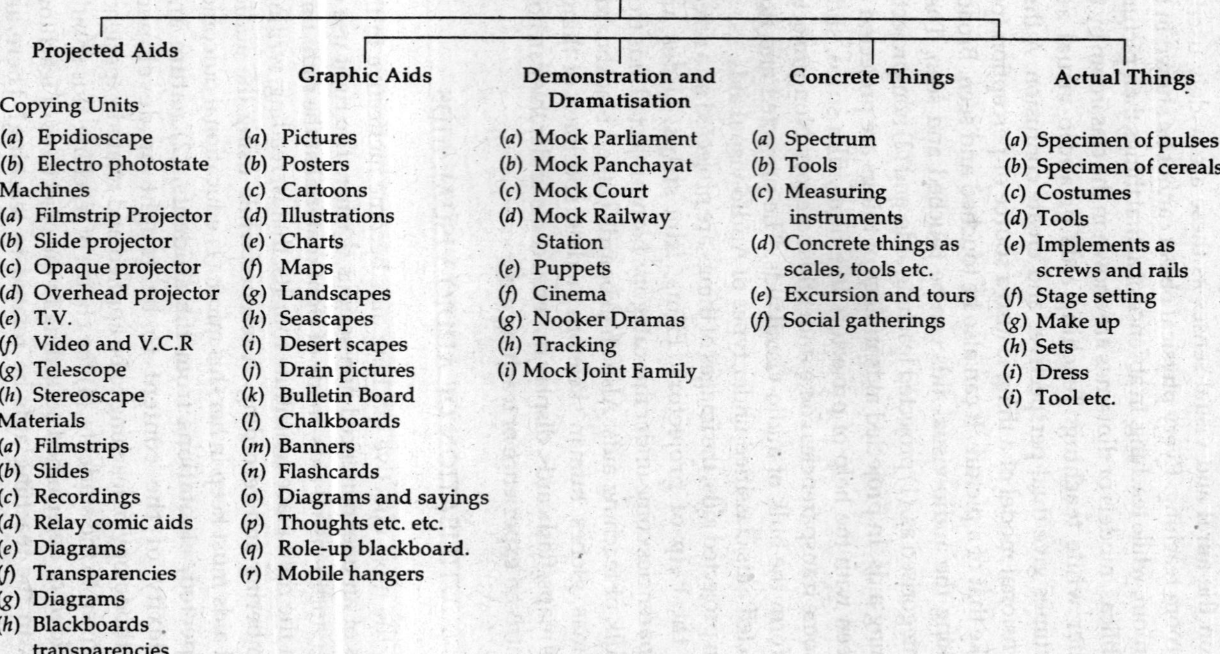

TYPES OF AUDIO-VISUAL AIDS
Projected Aids
1. Copying Units
(a) Epidioscape
(b) Electro photostate
2. Machines
(a) Filmstrip Projector
(b) Slide projector
(c) Opaque projector
(d) Overhead projector
(e) T.V.
(f) Video and V.C.R
(g) Telescope
(h) Stereoscape
3. Materials
(a) Filmstrips
(b) Slides
(c) Recordings
(d) Relay comic aids
(e) Diagrams
(f) Transparencies
(g) Diagrams
(h) Blackboards transparencies
(i) Flannel board
Graphic Aids
(a) Pictures
(b) Posters
(c) Cartoons
(d) Illustrations
(e) Charts
(f) Maps
(g) Landscapes
(h) Seascapes
(i) Desert scapes
(j) Drain pictures
(k) Bulletin Board
(l) Chalkboards
(m) Banners
(n) Flashcards
(o) Diagrams and sayings
(p) Thoughts etc. etc.
(q) Role-up blackboard.
(r) Mobile hangers
Demonstration and Dramatisation
(a) Mock Parliament
(b) Mock Panchayat
(c) Mock Court
(d) Mock Railway Station
(e) Puppets
(f) Cinema
(g) Nooker Dramas
(h) Tracking
(i) Mock Joint Family
Concrete Things
(a) Spectrum
(b) Tools
(c) Measuring instruments
(d) Concrete things as scales, tools etc.
(e) Excursion and tours
(f) Social gatherings
Actual Things
(a) Specimen of pulses
(b) Specimen of cereals
(c) Costumes
(d) Tools
(e) Implements as screws and rails
(f) Stage setting
(g) Make up
(h) Sets
(i) Dress
(i) Tool etc.

viability in different subjects. According to the writer the teaching aids should innovate and motivate the students to interact and respond without fear in the classroom. Getting some elicitations and enabling the students to learn should be the prime objective of the use of teaching aids. The teacher should not use more than one teaching aid at one time. This may create confusion in the minds of the students. Some teachers in order to avoid the trouble of displaying the teaching aids one after another, display the teaching aids material, such as role up blackboard, charts and maps in advance of teaching. This is not correct procedure. This creates confusion in the minds of the students.

While using projected aids like films, film strip and slides, the teacher should give an introductory talk about these to the students. After the projection of a particular aid is over, special points should be elucidated to the students, so that they may note down some special points about the topic which is being taught. Films are of generally of 8 mm, 16 mm, 35 mm and of 700 mm size, out of which 8 mm and 16 mm are generally used for making slides. A 16 mm film has pocket wholes on one side only, and sound track on the other side, therefore, it can be used as a sound film. A 16 mm silent film has pockets or teeth on both edges. As such, a 16 mm silent film should not be threaded into a silent projector as the pockets with teeth on both sides with totally damage the sound track and also the film. Only a sound projector should be used for sound film.

ADVANTAGES OF THE MOTION PICTURES

Both audio and visual aids appeal to; (1) both the senses at the same time, (2) because of presentation on an illuminated screen in darkness and semi-darkness, (3) the pupils generally identify themselves with the events presented on the screen appeal to the senses and emotions of the pupils, (4) these aids enable the pupils to witness the objects, places, events not ordinarily seen in their day-to-day lives. Films are close to real life and their motions contribute to realism. But the projectors and films are costly, as such, films suitably made for topics may not be readily available. Teachers sometimes use the films for mere relaxation from teaching and for enjoyment and entertainment and not for instructional purposes. Many teachers also do not try to know how to use the projectors and use the film in teaching. This attitude makes them dependent on those, who either live far from school or are few in numbers. In spite of all these limitations films, that is, motion pictures or TV programmes are very useful and very effective audio-visual aids. A teacher using these aids should guide the students to note down the important events. This should be done prior to the projection of the teaching aids. These points should be discussed in the follow up discussions.

FILM STRIPS

Film strips are useful teaching aids. One foot to three foot long film is used to prepare the film strips having a series of 30 to 50 picture or picture frames of 28 mm and 18 mm. A film projector is adjusted to project both kinds of frames. Film strips are cheap and easily transportable. Film strips negatives can be shot on camera and can be framed at home as per size of the film strip projector. For storing the card board racks can be made at home. These film strips can be projected easily for a desirable time again and again.

SLIDES

Slides are made from 35 mm films (2″ × 2″) and also by using plain glass (3.25″ × 3.25″). Film slides are photographic slides may be hand made. These can be used as photographic slides. These slides of 2″ × 2″ can be projected using a film strip projector after fixing in the slide gate.

The teachers can easily prepare slides with 3.5″ × 3.25″ or 2″ × 2″ glass plates using ink or cell phone paper having printed or written matter. The semi-transparent glass can also be used to prepare the slides. One surface of the glass, should be painted with their solution of gelatine. Writing should be made on this surface. Thereafter, it should be covered by another glass plate of the same size and glued using mixture of resistant glues. The slides are flexible aids, that is, sequence is not fixed. The teacher can arrange these slides serially according to teaching needs. This is the major advantage of the slides over the film strips. Slides needs storage space. The glass slides are breakable. The teacher has to be very careful while putting the slides into slide gates giving vertical and lateral inversion during projection.

NON-PROJECTED TEACHING AID

Graphic aids are non-projected aids. These are powerful media for teaching and learning. When these are shown and are visualised things simply convey epistemic facts and ideas. These aids represent a judicial spectrum of drawing, pictures and words. These are usually two dimensional and, many of these can be projected through an opaque projector (epidiascope). An easily shown chart, posters, diagram, illustrations, graphics, cartoons, flashcards, maps are some important graphic aids. "A chart is combination of graphic material and pictorial media especially, orderly and logically designed to represent the content and elicit knowledge from the students". Charts are useful to show relationship, classifications of the contents by means of pictorial media, figures or statistics to present the material systematically to apprise the students about the related problems and to stimulate and encourage them to think and respond charts can be classified as flow chart, time chart etc., etc. A poster is a pictorial devise to communicate and attract the attention to a story, a social fact or phenomenon, an idea or an image more quickly and clearly. A poster, though generally used for quick communication for publicising an important fact. It can be useful for communicating community's interests. It can also be useful to communicate a particular fact in teaching. A map is used to show the geographical boundaries of a country. It is also very useful for apprising the students about the geographical terrains. A graph is used to show representative, qualitative date showing comparisons, ratios and relationships. A cartoon is a kind of metaphysical representation of a thing or a person in the form of tainted pictures or posters. Comics are liked by the children. These can be used in teaching languages, social features and political happenings. In teaching, a map is an accurate representation in the form of diagrams of the surface of the earth or some part of it. The maps are always made according to scale. Maps vary in types and forms. These are universally used in teaching history, geography, political science and sociology. A flashcard is a small compact picturised card. It is flashed before the students to apprise them about a new idea, a new word and, a new thing. Generally the flash cards are used to teach language to the youngers. Photographs or pictures are used after sticking on a sheet of paper or on small cards, like flashcards are used in teaching. If the pictures are big, the big sheets of paper are used. These are also used like flashcards. These should not be used for a long time.

DISPLAY MATERIAL

Chalkboards, (moving and static), flannel boards, bulletin boards are some of the widely used display boards. Chalkboards are generally called blackboards, are extensively used in teaching. A class is incomplete without a chalkboard (blackboard). A chalkboard is the oldest and simplest 'eaching aids. It was developed during the Christian protestant religious movement under the leadership of Martin Luther in Germany. Later on it was adopted by the Church missionary schools in Europe. By the spread of colonialism, it became an universal teaching aid. Now there are various kinds of chalkboards as wooden chalkboard, slide chalkboards or movable chalkboards, role-up blackboard, glass chalkboard, slate chalkboard, rubber chalkboard, plywood chalkboard, cemented chalkboard etc., etc. As a teaching aid a chalkboard is an important teaching tool in the hands of the teacher these days. A teacher cannot proceed without a chalkboard in the classroom. So the chalkboard is a reliable friend of the teacher. But one of the deadliest drawback is that most of the teachers are not fully aware about the desirable qualities of the chalkboard. It is because, generally the teacher are not made aware about the chalkboard (blackboard) during the course of teacher's training. The teacher training institutes in many cases do not give proper important to the use of chalkboard during teaching. Following are the important features pertaining to the chalkboard which are to be kept in mind by the teacher while teaching:

1. The lower edge of the chalkboard should be at the eye level of the pupils.
2. The chalkboard or blackboard should be clearly visible to the students. There should not be light glare on the chalkboard.
3. There should be minimum 6 ft. distance between first row of the students and the blackboard.
4. The letters and other graphic material written on the chalkboard should be written in orderly manner. It should be written in straight lines.

5. Overcrowding and incomplete writing should be avoided.
6. Chalkboard writing should be done slowly so as to give chance to the students to follow the teacher.
7. The teacher should never stand before the chalkboard.
8. The teacher should never talk while she/he is doing the chalkboard work.
9. Never paste or nail any material on the surface of the chalkboard. It will spoil the surface of it.
10. The chalkboard is one of the most trusted friend of the teacher in the classroom. The teacher should also give it friendly treatment. The chalkboard should be kept clean and unhurt. It should be dusted after teaching.
11. The chalkboard dusting should not be left for the coming teacher.
12. The chalkboard is a mistake rectifier. The teacher should not be annoyed if any of her/his mistake is pointed by the pupil who noticed the mistake. The teacher rather should be thankful to the pupil who noticed the mistake and later on pointed out.
13. The teacher should advise the students to note down the chalkboard work. The students should be in tune to have pace with the teacher.
14. Necessary chalkboard accessories and material as good quality white and coloured chalks, good chalk duster, chalk tray, a piece of wet cloth and, also chalkboard equipments like templates, compass, set square, scale and enlarger should be used.
15. A teacher must be fully aware about the chalkboard (blackboard) paints. Generally all paints are made by (1) Pigment, (2) Binder and (3) paint vehicle. A pigment is a refined coloured clay. For a chalkboard, because blackboard paint is used, generally black pigment is used for making chalkboard black paint. A binder is made by double boiled linseed oil. The pigment and binder are mixed in a rotating machine. After this to make this mixture thin a thinner, usually turpentine oil, is mixed. The blackboard paint is ready. In blackboard paint the quantity of binder is very little just about ten percent of the whole mix. This is because the surface of the chalkboard should remain rough and not smooth.

16. The role-up blackboard is made of thick cartridge paper. On two sides of the paper round wooden strips with a binding chord are fixed so that the role-up blackboard may be rolled. The role-up blackboard should be used for making for advance blackboard work before teaching. And blackboard paint should be used for making a role-up board.
17. A flannel board is dynamic display board. The flannel cloth either can be stapled or tagged on an insulation board or glued on plywood sheet. The pictures which are to be fixed on the flannel board should have a sand paper background. The sand paper pieces of rough temper should be pasted on the back of the flashcards or on the pictures which is to be displayed. Generally the bulletin boards are used for displays. In teaching the young pupils, when the teacher uses the flashcards, it is necessary to use the flannel board, on which things can be fixed and removed easily on it.

A bulletin board is also used for displaying things and putting up notices. It can also be used for displaying students contribution in the field of artistic activities and literature. Bulletin boards are also generally made of insulation boards, as these are soft and drawing pins can be used on these. The bulletin board should be fixed where its visibility becomes common. As such, corridors of the school are most suited. At least one bulletin board should be fixed in one class. Picture clippings and other paper cuttings should be collected for bulletin board displays. At one time one thing should be displayed. Coloured pictures, photographs should have appropriate background. Lettering should be done if necessary. Bulletin board displays stimulate pupils' interests and motivate them to perform various artistic activities. Bulletin boards are very useful in introducing, explaining and reviving the topics to be taught in the school or else where as in social service. Bulletin boards are very useful in carrying out co-curricular activities in the school.

Besides the use of all these teaching aids, every teacher must at least know how to use the epidiascope for enlarging small drawings to big size on a drawing sheet. The teacher should also know how to use the overhead projector for projecting chalkboard transparencies. Also it would be good for the teacher to learn to learn to prepare film strips, slides and chalkboard work transparencies. The school should jointly arrange some seminars or workshops for apprising the teachers for such activities.

Besides these activities there are some activities or activity aids like arranging mock parliament, excursions, educational tours, inter-school debates and discussions on national burning issues like corruption, crimes against women, acculturation. And to check these group discussions, mélas, display and exhibitions should be arranged.

It is also necessary to apprise all teachers and students about the versatility of teaching aids in the field of education. The teachers and students should be motivated to prepare the necessary teaching aids themselves. The teachers should involve the students in the preparation of necessary teaching aids. This will motivate the students to do creative work. For this teachers have to be creative minded. The teacher should also involve the students in model making, in arranging displays and doing creative activities like alpana, rangoli and arranging exhibitions. The teacher should involve the students in making dioramas. A model is a true representation of a real thing which may be big like earth or very small thing like an atom. Diorama is a big model housing a multiplied spectrum of models. Also, there are situations when providing of contrived experiences, through models, dioramas, still models, topographic models or relief models are not necessary. Only samples of things as hand tools as hand saw, tools like hammer, speedometer and some other tools can be shown. In some cases, experience of touch and taste like knowing about *desi ghee* or *dalda ghee,* well be known by testing and smelling. Salty or sweety puddings will only be known by taste. It is also true that the use of audio-visual aids is necessary in sphere of teaching.

27

A Review

Aspirations for peaceful, happy and prosperous life, for better living is a natural, a logical and a common social feature. All living beings including human beings, that is, woman and man aspire to do so for living a happy, peaceful and sane social life. But, generally it is seen that, often it does not happen for all. Due to changed social scenario, generally women and men remain conflict ridden, which disturb their mental peace and also peace of the family members. This curbs the social homogeneity, harmony and integrity in the society. Even this trend promotes dys-functioning in social life. It reduces sociability, cooperation and sharing amongst the people. Because of this a lot of hurdles and difficulties emerge in the society.

Change is inevitable in every sphere of human life, in all living beings, in all physical atmosphere and flora and fauna. Greek philosopher Hereclitus said that "everything is in flux at every movement. So social change is also unavoidable. The present social change has occurred due to the development of science and technology in the world which brought affluency in the industrial societies. The woman and man though are rational beings but are greedy. Those who were not developed tried to acquire affluency by copying the developed industrial countries. They adopted the alien socio-economic and cultural norms and become totally accultured. They, more or less renounced their indigenous social, economical and cultural traits and adopted the foreign traits. This social change has very badly affected the Indian social life. It can be said that the reason for the social change is human greed. Generally, the social change which occurs due to extreme acculturation makes the social structure, which entails human sociability, economic, cultural and religiosity, topsy-turvy. The Indian society which was religious and theistic has now become materialistic, hedonistic, consumeristic, megalomaniac and self-centred. And now it is seen that mostly all have become self-centred, unsocial and inhuman. And it is also observed that most of the human beings—women and men are dys-functioning the old joint family system and Indian social structure. Due to acculturation the national culture is also being killed.

Many male members of the society have become so self-centred, egoistic, corrupt, uncivilised and barbarous that they behave with their life partners like animals. Women are physically weaker than men. They become the target of such persons. Many ladies are beaten, tortured and are badly maltreated by such persons throughout their lives. Many ladies face the heinous crimes like rapes, molestations, chain pulling and loots. Generally young ladies and minor girls are targeted for such crimes. This tendency of crimes against women has become a common feature. Even in the capital city Delhi the women are not safe. They cannot dare to come out of their homes neither early in the morning for walk or in the evening for having a stroll. Also in their own homes many innocent women becomes the victim of their own family members. In many cases, the fathers do not hesitate to rape their step-daughters and daughter-in-laws. Recent rape of Imrana, a Muslim lady, by her father-in-laws is a startling one. In August, 2005, a father raped his step-daughter aged 13 years. Also many nearest kiths and kins of the young girls do not hesitate raping their sibling sisters. What all this does indicate? The many men are becoming mad for illegal sex aspirations. They can be termed as *jungli* or barbarous. This also can be said a 'gender bias' against fair sex.

The girls, the future women, because of 'unity in bio-diversity' are to be married with the opposite sex, that is, with the boys and, are sent to the houses of the boys, they are considered 'anta-property' (पराया-धन). So, the girls are victims of gender bias. The birth of a girls is considered a bad omen in the present social situation because the girls are considered a liability. People do not realise that the genesis of the society lies in the girls, who are future women and mothers. When a girl is born in a family an atmosphere of sorrow spread. No joy and happiness are seen. People do not like the birth of a girl baby a good sign. They do not celebrate the birth of a girl as the birth of a boy is celebrated. It is the girls who are to be sent to another home. People do not realise that the girls and boys both are social necessity and, sending the girls to another's house is a social reciprocity. The girls are sent to another homes and girls are received and welcomed from another homes. This process of 'unity in bio-diversity' is must for social existence.

But it is unfortunate situation that because of sending girls to another house, they are considered anta-property (पराया-धन). And due to this anta-property (पराया-धन) the girls are not well-educated as boys are educated. The people think the girls well have to go another home, so there is no need to educate them well. Another reason of gender bias against the girls is that the boys side demand dowry at the time of 'unity in bio-diversity', that is, their marriage. And majority of the cases giving dowry becomes an ordeal for the girls parents. If the desired dowry is not given to the groom, his parents do not treat the bride well. And in many cases, the brides not only maltreated and tortured but murdered also. The dowry is also an alien system which we Indian borrowed from westerners. All this is happening due to men's greed for hedonism and consumerism which is going to cross all limits.

All these aspects of gender bias against women develop an unique psyche in the minds of the girls. In their childhood, the girls are convinced that they are 'anta-property' (पराया-धन) and they will have to leave their parental homes positively and go to another homes. So, the girls develop alienatory feelings and emotions in their childhood. They start to treat their parental homes as 'anta-homes'. This develop an unique psyche of alienation in them. They start thinking to achieve in their new homes (ससुराल) what was denied or slipped to them in their parental homes. They make up their minds to have full control over their husbands and enjoy hedonism in their marital life. Many girls just after their marriage separate from their in-laws and start living independently in nuclear families. This process does the dys-functioning of the institution of joint family. Dys-functioning of the joint family hampers the proper upbringing of their children and their enculturation. This also damages the spirit of sociability, homogeneity, cooperation in the society. It leads to hedonism, consumerism and acculturation.

Therefore, it is very important to look into all these aspects while educating the girls. The girls education should be for their life-building which could enable them to discharge their life roles properly. In this regard the lady teachers, the principals of the girls' schools will have to play an important role. The girls should be educated for social harmony, amity and homogeneity.

Bibliography

Andre Beabelle, Inequality and Social Change.
Cohen B.S., Society and Culture.
Durkheim Emile, On Education.
Etzioni Amati, Social Change.
Homman G.C., Social Behaviour.
Karl Marx and Engel Fredrick, The Class Struggle.
Karl Marx, Alienation.
कृष्ण कुमार, समाज और शिक्षा।
Linton Ralph, Culture.
Locke John, Essays on Human Understanding.
M.N. Srinivas, Sanskritisation.
Merriot, Social Structure and Change in U.P. Village.
Raymond Aron, Sociology.
Sermon, Modernisation.
Writer, Self Social Experience.